D1115053

AUKS

AUKS
An Ornithologist's Guide
Ron Freethy

Facts On File Publications
New York, New York • Oxford, England

Copyright © 1987 Ron Freethy

First published in the United States of America by Facts On File, Inc.
460 Park Avenue South, New York, New York 10016.

Library of Congress Cataloging-in-Publication Data

Freethy, Ron.
  Auks: An Ornithologist's Guide.
  Bibliography: p.
  1. Alcidae. I. Title.
QL696.C42F73 1987   598'.33   86-24327
ISBN 0-8160-1696-8

All rights reserved.
No part of this book may be reproduced
or utilized in any form or by any means,
electronic or mechanical, including photocopying,
recording or by any information storage and
retrieval systems, without permission
in writing from the Publisher.

Printed in Great Britain
10 9 8 7 6 5 4 3 2 1

CONTENTS

PICTURE CREDITS

The author and publisher would like to thank the following for kindly providing colour and black and white illustrations.

Colour Plates
Kenneth W. Fink/Ardea: 7, 8 and 9
S. Jonasson/Frank Lane Picture Agency: 3, 5
C.R. Knights/Ardea: 1
Leonard Lee Rue/Frank Lane Picture Agency: 6
P. Morris/Ardea: 4
Mark Newman/Frank Lane Picture Agency: 11
Roger Tidman/Frank Lane Picture Agency: 2
John Watkins/Frank Lane Picture Agency: 12
Winfried Wisniewski/Frank Lane Picture Agency: 10

Black and White Photographs
Ardea: p. 176
Will Bown: p. 76
Glen Elison/Frank Lane Picture Agency: p. 139
Kenneth W. Fink/Ardea: pp. 144, 160
Ron Freethy: p. 182
Eric Hosking: pp. 37, 65, 72, 85, 117, 187, 191
Eric & David Hosking: pp. 41, 90
Leonard Lee Rue/Frank Lane Picture Agency: p. 151
Mark Newman/Frank Lane Picture Agency: p. 120
Niall Rankin/Eric Hosking: pp. 57, 67, 187
Richard Vaughan/Ardea: pp. 100, 113, 167

Line Illustrations
Carole Pugh

1

CLASSIFICATION OF AUKS

There are more than 8,600 species of birds alive today and, although there is a broad consensus on the way they should be classified, there are still a few minor disagreements among taxonomists. According to the authority consulted, living birds are divided into 27 or 28 orders (see Table 1) and within these there are some 175 families, one of which is the Alcidae – the auks (see Table 2).

With the exception of the great auk (*Pinguinus impennis*), the family is made up of small, dumpy, short-winged birds confined to the sea and coasts of the Northern Hemisphere. They are well able to withstand wind, wave and cold weather and are found right up to the ice barrier of the high-Arctic seas. Their wings are small and the flight is direct and surprisingly fast but most species prefer to bob on the sea and be carried by the current. All their food is obtained by diving from the surface of the sea and consists mainly of crustaceans and small fish. Some species breed singly but others gather into huge colonies and their guano is responsible for the fertility of many small islands on which they breed. Fossil evidence suggests that auks are an ancient family. They probably evolved from a single ancestor which lived during the Eocene epoch (70–54 million years ago). Since 16 species breed in the North Pacific around the Bering Sea, this area would have been the most likely point from which the ancestral auks began to radiate and evolve into species. Five species breed in the North Atlantic but 12 are found nesting along the Arctic shores and this was probably the bridge along which auks moved from the North Pacific into the Atlantic. Before going into details of their classification, some discussion is required to explain the similarities in body shape between auks and penguins.

The 18 living species of penguin are all flightless and have evolved from ancestors which had the power of flight. We can tell this from the huge pectoral muscles attached to the breast-bone (called the *keel*). These drive the wings which function like powerful paddles. The efficiency of the wings is enhanced by the loss of the primary feathers. The webbed feet are trailed behind the bird as it swims and function efficiently as a rudder. Penguins walk ponderously but their strong toe nails enable them to get a firm grip on the ice. Adaptations to life in the cold Antarctic winters include curved overlapping down feathers and a thick layer of blubber under the skin which insulates the vital body organs. No species of penguin is native to the

Table 1 The Classification of Birds

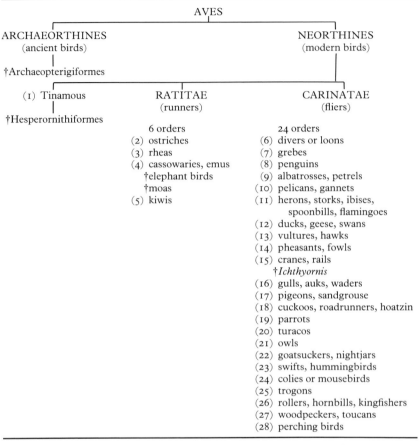

AVES

ARCHAEORTHINES
(ancient birds)

NEORTHINES
(modern birds)

†Archaeopterigiformes

(1) Tinamous

†Hesperornithiformes

RATITAE
(runners)

CARINATAE
(fliers)

6 orders
(2) ostriches
(3) rheas
(4) cassowaries, emus
 †elephant birds
 †moas
(5) kiwis

24 orders
(6) divers or loons
(7) grebes
(8) penguins
(9) albatrosses, petrels
(10) pelicans, gannets
(11) herons, storks, ibises,
   spoonbills, flamingoes
(12) ducks, geese, swans
(13) vultures, hawks
(14) pheasants, fowls
(15) cranes, rails
 †*Ichthyornis*
(16) gulls, auks, waders
(17) pigeons, sandgrouse
(18) cuckoos, roadrunners, hoatzin
(19) parrots
(20) turacos
(21) owls
(22) goatsuckers, nightjars
(23) swifts, hummingbirds
(24) colies or mousebirds
(25) trogons
(26) rollers, hornbills, kingfishers
(27) woodpeckers, toucans
(28) perching birds

Note only the living orders are numbered. Extinct groups are denoted thus †.

Table 2 Order Charadriiformes (Gulls, Auks, Waders)

Family	Common Name
Jacanidae	Jacanas
Rostratulidae	Painted snipe
Dromadidae	Crab Plover
Haematopodidae	Oystercatchers
Ibidorhynchidae	Ibis-bill
Recurvirostridae	Avocets, Stilts
Burhinidae	Stone curlews
Glareolidae	Coursers, Pratincoles
Charadriidae	Plovers
Scolopacidae	Sandpipers, Snipe
Thinocoridae	Seedsnipe
Chionididae	Sheathbills
Stercorariidae	Skuas
Laridae	Gulls, Terns
Rynchopidae	Skimmers
Alcidae	Auks

Northern Hemisphere and the equivalent niche in the Arctic regions is filled by the auks. The fact that there is a superficial resemblance between them is due to each group of birds finding a similar solution to the problems of feeding and breeding in icy conditions–a perfect example of what is termed convergent evolution. The smaller auks also show a remarkable resemblance to another group of Southern Hemisphere birds, the diving petrels.

An outline classification of the family Alcidae is given in Table 3 and it can be seen that we have either 22 or 23 species to consider, depending upon

Table 3 Classification and Distribution of Living Auks

Genus	Species	Sub-species	Distribution
Alle	*A. alle* little auk	*A. a. alle*	North Atlantic Ocean, New Jersey and western Europe
		A. a. polaris	Franz Josef Land, Barents Sea
Alca	*A. torda* razorbill	*A. t. pica*	North-east Canada and USA
		A. t. islandica	Iceland, Faroe Islands, British Isles
		A. t. torda	Baltic Sea islands
Uria	*U. lomvia* Brunnich's guillemot	*U. l. lomvia*	Arctic Sea and North Atlantic Ocean
		U. l. arra	Bering Sea and North Pacific Ocean
	U. aalge common guillemot	*U. a. aalge*	Labrador to Orkneys and Norway
		U. a. hyperborea	Bear Island
		U. a. spiloptera	Faroe Islands
		U. a. albionis	British Isles to Portugal
		U. a. intermedia	Baltic Sea islands
		U. a. inornata	Bering Sea and North Pacific Ocean
		U. a. californica	California
Cepphus	*C. grylle* black guillemot	*C. g. mandtii*	Arctic, Spitzbergen to north Greenland
		C. g. arcticus	North Labrador, south Greenland
		C. g. grylle	North Atlantic, Baltic and White Sea
	C. columba pigeon guillemot	*C. c. columba*	Bering Sea, North Pacific
		C. c. snowi Snow's guillemot	Kuril Island, north Hokkaido islands
	C. carbo spectacled guillemot	– – –	Kuril Island, Okhotsk Sea to north Japan
Brachyramphus	*B. marmoratus* marbled murrelet	*B. m. perdix*	Kamchatka to Kuril Island and Hokkaido Island
		B. m. marmoratus	Alaska to Canada
	B. brevirostris Kittlitz's murrelet	– – –	Bering Sea, North Pacific

* Some authorities classify Snow's guillemot as a separate species.

Genus	Species	Sub-species	Distribution
Brachyramphus cont'd	**B. hypoleucus* Xantus' murrelet	– – –	California and surrounding islands
	*B. craveri Craveri's murrelet		Gulf of California, Raza Island
Synthliboramphus	*S. antiquus* ancient murrelet or ancient auklet	– – –	Bering Sea, North Pacific Ocean
	S. wumizusume crested murrelet or Japanese auklet		Coast of Japan
Ptychoramphus	*P. aleuticus* Cassin's auklet	– – –	Aleutian Islands to southern California
Cyclorrhynchus	*C. psittacula* parakeet auklet	– – –	Bering Sea to North Pacific Ocean
Aethia	*A. cristatella* crested auklet	– – –	Bering Sea, North Pacific Ocean, eastern Siberia to Japan
	A. pusilla least auklet	– – –	Bering Sea, North Pacific Ocean
	A. pygmaea whiskered auklet	– – –	Kuril Islands, Aleutian Islands to northern Japan
Cerorhinca	*C. monocerata* rhinoceros auklet	– – –	Aleutian Islands and North Pacific coast
Fratercula	*F. arctica* Atlantic puffin	*F. a. naumanni* *F. a. arctica* *F. a. grabae*	Greenland to Novaya Zemlya North-east Canada to north Norway Faroe Islands, British Isles, southern Norway
	F. corniculata horned puffin	– – –	Bering Sea, North Pacific Ocean
Lunda	*Lunda cirrhata* tufted puffin	– – –	Bering Sea, North Pacific coast

* Some authorities place these two species in a separate genus *Endomychura*.
N.B. The great auk (*Pinguinis impennis*) has been extinct since the mid-nineteenth century.

which authority is consulted. Michael Walters (1980) in his *Complete Birds of the World* gives 23, allowing Snow's guillemot (*Cepphus snowi*) the full status of a species but points out that it may be a sub-species of the pigeon guillemot (*Cepphus columba snowi*), a view supported by Richard Howard and Alick Moore (1984). This is also the view expressed in the *Handbook of the Birds of Europe, the Middle East and North Africa* Volume 4 (Cramp *et al.*, 1984).

The simple mechanics of classification can easily be understood by reference to the Atlantic puffin, that attractive, colourful 'sea parrot' so beloved of coastal holiday makers, whether bird-watchers or not. Its scientific name is *Fratercula arctica*.

Each species is given a unique combination of two names so that it cannot be confused with any other organism. This name is universally used, whatever it may be called in the vernacular. In France, the species is known as *Macareux moine* and in Germany as *Papageitaucher* but all countries know it also as *Fratercula arctica*. Many birds vary slightly across their geographical ranges and these minor differences are often reflected by classifying them into sub-species. Thus we now recognise three sub-species of the Atlantic puffin. *Fratercula arctica naumanni* breeds from Greenland to Novaya Zemlya, *Fratercula arctica arctica* from north-eastern Canada to northern Norway and *Fratercula arctica grabae* from the Faroe Islands to Britain and southern Norway. Most taxonomists usually agree on what constitutes a species and it is at the sub-specific level that differences of opinion are likely to arise.

The second name should be written with a small initial letter – *arctica* – and is known as the specific name. The first name is termed the generic name and must be written with an initial capital letter as in *Fratercula*. Above the level of genus we have the family name. All auks belong to the family Alcidae. Family names end in -idae and are gathered together to produce an order, the name of which ends in -formes. The Alcidae belong to the order Charadriiformes (see Table 2).

Vertebrate animals are grouped into five classes: fish, amphibians, reptiles, birds (Aves) and mammals. Thus the Atlantic puffin found in Britain is classified as follows:

Class	Aves
Order	Charadriiformes
Sub-order	Alcae
Family	Alcidae
Genus	*Fratercula*
Species	*arctica*
Sub-species	*grabae*

As seen in Table 3, the Alcidae are classified into 12 genera. These are *Alle, Alca, Uria, Cepphus, Brachyramphus, Synthliboramphus, Ptychoramphus, Cyclorrhynchus, Aethia, Cerorhinca, Fratercula* and *Lunda*.

GENUS *Alle*

Only one species, the little auk (*Alle alle*) is contained in this genus. It breeds prolifically around the Arctic Ocean from Greenland to Franz Josef Land, the vast colonies of birds fighting for each nook and cranny in the towering cliffs. The rich summer vegetation on the tops of these cliffs is due entirely to the guano produced by the little auks. The wintering grounds are concentrated in the North Atlantic and, during abnormal weather conditions, 'auk wrecks' occur around the shores as far south as Britain. Two sub-species are recognised. *Alle alle alle* is widely distributed and is found for at least part of the year in the North Atlantic, western Europe and New Jersey. *Alle alle polaris* tends to be confined to Franz Josef Land and the Barents Sea. The little auk is described in Chapter 4.

GENUS *Alca*

At one time two species were included in the genus. The razorbill (*Alca torda*) is now the only species since the extinct great auk (*Pinguinus impennis*) was removed into its own genus. At one time its scientific name was *Alca impennis* and, on first sight, it does look like an enormous flightless razorbill. A full description of the great auk is given in Chapter 3.

The razorbill is basically a North Atlantic species which breeds in relatively small colonies on cliff ledges. Three sub-species are recognised at the present time. *Alca torda pica* is the variety found in north-eastern Canada and the north-eastern USA. *Alca torda islandica* is the species which breeds in the British Isles, the Faroe Islands and Iceland whilst *Alca torda torda* is confined to the islands in the Baltic Sea. The razorbill is described in Chapter 5.

GENUS *Uria*

Two species make up this genus: Brunnich's guillemot (*Uria lomvia*) and the common guillemot (*Uria aalge*). The former is found along the coasts and islands of the Arctic, North Atlantic and the North Pacific Oceans, nesting colonially on cliff ledges. Two sub-species are usually recognised namely *Uria lomvia lomvia*, which occurs in the Arctic and North Atlantic, and *Uria lomvia arra*, which is found in the Bering Sea and also in the North Pacific. Brunnich's guillemot, often also called the thick-billed murre, is described in Chapter 6.

The common guillemot (*Uria aalge*) is also known as the common murre. It occurs in both the North Pacific and North Atlantic Oceans and often collects in huge breeding colonies on the ledges of cliffs, as well as on the flat tops of stacks. The precise number of sub-species has been the subject of some difference of opinion, but most modern authorities settle for seven. *Uria aalge aalge* occurs from Labrador to the Orkneys and Norway. *Uria aalge hyperborea* is confined to Bear Island, although more work is necessary to establish if this is indeed a discrete breeding population. *Uria aalge spiloptera* breeds on the Faroe Islands, *Uria aalge albionis* ranges from the British Isles to Portugal, and *Uria aalge intermedia* is found on islands in the Baltic. *Uria aalge inornata* is found along the North Pacific and around the Bering Sea whilst the final sub-species occurs along the Californian coast and is appropriately known as *Uria aalge californica*. The common guillemot is also described in Chapter 6 and some effort is made to reduce the confusing number of sub-species to five.

GENUS *Cepphus*

This genus is represented by only three species, the first being the black guillemot (*Cepphus grylle*) which is known over most of its range as the tystie. It occurs in both the Arctic and North Atlantic Oceans and nests in quite small colonies, each pair seeking out a sheltered crevice in which the two eggs (most auks lay only one) are laid.

At present three sub-species are recognised. *Cepphus grylle mandtii* breeds around the Arctic but also around the coasts of northern Greenland and the island complexes of Spitzbergen. *Cepphus grylle arcticus* breeds in southern Greenland and northern Labrador whilst *Cepphus grylle grylle* is the species breeding in the North Atlantic, the Baltic and the White Sea. The black guillemot is the subject of Chapter 7, along with the two other species which make up the genus *Cepphus*. These are the pigeon guillemot (*Cepphus columba*) and the spectacled or dusky guillemot (*Cepphus carbo*).

The pigeon guillemot is a species breeding in the North Pacific from Kamchatka to California and, like the tystie, prefers to incubate its two eggs in a sheltered crevice of a cliff. Two sub-species are recognised. *Cepphus columba columba* is found in the Bering Sea and along the North Pacific coast whilst *Cepphus columba snowi* breeds on the islands of north Hokkaido and Kuril.

The spectacled guillemot, which has no sub-species, also breeds on Kuril Island, but spreads into the Okhotsk Sea to northern Japan.

GENUS *Brachyramphus*

This genus is made up of four species, usually referred to as murrelets, which are the subject of Chapter 8. These comprise the marbled murrelet (*Brachyramphus marmoratus*), Kittlitz's murrelet (*Brachyramphus brevirostris*), Xantus' murrelet (*Brachyramphus hypoleucus*) and Craveri's murrelet (*Brachyramphus craveri*).

The marbled murrelet is found along the coast of the North Pacific and also on the islands and, most unusually for an auk, prefers to nest on a branch of a forest tree. Two sub-species are recognised: *Brachyramphus marmo-*

ratus marmoratus is found from Alaska to California and *Brachyramphus marmoratus perdix* is distributed from Kamchatka to Kuril Island and also breeds on the island of Hokkaido.

There are no sub-species of Kittlitz's murrelet, which is found from eastern Siberia, the Aleutians as far west as Japan, the Bering Sea and the North Pacific Ocean. Its preferred nest site is on the bare rock high up on mountain cliffs.

Xantus' murrelet breeds along the Californian coast and particularly on its offshore islands, siting its nest in the shelter of bushes or in rocky hollows. There are no sub-species, as is also the case with Craveri's murrelet which breeds among rocks around the Gulf of California and on Raza Island.

GENUS *Synthliboramphus*

This genus is made up of two species of murrelets, which are described in detail in Chapter 8. The ancient murrelet (*Synthliboramphus antiquus*) sites its nest in cracks in rocks and small burrows, the colonies of birds being quite small. These occur from the Bering Sea as far south as California, Japan and on islands in the North Pacific. It is sometimes called the ancient auklet and there are no sub-species. The crested murrelet (*Synthliboramphus wumizusume*) breeds around the coast of Japan. It is often called the Japanese auklet and there are no sub-species.

GENUS *Ptychoramphus*

The auklets which make up this and the following three genera are species which merit a deeper study than they have been given hereto. They are five or six species altogether, according to the authority consulted, and five are described in Chapter 9.

Cassin's auklet (*Ptychoramphus aleuticus*) is the only representative of the genus and there are no sub-species. It breeds on the Aleutian Islands and along the Pacific Coast of North America as far as southern California, nesting in burrows and cracks in rocks.

GENUS *Cyclorrhynchus*

Again there is only one species in the genus. The parakeet auklet (*Cyclorrhynchus psittacula*) is basically a bird of the North Pacific and the Aleutian Islands. No sub-species have been recognised although it is also known as the parrakeet auk. It sites its nest under driftwood and stones but it may also choose crevices in rocks. The species is described in Chapter 9.

GENUS *Aethia*

Three species make up this order of auklets. These are the crested auklet

(*Aethia cristatella*), least auklet (*Aethia pusilla*) and the whiskered auklet (*Aethia pygmaea*). None of the three have been separated into sub-species.

The crested auklet breeds throughout eastern Siberia southwards to Wrangell Island and winters as far south as Japan. The chosen nest site is usually among stones or cracks in rocks. The least auklet occurs around the Bering Sea and the North Pacific and is another typical auk in seeking out rock crevices in which to breed. This is also true of the small colonies of the whiskered auklet which occurs on Kuril and the Aleutian Islands and as far as northern Japan. This species also breeds on the Commander Islands and Kamchatka. All three are described in Chapter 9.

GENUS *Cerorhinca*

Only the rhinoceros auklet (*Cerorhinca monocerata*) is included in this genus and its range extends from the Aleutian Islands down the coastline of the North Pacific where it breeds in burrows in the coastal soil. There is no doubt that this bird should be regarded as a puffin rather than an auklet and it is therefore described in Chapter 10.

GENUS *Fratercula*

This genus includes two of the three species of puffin, all of which are described in Chapter 10. These are the Atlantic puffin (*Fratercula arctica*) and the horned puffin (*Fratercula corniculata*). The Atlantic puffin is found throughout the Arctic and North Atlantic Oceans and breeds often in huge colonies sited in burrows which they are able to dig themselves if a suitable site is not available. There are three sub-species: *Fratercula arctica naumanni* occurs from Greenland to Novaya Zemlya; *Fratercula arctica arctica* occupies nest sites from north-east Canada to northern Norway and *Fratercula arctica grabae* occurs in the British Isles, the Faroe Islands and southern Norway.

GENUS *Lunda*

The tufted puffin (*Lunda cirrhata*) is the only species in the genus and there are no sub-species. It occurs around the Bering Sea and along the coast of the North Pacific. It may also be found in Arctic Siberia, east as far as the Aleutian Islands and the south-east of Alaska. The tufted puffin is described in Chapter 10. Like the Atlantic puffin, this species lays its single egg in a substantial burrow.

Thus we have 23 species to describe, but before doing this it is necessary to devote a chapter to the biology and ecology of auks in general.

2

BIOLOGY AND ECOLOGY

Auks and their eggs have been part of the human diet for centuries but it is only in recent years that so many features of their often bizarre life-style have been discovered. The word 'auk' derives from the old Norse word (*ālka*) for some of the species and reflects the noise they make with a fair degree of accuracy.

EXTERNAL ANATOMY OF AUKS

As we have seen, auks are the ecological counterparts of the Southern Hemisphere penguins – both groups have greatly reduced wings which they use to swim under water in pursuit of prey. Auks are small- to medium-sized birds with short tails and small, but still functional, wings. Unlike penguins, all modern auks can fly, although the much larger great auk could not. In fact the size of their wings is a compromise. They are large enough for flying but small enough to work efficiently in the much denser medium of water. This accounts for the rapid wing beat and whirring flight which are common to all of them. A look at the skeleton of the wing reveals that the humerus is significantly longer than the ulna. Although the wing is short, the tip is comparatively long and pointed, and this makes it efficient as both a flying and a swimming organ.

The legs of the majority of auks (see accounts of individual species) are positioned towards the rear of the body which accounts for their upright posture. Some species, including the puffins, walk on their toes, as do most birds, but the murres (guillemots) and razorbills walk on their tarsal bones. In the four genera of *Cepphus*, *Aethia*, *Fratercula* and *Lunda*, the post-acetabular portion of the pelvis is broad. This provides a firm base to allow efficient running but also gives enough leverage to make digging, using the sharp claws, very efficient indeed. The legs of auks are slightly compressed laterally, an adaptation for swimming, although this feature is much more evident in the shearwaters and grebes. The three toes are connected by webs, thus increasing swimming efficiency.

Bill shape also varies a great deal in the auks which is clearly a reflection of diet and feeding methods. It is a well-established rule that no two species can survive in the same habitat and eat the same food without one or the other becoming extinct. Each auk therefore ensures its own ecological niche by having a bill adapted to handling prey items different from those of other auks. The large and colourful bill of the Atlantic puffin also plays an important role in the formation of pairs. Close examination reveals that the bill is made up of nine plates which, most unusually, are shed each year during the moult. Outside the breeding season, the bill is therefore a lot smaller and less colourful, a fact which often leads to some confusion regarding identification. It does not, however, result in any loss of feeding efficiency since the tongue is covered with spines and the inside of the upper mandible of the bill is serrated. This combination allows up to 50 sand-eels to be carried crossways in the bill, a feat often witnessed at the breeding colonies when the adults are returning to feed their young deep in their burrows.

All auks have distinctive winter plumages, some of which can be startlingly different. Both the black guillemot and the pigeon guillemot are black with a prominent white wing patch in summer but, during the winter, they are grey and white, although still very attractive. Some of the auklets, the whiskered auklet for example, have long head plumes during the breeding season from which they derive their vernacular names. These plumes are lost during the winter. Both Kittlitz's murrelet and the marbled murrelet have a dull brown breeding plumage which gives a good measure of protection to the incubating birds whilst, in the winter, the birds are dark grey above and white below. It is interesting to speculate why a similarly even brown plumage would not suffice for winter. I believe that fish looking up are less likely to see the murrelets' pale underparts against the sky and thus the feeding efficiency of the birds is substantially increased which must, in turn, increase the survival potential. The dark grey upper plumage blends well with the sea and any potential avian predator hovering above the sea will be less likely to spot the birds in the water. Thus the two separate plumages have great survival value.

MOULT AND FEATHER MAINTENANCE

Most auks enter the period of moult soon after the breeding season has ended, the largest members of the family being flightless during the time when the flight feathers are moulted. In contrast, the smaller auks are able to moult their flight feathers one at a time without losing too much efficiency. The reason for this difference can be explained in terms of wing loading (the ratio of body weight to wing size). In the larger, and therefore heavier, auks, which include the guillemots and razorbill, the birds are flightless for as long as 6 weeks, during which time all the flight feathers are moulted together. The smaller auks follow the more usual avian pattern of undergoing a *sequential moult* during which the flight feathers are replaced one by one, enabling the birds to retain the ability to fly. For the larger auks, flight is already very demanding in terms of energy expenditure and any further reduction in efficiency would be far too expensive in terms of food (energy).

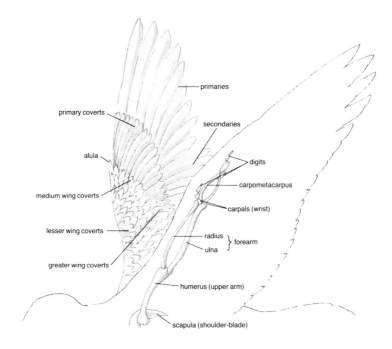

primaries

primary coverts

secondaries

alula

digits

carpometacarpus

medium wing coverts

carpals (wrist)

lesser wing coverts

radius

forearm

ulna

greater wing coverts

humerus (upper arm)

scapula (shoulder-blade)

Bird's wing showing feather structure and bones.

Flight is not the only function carried out by feathers and there are four basic types, namely contour, down, plumes and bristles. *Contour* feathers include both those which give the body its shape and the *flight* feathers which are carried on the forelimbs. The *primary* feathers are supported on bones equivalent to the human hand whilst the *secondaries* are attached to the area of the ulna bone between the elbow and the wrist. The bird's wing is a much more flexible structure than is often imagined. Each feather has a tapering shaft, called the *rachis*, bearing a flexible *vane* on each side. The base of the feather is called the *calamus* and it has a hollow bottom called the *lower umbilicus*, through which the blood supply enters the feather during its short growing period. When growth is complete, the feather is sealed off and is then dead, although each feather can be moved by its own muscle buried in the skin. During the moult each feather is pushed out by the new feather growing from the follicle below it. The solid rachis carries the vanes of the feather, each of which is composed of a row of *barbs* which are linked together by tiny hook-like structures called *barbules*. These can be linked together to produce a smooth surface or 'unzipped' to allow the bird to get at the feather during preening, which is essential if the feathers are to do their job effectively and keep the bird alive. Auks have 11 primary feathers on each wing but the last is so minute that it has little function. There are between 16 and 21 secondary feathers, the primaries and secondaries together being called the *remiges*, whereas the tail feathers, of which auks have between 12 and 16, are called the *retrices*. The genus *Cerorhinca*, i.e. the rhinoceros auklet, is unique in having 18 tail feathers.

The *down* feathers are vital to protect the bird against cold and the efficient insulation they provide enables auks to withstand the often freezing conditions in which they thrive. All down feathers have a rachis but they lack barbules and are not zipped together like the contour feathers. In the auks and the wildfowl, the down feathers are packed tightly together and air is trapped between them, adding to the efficiency of the insulation they provide. They are kept in first-class condition and their waterproofing is maintained by the application of 'preen oil' produced from a gland situated above the tail. This gland can be seen in a chicken and is known as the parson's nose. Auks have such efficient *uropygial glands*, as the oil stores are technically called, that their bodies gleam. Whilst watching a raft of common guillemots diving off the Farne Islands in Northumberland, England, the water was clear enough for me to see the silvery bubbles of air trapped beneath the sleek well-oiled feathers of the birds as they dived.

As you would expect, the oil glands of auks are quite large. They are tuft-shaped structures with at least three openings on each side, allowing liberal doses of oil to be delivered quickly. It has been suggested that the oil gland could have a second function, namely the provision of Vitamin D. This is an anti-rickets sterol which is found in fish-liver oils and requires to be irradiated with ultra-violet light (which is present in sunlight) to be effective. It is essential for the proper formation of bones and the suggestion is that birds, in the process of spreading the oil on the feathers, may ingest Vitamin D or may even consume it on purpose after the oil has been exposed to sunlight. The main function of the oil, however, must surely be as a water repellent.

There are two types of *plume* feathers. *Semi-plumes* are intermediate between contour and down feathers, the rachis always being longer than any of the barbs. They occur between the tracts of contour feathers and seal any gaps through which heat could be lost. The *filoplumes* look like hairs and act rather like triggers, telling the bird when other feathers are out of position and thus initiating the preening process. *Bristles*, which are even more hair-like, are specialised feathers which have a stiff rachis and few if any barbs. They often function as eyelashes.

INTERNAL ANATOMY OF AUKS

Birds which dive into water and often land on it at high speed must have other anatomical features in addition to feathers to allow them to cope with the stresses of this jarring impact. How, for example, does the body handle the shock of landing, and how do the internal organs cope with the increased pressure as the bird dives?

Watch an auk skim across the surface and then plunge clumsily into the water. I've seen this many a time and wondered why no bones are broken. Certainly a mammal would never cope with these stresses, but then they have a far greater number of separate vertebrae making up their backbone. In birds, the vertebrae are fused together to produce a resiliant rod. This is attached to the pelvic girdle and so provides an even greater resistance to the shock of landing. The *sternum* (breast-bone) is also much stronger than the equivalent bone in a mammal. The avian sternum is drawn out into a deep structure called the *keel* to which are attached the powerful flight muscles. These muscles, which in chickens form the breast meat, are so large that they function very well as a second shock-absorbing system during landing.

Now we come to the second problem faced by the auks. Having survived the sudden blow of the impact of landing how can they cope with the slow squeeze of water pressure as they dive and swim in search of food? Seals have solved this problem by having a very flexible rib cage which 'gives' under pressure and springs back as the animal comes towards the surface with the subsequent reduction in pressure. In the auks, the solution to the problem is quite the reverse. The ribs connect the sternum to the vertebral column and the strength formed by this box is increased by structures called *uncinate processes* which look rather like miniature deer antlers. They fold back from one rib and overlap the next, being held in place by strong muscles. These uncinate processes are a unique feature of birds and, in the auks, they are particularly effective and provide a very rigid box inside which the heart and lungs can continue to function efficiently at depths where the water pressure is very high. The auks are therefore able to pursue their food in areas which other families of birds are unable to penetrate. Thus the auk family has its own niche and the variation of bill shape discussed earlier in this chapter ensures that no two species are in direct competition.

FEEDING

Watching auks feed at depths is obviously an almost impossible task and most of what we know of their diets has been obtained by direct observations on adults bringing food to their young. This is obviously time-consuming and some insight into diet has been obtained more quickly by killing birds on the feeding grounds and analysing their stomach contents. To many of us in this conservation-minded period these short cuts are not to be encouraged unless the knowledge so obtained can be used to preserve more birds than have been killed.

Auks seem to be either plankton-eaters or fish-eaters. Only the little auk in the North Atlantic feeds exclusively on plankton whilst, in the North Pacific, the number of species tapping the plankton supply is six. It is interesting to note that plankton-feeding whales are also more numerous with regard to both species and populations in the North Pacific than they are in the North Atlantic. Biologists have analysed the plankton in both

The common guillemot (right) carries its food headfirst whilst both the spectacled guillemot (left) and the razorbill (centre) transport prey to their young held cross-wise in the bill.

regions and found a far greater quantity, which they refer to as the *biomass*, in the Pacific. With more food to go round, the auks have not been slow to evolve more species to utilise the resource. Bedard (1969a) suggested that auks may have had a plankton-feeding ancestor from which the larger fish-eaters evolved. Because they dive, the fish-eaters have thicker more power-ful skeletons and a larger body size typical of the guillemots. If the plankton-eaters are to provide food for their young they require pouches to carry it in. Both the ancient murrelet and Xantus' murrelet lack this pouch and this may well account for the comparatively short nestling stage. No other sea birds take to the sea as early as their second day out of the egg, as is the case with the murrelets.

It is tempting to suggest that a combination of body size and bill shape ensures a clean-cut feeding niche for each species without any competition at all. This may well be the end result of evolution, but the process is on-going and, at present, there may be some competition between the fish-eaters. This is particularly apparent where the range of the common guil-lemot overlaps with that of Brunnich's guillemot, otherwise known as the thick-billed murre.

A journey from the open sea will tell us a great deal about the preferences of feeding auks. With huge waves breaking over the prow of the boat, and the swell rolling her, our binoculars pick out shearwaters and petrels sweeping low over the water, but very few auks diving from the surface. As the boat approaches the shelter of island and coast, the auks are found feeding in the coastal waters. Those which are not in pursuit of plankton soup are chasing fish in order to build up their energy reserves and to face the pressures of the breeding season followed by the moult and, beyond this, in preparation for the tough northern winter.

Eating is one thing but what about drinking? How do sea birds like the auks cope with having to drink sea water since they never come in to contact with supplies of fresh water? Many birds have a salt gland sited just above the eye which is able to extract salt from the blood and excrete it *via* a duct through the nostril. This means that, if the bird drinks sea water and excretes concentrated sea water, it can maintain its salt balance and does not need to have a supply of fresh water. The salt gland is nature's own desalinating plant. Birds do not normally sneeze and they get rid of the liquid by vigorously shaking their heads.

THE BREEDING CYCLE

Birds in general, and auks in particular, have been forced to adopt either a solitary nesting habit aimed at concealment or a 'safety in numbers' strategy which enables them to face their predators. Auks seem to have decided on the latter policy and only the marbled murrelet and Kittlitz's murrelet breed as solitary pairs, although in other species the colonies may be small and rather loose, as is the case with both the black guillemot and the pigeon guillemot. These species must breed inshore and be as close as possible to a predictable supply of food. The colonial species can afford to hunt further afield since there are many more individuals available to search, and a successful hunter will soon attract others to share in the bounty. Around the breeding colonies, it is often possible to trace flight lines of birds leading out to the feeding grounds. I have watched this with the puffins of St Kilda and the guillemots of the Farne Islands and it is especially true of the little auk in the high Arctic where the colonies consist of millions rather than thousands of birds.

After the breeding season, young auks disperse widely from the colony and do not return to breed themselves until they are a minimum of 3 years old. Providing the ice has receded, auks often return to their natal colony months before breeding actually begins, spending the time in finding last year's partner and, in the case of some of the auklets and the puffins, by tidying up the nest burrows. Although a pair of auks do not spend the winter together, it is quite usual for the same pair to breed together for many years, each remaining faithful to the nest site. This is quite understandable in the

Where auks are found breeding in the same area, various species select a particular niche. Puffins (top) show a preference for the grassy tops of cliffs into which they can burrow. Common guillemots (second row, left) are able to breed on surprisingly narrow and exposed ledges. Black guillemots (second row, right) seek out crevices in the rocks while the razorbill (third row) selects sites under overhanging cliffs and does not like being splashed by spray. Members of other families, including the shags (bottom) do not seem to mind being soaked with spray.

case of the auklets and puffins which nest in burrows with recognisable physical features, but much more confusing in the case of thick-billed murres and guillemots where, to human eyes at least, the site is a small area of cliff top or rocky ledge. The act of mating is often a very noisy affair and occurs frequently. In the puffins, copulations may occur at sea, but it is more usual among auks for this to occur at the nest site itself.

Just as we saw when considering feeding niches, there is both inter- and intra-specific competition for nesting sites which, in the case of auks, can be very much at a premium.Cliffs towering out of the sea offer several types of possible nesting habitat. Auks searching for sites will find the lower reaches, with flat-topped stacks splashed by waves, already commandeered by the much larger shags (*Phalacrocorax aristotelis*) whilst higher grassy areas are taken by colonies of cormorants (*Phalacrocorax carbo*), which can be distinguished from the shags by the white thigh patch present during the breeding season, white on the throat and the lack of either a crest or yellow around the mouth. The huge gannets (*Sula bassana*) are much too aggressive to be challenged but the presence of the much more docile kittiwakes (*Rissa tridactyla*) and fulmars (*Fulmarus glacialis*) will allow the auks to prospect quite close to their sites.

Common guillemots gather along ledges and on the top of rocky stacks in huge numbers and the tighter they are packed the more successful they seem to be. If Brunnich's guillemots are found in the same area, they tend to seek out much smaller ledges and the colonies are much smaller. This strategy is also followed by razorbills which seek out tiny projections, ledges and cracks so that they do not always seem to be colonial and are more difficult to count than many other auk species. This is even more true of the enchanting black guillemots which seek out holes in rocks and scree or select a small overhang away from the hordes of competitors for space. In their breeding grounds of the high Arctic, millions of little auks seek out crevices in which to lay their egg away from the wind, which can be strong and cold, even in the summer. The puffins have tapped yet another niche and dig burrows with their powerful feet and lay their egg underground.

The eggs of auks are huge and are never less than 10% of the female's body weight and are frequently over twice this figure, up to a maximum of 23%. Watching a common guillemot hatching its egg one is left wondering how the female was able to deliver the egg without severe injury! Auks which nest in burrows produce mainly white eggs with an occasional individual with dark markings indicating that the ancestral bird laid its egg in the open. This is still the case with both the marbled murrelet and Kittlitz's murrelet which produce olive-green eggs blotched with dark brown. Both these species nest out in the open and the eggs do need a good degree of camouflage. The clutch size of all sea birds is to a large extent determined by the availability of food. The black and pigeon guillemots lay two eggs and, as they breed close to the shore, can manage to keep the young supplied with regular supplies of food.

The young are often hatched at an advanced stage of development and can soon make their way out to sea and find food. In the Pacific, the young of the four murrelets (crested, Craveri's, ancient and Xantus') leave the nest when only 2 days old and follow their parents to the feeding grounds. This may very well account for the large size of the eggs which provide sufficient food to supply a very large youngster. It is interesting to note that the feet of these youngsters are huge and no doubt act as very efficient paddles which do a great deal to help them swim against powerful currents and into large waves.

Some birds are hatched naked and remain helpless in the nest for a long time, as is the case with the song birds such as the blackbird (*Turdus merula*) and the American robin (*Turdus migratorius*); this condition is termed *nidicolous*. Others, the wildfowl for example, hatch from the egg with good vision and covered with down. They are termed *precocial*. Where do auks fit in this scheme? No other family shows such a range from the nidicolous stage to the almost totally precocial, as is the case with the Pacific murrelets. The majority of auks, including the black guillemot, auklets and the puffins, produce young which are *semi-precocial*. They have an ample covering of down and do not therefore require their parents to brood them and their eyes are also fully functional on hatching. They do, however, require food from their parents for periods of between 1 and 2 months, depending upon the species. The razorbill, common murre and the thick-billed murre show an intermediate condition where the young leave the nest site after a period of around 3 weeks and set off to the open sea, usually with the male in attendance, when only around one quarter of the adult size. This saves the parents the tiring and energy-consuming journey between the feeding area and the nest site. The period during which the young abandon the breeding cliffs is one of the most exciting for naturalists with the time to sit around and watch the chicks as they prepare to leave the site, which can be 300 metres (1,000 feet) above the rocks washed by the sea. It is always dangerous to ascribe human emotions to birds, but whilst I was watching young razorbills preparing to set off for sea around the Treshnish Islands off Mull, they seemed to be calling 'Weel-go, Weel-go' and then, suddenly, they went. As they plummeted down, they fluttered their tiny wings which proved efficient enough to at least break their fall, although the anatomical adaptations discussed above are certainly given an early and stringent test.

Once independent, young auks seldom make any effort to return to their natal colony before their third summer. This, plus the fact that they lay only one egg or, at the most, two, means that auks must be particularly vulnerable should any catastrophe overtake them. If a catastrophe, such as a large oil spill, should affect the breeding grounds, it may take as long as 20 years for the numbers to recover. Song birds, which produce large clutches and may produce two or three broods in one season, are able to recover from population declines of up to 50% in the following two breeding seasons. Auks do, generally speaking, live for a long time, occasionally as long as 40 years.

There are records of thick-billed murres and common murres ringed as chicks and still breeding in their natal colonies over 20 years later.

RINGING

The contribution made by bird-ringers to the knowledge of bird movements, population make-up and life-span cannot be overestimated. Ringing (or banding) has been organised on a scientific basis since the early years of the twentieth century. Each ring consists of thin strips of a lightweight alloy, usually with an aluminium base for small birds or a nickel one for larger species, including the auks. The ring is secured around the leg by gentle pressure from specially designed banding pliers. Each ring is individually numbered and bears the address of the ringing scheme to which it is hoped the ring will be returned.

A great deal of research has been done, and remains to be done, on the correct metals to use for the rings and where to attach them. In the case of auks, which spend most of their time in the sea, the solutions are even more difficult to find than usual because sea water has a corrosive effect on the rings, due to the electrical current set up between the metal and the chemicals in the water. The ring also needs to be hard-wearing to withstand the friction of scrambling over rocks whilst territory is being established and successful breeding accomplished. Research workers are now ringing not just one leg but both. They always use the metal ring, but also they often add coloured rings of tough plastic. By using a combination of colours and ringing both legs, the researcher can indicate the year of ringing, the sex of the bird and the colony at which the bird was banded. This can allow birds at sea to be identified even if the individuals are not handled. Some birds may be caught alive either at the nest site or perhaps oiled, or caught in a fishing net. These are called 'controls' in contrast to birds found dead and bearing a ring. The more publicity which can be given to the value of ringing the better, since anyone finding a dead bird bearing a ring will be encouraged to return it. Many beachcombers find dead auks and read the ring number and send it to the correct address. Ideally the ring should be removed, wrapped in tissue and sent with the letter. This will give ring designers a chance to assess the wear and tear on the ring and, when sufficient data is to hand, enable them to improve the design. The finder of the ring should always include details such as how the bird died (if known) and whether it was freshly dead or decayed, as well as their own address. In exchange for the trouble taken, the finder receives details of where the bird was ringed, its age, sex and the name of the ringer.

The only value of ringing comes from *returned* rings and it is essential to the study of distribution and migration routes. The time lapse between ringing and recovery gives an indication of how long birds live. During the process of ringing, the bird is held in the hand and it can be accurately weighed and measured. Fortunately the handling and banding of birds is strictly controlled and a ringing permit and licence are essential. Most ringers are amateur ornithologists, although a number of universities are also actively engaged on ringing programmes. No other branch of ornithology demonstrates the interdependence of amateurs and professionals of all countries so much as ringing. Even during the last war there was an exchange of rings between German and British bird scientists *via* the diplomatic bags going in and out of Dublin in the Irish Republic.

A knowledge of the biology and movements of auks is essential if the family is not to lose some of the more vulnerable species. Birds which nest in such packed masses can be vulnerable and this was certainly the reason for the demise of the great auk. My own love of auks stemmed from the amateur side of ornithology. Sailing in small boats around these sea-bird cities, with the smell of guano mingling with the brine of the sea and the sound of wings and birds arguing over space, leads to an irresistible urge to sit among them and study their every movement. This in turn leads to an even more irresistible urge to protect them.

3

GREAT AUK

It is perhaps surprising in view of our recent attitude to conservation that only one species of bird in western Europe has become extinct during the last 150 years. This is the great auk, once known as the garefowl. In Yarrell's *History of British Birds*, first published in 1843, and the *Manual of British Birds Complete* by William Macgillivray of 1846, the species is described as rare.

It was Macgillivray who first stimulated me to begin a serious study of auks, especially the fascinating folklore which surrounds them. I had purchased a first edition in a book shop in Oban just before setting off on my first visit to the island group of St Kilda, calling in on many of the isolated seabird cities *en route*. The trip from the Sound of Harris took over 6 hours, even in our comfortably re-fitted trawler. The day was mild, the grey sea still but a mist hung low over the water, making bird-watching impossible. I therefore opened my book and read Macgillivray's fascinating account of *Alca impennis*, as he called the garefowl from its superficial resemblance to a very large razorbill (*Alca torda*). He noted that:

This species is met with in high latitudes, along the coasts of both continents, but not in great numbers. A few individuals have been seen about the Islands of St. Kilda and our north-eastern islands. One was captured in 1822, but made its escape. The habits of this remarkable bird are little known. It is supposed rather than observed to be incapable of flying.

I had just finished reading the section when a call from the skipper announced that the freshening breeze had driven away much of the mist and there, rising out of the sea, were the craggy stacks and islands which make up St Kilda, one-time home of the garefowl, which more closely resembled a penguin than any other species of auk. Indeed the word penguin was first used to describe the garefowl and was then applied to the penguins of the Southern Hemisphere by sailors who had sailed the northern seas and saw their similarity to the great auk.

Abandoned by its human population in 1930, St Kilda, grouped with the main island of Hirta, once supported a thriving community. The outlying islands are Soay, Dun, Levenish and Boreray overlooked by the towering stacks of Lee and Armin. All these and the main island itself abound in sea birds. The seas around are treacherous and it is not surprising that the islanders' economy was based totally on sea birds. Gannets (*Sula bassana*) and fulmars (*Fulmarus glacialis*), as well as the huge populations of auks, were eagerly farmed and the St Kildans became very adept cliff-cimbers. When Victorian tourists discovered the islanders it was said that the 'natives' had an extra 'prehensile toe' which enabled them to climb the steepest of cliffs. They always seemed to be able to catch sufficient for their needs, despite the fact that the birds are such mobile creatures. There were many island economies based on sea birds on both sides of the Atlantic and it is no wonder that the large flightless garefowl with its tasty flesh and huge nutritious egg was hunted to extinction. There is every reason to suppose that it was once present in large numbers and the historian-traveller Martin Martin, writing in 1697, was able to report that the garefowl was suffering from over-exploitation. He mentions its value not only as food, but also as a source of valuable feathers. In addition, its fatty body could be rendered down and used in oil lamps during the long northern winter nights.

A very comprehensive account of the garefowl was given by William Yarrell in 1843 and it is on this that the following account is based. Yarrell's *History of British Birds* was updated by Howard Saunders, who edited the fourth edition of the work published in 1885. He observed that:

The great auk was described as a very rare British Bird when the 1st Edition of this work was published in 1843, but in all probability neither the Author nor the majority of the ornithologists of that generation suspected that the destruction of the last-known individuals of the species was even then on the point of accomplishment. Another forty years have elapsed since the latest authenticated examples were obtained on Eldey near Iceland, and there can now be little doubt that this species must be added to the number of those which have been exterminated by the agency of man; but inasmuch as the species, so long as it survived, was thoroughly entitled to a place on the British list, the present Edition would be incomplete without a notice of it, albeit 'In Memoriam'.

Field Description

Macgillivray (1840) provides us with a description which reads as if he had observed a living specimen or at least communicated with a keen and competent observer.

Length about thirty inches; wings diminutive, with the quills scarcely longer than their coverts; the tail short, of fourteen feathers; bill rather longer than the head, black with eight or nine white grooves on the upper, ten or twelve on the lower mandible; the head, neck and upper parts black, the throat and sides of the neck tinged with chocolate-brown, the wings with greyish-brown, the upper parts glossed with green; the lower parts, and a large oblong spot before each eye, with the tips of the secondary quills, white.

The great auk, extinct since the 1840s, looked more penguin-like than any other auk species.

In his account of his visit to St Kilda in 1753, Martin Martin writes that the garefowl is 'of a black colour, red about the eyes'. This would seem to suggest that red eye rims were part of the breeding season's ornaments. In his plate of the species in *The Birds of America*, Audubon does show a dark orbital ring, but doubtless he worked from skins in which the red colour may well have faded.

The remains of the great auk have been discovered by archaeologists in kitchen middens and cave deposits all around north-western Europe and even as far south as the Mediterranean, and there is no doubt that the species was once a very important source of food. Researches have so far revealed only eight positive breeding sites although the addition of possible breeding sites gives us at least 20 colonies, some of which seem to have been very large indeed. The main congregations appear to have been around Newfoundland and, in 1534, the explorer Jacques Cartier and his men must have found the fresh food supply most welcome. There are later accounts which describe the flightless birds being driven onto vessels and kept alive to provide food for the crew during long voyages. The supply was so ruthlessly exploited that the garefowl had disappeared from Newfoundland by 1800 while, on the European side of the Atlantic, its fate had been sealed. In 1939, Kenneth

Williamson traced the history of the great auk on both sides of the Atlantic and his work was published in the *Journal of the Manx Museum* (Volume 61).

Williamson's detective work began with a viewing of two crude colour-wash drawings of birds, one clearly of a gannet, the other of a great auk. These pictures were copies of original sepia drawings now in the possession of the British Museum (Natural History). The drawings have been reliably dated to 1651 or 1652 and, as such, this is the earliest delineation of the great auk. Williamson pointed out that, although misshapen, there is no doubt that the picture shows the species in breeding plumage.

The distinguishing features – the shape of the bill and the transverse grooves on both mandibles, the white oval patch (here almost triangular) between the bill and the eye, the dark upper and white underparts, and the extremely small wing – have all been faithfully emphasised by the artist, who, however, appears to have overlooked the white tips to the secondary wing-feathers, whilst the normal carriage is said to have been stately and very erect.

The caption to the figure originally read 'Theis kind of birds are aboute the Isle of Man', but the two words 'Theis' and 'aboute' were altered (apparently by the same hand) to conform with a more orthodox spelling. Three lightly pencilled words are written on the drawing, two in relation to the bill and one to the legs, all denoting colour. 'Yellow' and 'red' refer to the bill, the latter indicating the grooves, and 'black' to the feet. No colours appear in the original sepia drawing, and Mr E. G. Millar, Deputy Keeper of MSS. and the British Museum, is of the opinion that the pencilled indications were probably put in by some early nineteenth century antiquary.

There can be no doubt that these additions were made by someone who thought that the bird depicted was a puffin and this misled many who looked at the colour copies and had no access to the original. In his *Birds of the Isle of Man*, P.G. Ralfe (1905) fell into the same trap – or did he – since he did mention that the picture showed 'the white spot before the eye, something after the fashion of the Great Auk'.

It is known that Daniel King was the engraver of the plates, although his ornithological skill leaves much to be desired. A much better attempt was made by the Danish naturalist Olaus Wormius. His drawing was made from a captive bird taken in the Faroes and first appeared in his book which was published in 1655 and entitled *Museum Wormianum Historiae Rerum Rariorum*. This picture was reproduced in Willoughby's *Ornithology* which was published in Latin in 1676 with an English translation overlooked by Ray in 1678. It is interesting to note that Wormius labelled his figure *Anser magellanicus*, a name also given to the Southern Hemisphere penguins and indicating that confusion with the great auk had already begun. Willoughby describes the great auk from the Faroes under the heading 'Penguin'. Johnstone's *Die Avibus* carries the confusion one step further by having a picture labelled *Anser magellanicus* which is very obviously a true penguin.

From this it is easy to see why the Linnaean system described in Chapter 1 should have received such an enthusiastic welcome.

Pictures of the great auk from North America may possibly predate those from Europe. In 1605 Jacobus Plateau sent pictures of a gannet, and almost certainly a garefowl, from North America to Clusius, who used the latter in his *Exoticorum Libri Decem* but some workers have expressed doubt about its authenticity. The present author feels inclined to ask, if Plateau's picture is not of a great auk, what is it? The fact that it was presumably drawn at the same time as the gannet is also, I feel, very significant since the two could well have shared the same habitat and lived very close together without the slightest competition. Great auks are also figured in at least three other publications, including the fourth volume of John Seller's *English Pilot*. In the 1728 London edition (page 17) is a woodcut of a great auk which, although in no way skilful, is quite obviously of a garefowl. A rather better effort, of a swimming bird, is found in Pennant's *Zoology* (Volume 2, page 146) which was published in 1793. There is also a good likeness to the great auk in Volume 9.

Distribution

Williamson's researches suggest that the historian has a more important role to play in the unravelling of the great auk story than the natural historian and a watchful eye should be kept upon archaeological digs and newly discovered documents. Remains of garefowl have been unearthed from kitchen middens at Keiss in Caithness (1864), in shell mounds at Oronsay in the Outer Hebrides (1881) and in cave deposit at Whitburn Lizards, Durham, in 1878. Irish deposits also revealing remains of the garefowl have been found in the counties of Antrim, Clare, Donegal and Waterford. The indication is that garefowl occurred south to latitude $53°S$ on the eastern side of the Atlantic. In North America the most southerly latitude in which the species was thought to occur was $45°S$. Williamson proves almost certainly that the species was present on the Isle of Man and he pointed out:

... that the Great Auk should have occurred in Manx waters in the middle of the seventeenth century is not at all surprising in view of what is known of its distribution in the British Isles in this and subsequent periods. It is difficult and even dangerous to attempt an explanation of its true status in Man from the evidence provided by a single early portrait, for, so far as is known, there is no reference to the species in Manx historical literature. Nor have any archaeological remains of this bird been discovered, although in future investigations of cave-deposits and 'kitchen middens' Manx archaeologists would be doing a great service if they would bear the possibility of such discovery in mind.

It may be well, however, to explore this question of status, for it is not without an important bearing on present knowledge of the distribution of the Garefowl in the British Isles. The fact that the bird depicted is in full breeding plumage, and is standing on a low, flat rock near the water's edge, is suggestive. The Great Auk was a pelagic bird, a strong swimmer and powerful diver, and appears to have come to land rarely except for breeding purposes. Being flightless and by no means agile ashore, it selected for its breeding place such rocks as were most easily accessible to it – low, flat shelves near the sea of a type similar to that seen in the drawing. In passing it may be worth while noting that a considerable area of the Manx coastline on the south-eastern side from Cassiny Hawin to Kione ny Ghoggan has a geological formation of this kind.

The nearest known breeding-place to Man was St. Kilda, where in the seventeenth century there must have been a fairly considerable colony. It is possible from archaeological evidence that in earlier, but historic times, the Great Auk bred also at Colonsay and Oronsay in the Hebrides, and also on the south-eastern Irish coast: a bird with such powerful abilities of swimming and diving is hardly likely to have been killed for food in any numbers except ashore, and that the remains discovered represent only a tithe of the birds taken for food we may be sure. Although the Great Auk does not appear to have been to any extent migratory, it is probably safe to assume that, outside the breeding season, a number might regularly have reached the Irish Sea and visited the Manx coast – even if, as is likely in the mid-seventeenth century, St. Kilda was the only remaining colony in the west of Britain. The caption 'These kind of birds are about the Isle of Man' contains no hint of breeding, but it does suggest that the bird was a not uncommon one in Manx waters. Thus, whilst there does appear to be some likelihood of breeding, it is also equally probable that the Manx birds were only visitors in the spring and autumn and winter months.

When William Yarrell published his four-volume *History of British Birds* in 1843, the great auk was still a living beast but, by the time Howard Saunders completed his revision of the fourth volume in 1885, he was writing a description of the last rites being administered to the species and attempting to piece together as many accounts as possible. I have drawn heavily on this account in the following pages. The earliest reference to the species under the name of garefowl is the *Account of Hirta (St. Kilda) and Rona etc by the Lord Register of Tarbat* which was printed in 1864. Martin Martin's visit to St Kilda in 1697, which lasted 3 weeks, has already been mentioned and, in 1758, the same island group is referred to in the writings of the Reverend Kenneth Macauley. He was interested in the bird-based economy of the residents who told him that the garefowl was no longer an annual visitor, a sure indication of the increasing rarity of the species.

Lowe, whose work was published after his death in 1795 under the title *Fauna Orcadensis*, noted that the species did not occur in the Orkneys. This view was contradicted following Bullock's visit in 1812 when he wrote of his observation to Montagu who referred to the letter in an Appendix to the *Supplement to the Ornithological Dictionary*:

The natives in the Orknies informed Mr. Bullock on his tour through these islands several years ago, that only one male had made its appearance for a long time, which had regularly visited Papa Westra for several seasons. The female (which the natives call the Queen of the Auks), was killed just before Mr. Bullock's arrival. The King, or mal, Mr. Bullock had the pleasure of chasing for several hours in a six-oared boat, but without being able to kill him, for though he frequently got near him, so expert was the bird in its natural element that it appeared impossible to shoot him. The rapidity with which he pursued his course under water was almost incredible. About a fortnight after Mr. Bullock had left Papa Westra a bird, presumably the same, was obtained and sent to him, and at the sale of his collection was purchased for the British Museum, where it still is.

When Robert L. Stevenson carried out his inspection of lighthouses in 1822, he was accompanied by a Dr Fleming, who wrote a fascinating account of their encounter with a live garefowl. The account was published in the *Edinburgh Philosophical Journal* (Volume 10, page 96) and Fleming obviously enjoyed the experience of watching the bird which had been captured by a Mr Maclennan off St Kilda:

It was emaciated, and had the appearance of being sickly; but, in the course of a few days, it became sprightly, having been plentifully supplied with fresh fish, and permitted occasionally to sport in the water, with a cord fastened to one of its legs, to prevent escape. Even in this state of restraint it performed the motions of diving and swimming under water, with a rapidity that set all pursuit from a boat at defiance. A few white feathers were at this time making their appearance on the sides of its neck and throat, which increased considerably during the following week, and left no room to doubt that, like its congeners, the blackness of the throat-feathers of summer is exchanged for white during the winter season.

In May 1834 another live specimen was taken close to Waterford harbour in Ireland by a local fisherman near Kirby. He must have recognised its rarity and also its potential value. Tossing a number of sprats he managed to attract the bird close enough to catch it in a net. The bird was sold to Francis Davis of Waterford and observations of its behaviour were made throughout the summer when it 'stood very erect, was a stately-looking bird and had a habit of shaking its head in a peculiar manner particularly when it recognised its favourite items of food which apparently was mainly trout. It was however, dead by September and found its way via a Dr J. J. Burkitt to the museum of Trinity College Dublin where the stuffed skin still resides.'

A living garefowl was captured in 1844 on Stac an Armin by the St Kildans, who blamed the bird for a particularly severe storm. They tried the great auk, found it guilty of witchcraft and stoned it to death.

These are the only three records of living birds but there are several other records which should be mentioned, although they are difficult to substantiate scientifically. Records from Irish sites, including Belfast, Lough and Cork, as well as on the sea near Lundy Island in the Bristol Channel, have not been properly documented and must remain no more than speculation. In June 1798, a garefowl was recorded between the Orkneys and Shetland just off the coast of Fair Isle and this seems to be a more acceptable record. A bird washed up at Gourock on the Clyde Estuary would appear to be an authentic record.

The 1769 edition of Wallis's *Natural History and Antiquities of Northumberland* gives what seems to be an acceptable record of:

. . . The Penguin a curious and uncommon bird presented to John William Bacon Esq. of Etherstone, with whome it grew so tame and familiar that it followed him, with its body erect, to be fed.

Although it is possible that this bird may have been a Southern Hemisphere 'true penguin' it seems to the present author more likely that this is a genuine record of a garefowl. However, as there are no details of the donor or from whence the bird was obtained, it cannot be accepted as a recording for Northumberland.

Debbes writing of the avifauna of the Faroes in 1673 states that the *Garfogel* was very easy to tame, but seldom survived for very long away from the sea. The writings of Mohr in 1786 record that some specimens were still obtained in most summers, but it is significant that he writes *most* rather than *all*. The decline was confirmed in 1800 by Landt who wrote that the great auk was then something of a rarity. This rarity, of course, heightened the interest in and the value of the remaining individuals. Writing in the 1872 edition of *The Zoologist*, Major Feilden records an interview with Jan Hansen, who was then a very old man but who could recall the capture of a 9 pound great auk at the foot of the Great Dimon on the 1 July 1808.

Iceland, where the population of garefowl had always been healthy, was now under pressure to provide skins, for which there was an insatiable demand from ambitious curators of European museums. The best-known breeding sites were the Geirfuglaskers, three skerries which had been harvested for food by the native people for centuries. In 1808 the pick of these breeding skerries off Reykjanes was visited by a British ship and the crew 'amused' themselves for a whole day clubbing down the adults and crushing the eggs and young in a frenzy of killing. As explained in Chapter 2, auks tend to live a long time but have a low reproductive rate and therefore recover from such devastation very slowly. The population of garefowl would not have recovered by 24 August 1813 when the inhabitants of the Faroes were having a hard time finding sufficient food. Lobner, the Governor, sent a schooner to bring back some nutritious garefowl from Iceland. One of the crew was Daniel Joensen and, in 1858, in his 71st year, he was interviewed by the indefatigable Major Feilden and mentioned that they had killed either 11 or 14 adults although a larger number than this escaped to sea.

Although birds were still being killed on the Icelandic mainland, Faber, who visited the Geirfuglaskers in 1821, failed to find a single bird. This was perhaps just as well because, in the spring of 1830, there was a tremendous undersea movement and the Reykjanes skerry disappeared beneath the waves. Subsequent events make the present writer suspect that there had still been a few breeding pairs on the skerry because, soon after its submersion, the garefowl established a completely new colony on a rock known as the Meal-sack, or more usually as Eldey, a spot in which they had shown no previous interest. It is situated between the mainland and the sunken skerry and it was to here that the greedy hunters now turned their attention.

Between 1830 and 1844, regular and very systematic expeditions were made to Eldey and, during this time, a large number of eggs were taken and 60 adults killed and sent off mainly to satisfy the chair-bound curators at Copenhagen and Hamburg. The last two living Icelandic garefowl were sent to the Royal Museum in Copenhagen in June 1844, after which the breeding grounds were empty and only the slapping of the waves on deserted rocks could be heard. These two pathetic corpses are still to be seen preserved in spirit in the museum collection. Even when Saunders was carrying out his revision of Yarrell's work in the 1880s, and it was almost certain that the garefowl was extinct, his writings do give a faint glimmer of hope which was, alas, unfounded. Referring to the two 1844 birds taken on Eldey he writes, with what I like to feel is a tear of remorse in his eye:

Since that date no examples are known to have been obtained and the faint hope may now be abandoned that a remnant may have taken refuge on the Geirfug-ladranger, a lonely islet hitherto protected from the invasion of man by the dangerous surf which surrounds it.

We can be quite sure that if a remnant population had been present, then, however dangerous the surf may have been, the speculators would have surmounted the obstacle.

The idea that the garefowl was a bird of the high Arctic does not seem to be true, although there would seem to be no doubt that the bird was at one time found on the east coast of Greenland with occasional records on the west. Danell's Islands (also known as Graah's Islands) are situated in latitude 65°20'N and, around 1574, an Icelander was reported in the writings of Preyer to have loaded his boat with garefowl. Since then, however, drifting of polar ice has changed the face of the coast of Greenland and it is highly unlikely that the species ever bred, or even occurred very often, north of the Arctic circle.

Despite recent suggestions that a great auk has been spotted around the Hebridean islands off Scotland, it seems certain that the species has been extinct since the 1840s.

There is no argument, however, regarding the ancestral stronghold of the great auk which was found, often in immense numbers, around Newfoundland. Early explorers called it a penguin and there has been lively debate over many years regarding the derivation of the name. The popular opinion has always been that it derives from the Latin *pinguis* meaning fat, but the early voyagers to Newfoundland called them pin-wing because of the tiny 'pin-like' wings.

Persecution of the great auk on the North American side of the Atlantic was, if anything, even more catastrophic. The scale of the destruction was shown in the writings of Hanklyut published in London in 1600. Writing of the voyage of a Mr Hore, he tells of a visit to the appropriately named Penguin Island which was:

... full of great foules, white and grey, and big as geese, and they saw infinite numbers of their eggs. They draue a great number of the foules into their boates upon their sayles, and took many of their egges, the foules they flead, and their skinns were very like hony combes full of holes; being flead off, they dressed and eate them, and found them to be very food and nourishing meate.

Soon the pattern of stocking up with garefowl which were salted down for the voyage was established by the French travellers, and especially the fishermen whose activities were also described by Hankluyt who said that:

... there is more meat in one of these than in a goose; the Frenchmen that fishe neere the grand baie, do bring small store of flesh with them, but victuall themselves always with these brides.

It is written that Jacques Cartier and his crew killed more than 1,000 'penguins' at a single colony. Observers reported that, even after this carnage, there were enough birds left to have filled 40 more rowing boats. Despite these numbers present in the mid-sixteenth century, the writing must have been on the wall for the garefowl of Newfoundland.

In 1620, Captain Richard Whitbourne of Exmouth in the county of Devon, England, published his *Discourse and Discovery of Newfoundland* in which he pointed out that among the plentiful waterfowl is a species called the penguin which as he charmingly put it:

... are as bigge as Geese, and flye not, for they have but a little short wing, and they multiply so infinitely, upon a certain flat Iland, that men drive them from thence upon a boord, into their boates by hundreds at a time, as if God had made the innocency of so poore a creature, to become such an admirable instrument for the sustentation of man.

In the event, the garefowl proved to be far too vulnerable to stand any chance of survival and, by the time Anspach reported on the area in 1819, he records its extinction. In 1841, Stuvitz visited Funk Island which is around 30 miles (50 kilometres) off Newfoundland and observed the grisly piles of bones in the remnants of the stone slaughterhouses into which the auks were driven for butchering and salting down. This slaughter was a part of a mariner's life along the coast of Labrador and, in his *History of Carolina*, Catesby lists the 'penguin' as a winter visitor to that state. Garefowl bones have also been disinterred from the middens there.

Thus the largest of the auk family became extinct on the North American coast a little before its European cousins were finally slaughtered and we must conclude with a description of what were probably the last great auks to be seen alive. In 1844 an Icelandic bird-dealer named Carl Siemson persuaded a fisherman named Hakonarsson and his crew of 14 to make a last desperate search for the by then very valuable garefowl. He decided to try Eldey Island and, despite mountainous seas, three men struggled to row their skiff ashore. Let the evocative writing of Kenneth Williamson provide the epitaph to a magnificent species sacrificed on the altar of human avarice.

These were the last three men to see the Great Auk alive. The only remaining pair rose from the rocks of Eldey and made their way clumsily towards the sea and safety but the men caught them before they could escape. It is said that one of them also found the egg but the shell was chipped and so he threw it away. When it vanished in the swirling water the life history of the garefowl was at an end.

During the summer of 1986, it was suggested that a great auk may be alive in the Hebrides and a Brathay expedition set off to investigate. Experts quite correctly remain sceptical, but is the garefowl about to do a Phoenix and rise from the ashes?

4

LITTLE AUK

It was like 'a vast opera house, packed with crowds of people in white shirt fronts and black tails, all whispering comments on each other and rustling their programmes'. This delightful, if anthropomorphic, view of the ecologist Charles Elton perfectly describes the cliffs which fringe the islands of the high Arctic and which are thronged with colonies of razorbills, guillemots and, the most numerous bird of all, the little auk. The species has also been known as the dovekie or common rotche. Dovekie was a term coined by the Scandinavian whalers and it meant 'little dove'. They also used this term for the black guillemot (*Cepphus grylle*), but the description well suits both species. The small auks they referred to as rotche. Black guillemots were called sea pigeons by New World fishermen who used dovekie for the little auk, by which name it is still affectionately known in North America. Its scientific name has also been altered since Linnaeus first named it *Alca alle*. This was changed to *Mergulus alle* and it was also described under the name of *Plautus alle* before its present name of *Alle alle* was settled upon.

Habitat

The little auk is a truly oceanic species and is confined to the Arctic apart from the times when it is searching for a suitable breeding area or winter food, or on occasions when it is driven before gales (see page 41). Outside the breeding season the favoured location is close to the pack ice where upwellings of plankton-rich water occur. As the average temperature of the earth is at present rising, the pack ice is gradually melting and the little auks are faithfully following this retreat. Some individuals occasionally get their timing wrong and are cut off by ice as winter closes in and groups are often seen using ice floes as rafts and staining the surface with their characteristically red guano. These droppings may well be responsible for the surprising fertility of some of the islands on which they breed. In 1981 Evans found lush mats of mosses of the *Dicranum* genus as well as higher plants, such as the grass *Alopecurus alpinus*, scurvy grass (*Cochlearia groenlandica*) and chickweed (*Cerastium alpinum*), flourishing around the vast little auk colonies. This in turn provides cover for other Arctic fauna including the ptarmigan (*Lagopus mutus*) and the Arctic fox (*Alopex lagopus*) which often preys upon the little auk, and especially upon its eggs. There can be no doubt about the vital role played by the guano-producing birds in the Arctic food web. The nest sites may well be covered with snow by the time the birds return to breed. The majority of birds select sites facing the sea (perhaps these areas are the first to thaw out), although a minority are found around inland valleys. Sheltered crevices or gaps in the scree are favoured sites obviously because they provide shelter from chilling winds, driving sleet and also predators, including the piratical and ever-hungry glaucous gull (*Larus hyperboreus*).

Description

It is quite amazing how a bird about the size of a starling can hold sufficient heat in the core of its body to withstand the Arctic cold. The little auk, which measures just less than 20 centimetres (8 inches), not only survives but thrives. Its dumpy body has good fat deposits and its dense covering of feathers provides efficient insulation. The bird appears to be snub-nosed because of the tiny bill which measures only 1.5 centimetres ($\frac{5}{8}$ inch) and this feature also cuts down the area over which body heat is lost. I have

Little auks or dovekies seem to find the icy waters of the Arctic much to their liking.

Little auks showing display patterns.

watched little auks bobbing on the sea and they not only appeared to have no bill at all but also seemed to be lacking a neck. These characteristics, combined with the little auk's ability to rise easily from the water and skim across the waves, can be confusing to bird-watchers familiar with Atlantic auks but not with the little auk. When they are angry, preening or displaying the short neck and bill (which is very like that of a finch) can be seen. The sexes are similar in appearance but their summer and winter plumages are very different.

The mature adult is a strikingly black-and-white bird, but a close examination shows that the head, short neck, dorsal surface and tail are all glossy black. So is the chest and one can see the truth of Elton's 'dinner jacket' description. It seems to the present writer that the shape of the black chest against the white belly is unique to each individual little auk. I also feel that other species could also be separated into individuals, according to plumage-pattern variations in the case of the common and Brunnich's guillemots and differences in bill patterns in the Atlantic puffin and razor-bill. In view of the complex mixing of genes which occurs during reproduction, the fact that each individual is distinct should not surprise us – indeed we should be surprised if it were not so. It has already been demonstrated by Peter Scott and his co-workers at the Wildfowl Trust in Slimbridge, Gloucestershire, that the bill pattern of each Bewick swan (*Cygnus bewickii*) is unique. They were able to show this because large numbers of swans were gathered at a predictable place at a predictable time. This is just as true with the auks and I am convinced that ornithologists with enough time to spare to pay regular and prolonged visits to the colonies would soon learn to recognise individual birds by colour patterns. In any event further researches are necessary and ringing will show if plumage differences are continuous from one moult to the next.

A close examination of the little auks' summer plumage will reveal that the shiny black fades to a duller brown on the chest and face and that there is a small white patch above the eye which adds to the bird's often quizzical expression. Evans (1981) is of the opinion that this patch plays a part in the bird's display at the nest side (see page 52). The secondary feathers and also those along the sides of the back (the scapulars) are fringed with white and are occasionally visible when the bird is swimming or standing on land. The flight feathers and coverts are silvery on part of the lower surface and this, combined with a white patch in the middle of the wing pit, give the flying bird a somewhat paler appearance than expected when compared with the upper surface.

An interesting letter by Dave Braithwaite was published in Volume 72 of *British Birds* and clearly points out the difficulties which can be encountered in the field when trying to identify flying auks.

Identification of small, solitary auks over the sea can sometimes cause problems. Gibson-Hill (1947) mentioned that juvenile Puffins Fratercula arctica, *which are smaller and have much smaller bills than adults, might be mistaken for Little Auks* Alle alle. *In strong winds, Puffins can indeed look small and 'quick', especially if flying with the wind; inexperienced observers have sometimes identified them as Little Auks. The reverse, however, should not occur, since, when actually seen, Little Auks appear extremely small and are recognisable on this feature alone.*

One point worthy of note that does not find its way into the text of the popular field guides, and was in fact erroneously depicted by both Fitter and Richardson (1952) and Brun and Singer (1970), is the colour of the underwing. Inspection of over 50 little auk skins at the British Museum, Tring, showed that, regardless of origin, age or seasonal plumage, all had dark brown underwings. Some did appear more mottled than others, but this was apparently an individual variation and the general effect was still dark, in contrast with the underwing of the puffin, which is pale. Johnsson (1978) noted that:

The undersides of the wings, if one has time to see them, are black, unlike those of other auks, and illustrated this difference well, but depicted an 'underwing bar', presumably caused by white endings to the median underwing-coverts, which was shown by none of the specimens examined at Tring. The underwing colour was illustrated, but not mentioned in the text, by Heinzel et al. *(1972); it was neither illustrated nor described by Peterson* et al. *(1954).*

In my experience, the underwing of Little Auk looks extremely dark, contrasting with the white belly, in the field and recalls that of Green Sandpiper

Common puffin and little auk in flight show differing wing patterns.

Tringa ochropus. The dark underwings of Little Auks should prevent the misidentification of Puffins, which show pale underwings, and also have grey cheeks, a complete breast band and lack white endings to the secondaries.

Whilst I agree with Braithwaite's note that the puffins wing is on the whole much lighter, some little auks do show the patch of white on the wing pit referred to in some (but not all) field guides.

In winter, little auks are also glossy black on the upper surfaces but the brownish summer feathers on the cheeks, chin, throat, sides of the neck and the breast are replaced by white. The ear coverts are still dark, however, and stand out clearly from the surrounding feathering. The nape has a varying amount of white which sometimes, but by no means always, forms a collar. Throughout the year the bill is black, as are the irides (singular iris) around the eye. The legs and feet are brownish grey and both the webs and joints are etched with black.

The young are born with a thick almost black down, paling gradually along the flanks to a pale brown on the underside. P.G.H. Evans (1981) noted that there is a variation in colouration from almost black to a very light grey, depending upon the individual, and, in consequence, the field guides may often be too dogmatic with regard to colour. The juvenile little auk resembles the breeding adult but the white eye patch is lacking, the throat is paler and the upper plumage lacks the shining elegance of the adult. The bill of the juvenile is also browner than that of the adult. There is little information on the precise sequence followed as one plumage gives rise to another. There appears to be a complete moult following breeding, the body feathers being the first to be replaced followed by the flight feathers and tail. The process is usually completed by the end of September. Prior to breeding there is often a partial moult involving the body, but never the flight feathers.

Distribution of Breeding Sites and Movements

Most workers accept that the melting of the polar ice caps, due to gradual, but still significant temperature rises, has led to the abandonment of some of the more southerly breeding sites and a corresponding extension to the north. The breeding range is from latitudes around 60°N to as high as 79°50′N, 99°50′E at Severnaya Zemlya in northern Siberia and down to Ellesmere Island, Canada, which is at 76°10′N, 81°20′W. There is no doubt, however, that the headquarters of the little auk is in Greenland. The population here is at least 8 million pairs and could even be as high as 25 million pairs, but with numbers like this it is very difficult, indeed probably impossible, for field-workers to be really accurate. I would, however, be inclined to prefer the higher estimate. The present distribution of colonies in Greenland is centred around Thule and Scoresby Sund but the fact that this may not always have been the case was noted by Salomonsen in 1950 who pointed out that climatic amelioration had led to the abandonment of sites in southern Greenland in favour of those in more northerly regions. This may also account for the abandonment of former Norwegian colonies, although there

Little auk: adult in summer plumage (top); adult in winter plumage (bottom right); downy young (bottom left).

Distribution of the little auk (*Alle alle*).

has been a suggestion of breeding at Finnmark during 1981–2. The Icelandic colonies, once heavily populated, have also been gradually abandoned since the mid-nineteenth century. Only the Grimsey Island colony remains. In 1905 Hantsch postulated a minimum population of 105 pairs, but this has recently declined to less than 10 pairs. Since this has not been due to over-exploitation or human-introduced predators, but is merely a function of the weather then we need not grieve about the loss of the Icelandic colonies.

There are still millions of pairs breeding in the USSR, especially on Franz Josef Land, with smaller colonies on Novaya Zemlya where there were, according to W.R.P. Bourne (1972a), around 5,000 pairs in 1969. Large colonies still breed at Spitzbergen, although there has been some northerly movement of the once vast colonies in recent years, but there may still be over 1 million pairs. Counts made on Bear Island in 1980 by Luttik indicated around 10,000 pairs and a census of the colonies on Jan Mayen by J.A. van Franeker and C.J. Camphuijsen found them to exceed 100,000 pairs in 1983. As we saw in Chapter 1, there are two sub-species of the little auk. *Alle alle alle* is the nominate race which is slightly smaller than *Alle alle polaris* which occurs on Franz Josef Land. Two specimens of *Alle alle polaris* have, however, been recovered from the Shetland Islands. This is the only criterion on which the two are separated and it has still not been established whether the birds from Severnaya Zemlya and the North Pacific should be given sub-specific rank, a decision dependent upon the necessary measurements being made in the future.

Once the breeding season is over, the little auks from Greenland moult and, whilst they are unable to fly, they are carried by westward currents across the north of Baffin Bay and, by September, have reached the east coast of Arctic Canada. They then drift south into the Labrador Sea, which they reach in October, and they remain around the north-western Atlantic until April and early May, when it is time for them to return in order to find out whether the breedings grounds have been relinquished by the relentless grip of the winter's ice. An immense ringing project by Norderhaug in the late 1960s resulted in the banding of 11,000 little auks on Spitzbergen. His returns proved that these birds wintered off the south-west coast of Greenland and also that, although the breeding pair may not winter together, they meet up at the same site for several years, and possibly for life.

There is always a tendency for little auks to seek out cold currents, no doubt because of the rich plankton which they support and on which the species feeds (see page 55). There are occasions when the autumnal gales blast the birds completely off course and, tired and often emaciated, little auks are stranded in the West Indies whilst others are driven across the Atlantic and dumped as far south as the Mediterranean. Minor 'wrecks' occur almost every year but, in some years, thousands of birds are involved. It seems that heavy and continuous gales force the plankton into deeper water and out of reach of the diving abilities of the little auk and the hungry birds must drift downwind and are pushed onto beaches, and even far inland, by the continuing storm. These 'little auk wrecks' have been documented over many years and one of the most dramatic was recorded by Howard Saunders in his revision of Yarrell's *History of British Birds* published in 1885.

A remarkable instance of this sort occurred in the month of October, 1841. Dr. Edward Clarke, of Hartlepool, sent the Author word, that after a violent storm of wind from N.N.E., which lasted several days, his attention was directed by pilots and fishermen on the look-out, to various flocks of small black and white birds, then close in shore. There were several hundreds of them, which were unknown to these seafaring men, but which proved to be the Little Auk. Many were obtained, five or six being killed at each shot, the birds were so numerous. The same thing happened at the same time at Redcar, on the Yorkshire coast, but after two or three days, the wind abating, they were seen no more. About the same time the Author heard from various friends of other examples being taken in many different counties, – in Lincolnshire, Norfolk, Suffolk, Essex, Kent, and Sussex. During the early part of November, 1841, a few of these birds were sent for sale to the London markets. Some were taken at unusual distances inland. Mr. Thrale, a collector in Hertfordshire, sent notice of one that was obtained on the mill-head at Wheathamstead; and another, which was picked up alive between Baldock and Royston, is now preserved in the Museum at Saffron Walden. The Author heard of others taken near Birmingham; Strickland recorded nine taken in Worcestershire; three in Shropshire; some at Bristol, and other parts near the Severn. Since the above was written the Little Auk has been obtained all round the coast of England. In Scotland it is tolerably common on the east side, but decidedly a straggler, according to Mr. R. Gray, on the west; and in the Shetlands and Orkneys it is observed almost every winter. In Ireland, its appearance in Wexford and Kerry has been noted by Thompson; and it has been observed on other parts of the coast. There is no evidence that it has bred in any part of the British Islands, although examples are occasionally obtained in full summer plumage. Mr. F. Bond has a fine specimen with full black throat, picked up dead in the Solent.

North American observers also refer to inland records during periods of autumnal storms, especially during November. Snyder reported a heavy mortality in the USA in 1960 when the dovekies died of starvation, or were eaten by gulls or other predators, including pet cats and dogs. It was reported at this time that many tired birds were 'adopted' by well-meaning people and kept as 'little penguins' until they died. The kindest thing to do is to return them to the coast as soon as possible and let them take their chance in their natural habitat.

Fisher and Lockley, in their classic work *Sea Birds* published in 1954, had some fascinating observations to make on little auk wrecks on both sides of the Atlantic which, to the superficial observer, might well seem to threaten a catastrophic fall in population. They made a distinction between what they called 'flights' and 'wrecks'. Flights they defined as rafts of birds drifting along close enough to the coast to be observed by land-based observers but showing no real physical distress. Wrecks on the other hand were typified by dead and dying birds along coasts and also at inland areas. Fisher and Lockley further postulated that these wrecks were irregular and very unlikely to have any effect at all upon population levels. They also occurred at the most southerly extremity of the normal wintering range and the birds found here would already be weakened, possibly by shortage of food, before they were hit by the storm. Wrecks occur involving other sea birds, including the larger auks, but it is those involving the little auk and also Leach's petrel (*Oceanodroma leucorrhoa*) which are the most spectacular and well-documented. Most birds return to the breeding grounds as the ice begins to recede, which can be as early as early March in Franz Josef Land, April in Spitzbergen but towards the end of May in the north of Greenland.

Behaviour and Breeding

Little auks are gregarious throughout the year, even in the wintering areas, when it is an advantage to have as many individuals as possible on the look-

A colony of little auks.

out for rich drifts of plankton. These rafts contain both adults and adolescents but, as the time for breeding draws near, the adolescents withdraw and huge congregations of adults move into the breeding grounds. They then make periodic landings to explore the nest site, possibly locating that of the previous year and making contact with their sexual partner. It does seem that little auks are monogamous but there is certainly a need for more studies to be made, although the work of P.G.H. Evans on the west coast of Greenland has done much to lighten our darkness. The whole breeding cycle, from the formation of the pair bond to the young leaving the nest, takes from 12 to 14 weeks, which compares with 16 weeks for the razorbill and Brunnich's guillemot and 18 weeks for the Atlantic puffin and the black guillemot. It would seem that the relatively short reproductive cycle may be a significant factor accounting for the little auk's ability to breed in the high Arctic, which is only free of ice for a limited period. It is significant that those little auks in the south of the range spend more time in precopulatory display than those in the north where time is of the essence.

For 4 or 5 weeks before the nest is selected and the egg laid there is a period of intense feeding activity, especially by the females which produce very large eggs. Evans has shown that, in Greenland at least, newly hatched little auk chicks weigh 13.5% of their parents' body weight whereas, for other auks nesting in the area, such as Brunnich's guillemot and the razorbill, the comparative figure was between 8 and 9%. There is certainly sufficient food available during the reproductive period to make rapid growth rates and weight increases easily achieved.

Little auks site their nests in eroded crevices of cliff faces, among slopes of scree or in the talus (a term used to describe the pile of boulders at the base of the cliff). Sometimes the pile of talus can be quite high and, as a rule, the dovekie prefers to site its nest some distance from the ground and even inland cliffs have supported quite substantial colonies. Should the site require adapting, the pair are quite able to dig out the soil from between the stones and arrange a neat mat of pebbles about 1 metre (3 feet) from the entrance to the nest where the single egg is laid. It should be admitted that this suggestion of little auks constructing a nest may be controversial and in the *Handbook of British Birds* (Witherby *et al.*, 1938–42) it states categorically that no nest is built. The work of Ferdinand published in 1969 might, I feel, be significant. He noted that a bird presented a stone to its partner on five or six occasions. On one of these occasions a bird hopped down from its rocky perch, picked up the stone and carried it to its partner before dropping it in front of the other bird. The sequence was then repeated and was listed as site-prospecting. The performance was, however, continued by one bird, which retained the stone for a period of between 5 and 10 minutes. The stone-carrier was then observed to spread itself on the ground and produced a rapid sequence of calls, resembling a snarl, which Ferdinand associated with birds prospecting for nest sites. After standing together, the two birds disappeared among the rocks. I am left wondering if pebble-collecting could not have the dual function of site selection and nest-building. In the *Handbook of the Birds of Europe, the Middle East and North Africa* the work of Norderhaug (1980) and Stempniewicz (1981) is summarised and suggests that nests are built and even lined with small pebbles, lichen and dry grass.

Only one egg is laid and, when two occur in the same nest, it is probably that two females are responsible. Only one brood is attempted, apart from in Iceland where a replacement egg may be laid if the first is lost. At points further north, however, there is just not sufficient time to allow either for a second brood or a repeat clutch. Each egg, which averages 4.8 by 3.8 centimetres ($1\frac{29}{32}$ by $1\frac{1}{2}$ inches) and weighs 29 grams (just over 1 ounce) is of a dullish pale blue. The occasional egg is streaked with spots and scribbles. This may indicate that the ancestors of the little auk nested in more exposed sites and the loss of pigment is related to the tendency to nest further away from light in more recent times. In Greenland, most eggs are laid at the end of June with an earlier date in more southerly colonies.

The incubation period is shared by both sexes, the female having a tendency to take the day shift, the male taking over at night. Doubt has been expressed with regard to the incubation period which is normally quoted as 24 days, a figure first postulated by Faber way back in 1825 and freely plagiarised ever since. A period of around 30 days would seem to be nearer the truth. In areas where the weather is so unpredictable it would not be surprising if there was some associated variation in incubation period.

Both parents care for the single young which is semi-altricial and requires constant brooding for the first few days, until its down develops and there is some control over body temperature. The male may well do most of the feeding, especially as the chick gets older. The fledging period, once given as around 20 days is now known to be nearer to 30, the work done by Evans (1981) on the Greenland colonies suggesting an average of just over 28 days. The young are fed by both parents on planktonic crustaceans which are generally obtained mostly at night when the organisms move closer to the surface, although at Spitzbergen for some unknown reason this does not seem to be the case. The feeding grounds are often some distance from the breeding colonies, but large amounts of food can be carried in a gular pouch which proves to have surprisingly elastic walls.

The period during which the young are left whilst the adults are foraging for food is full of hazards and the Arctic fox and glaucous gull can destroy large numbers. Despite this Stempniewicz (1981) working in Spitzbergen found that 65.3% of eggs were successfully hatched and, of these, 80% of the chicks fledged, which compares with Evan's figures for Greenland of 65% and 77% respectively. It should be pointed out, however, that both samples were small – 98 and only 20 eggs – and, once more, we find the need for more researchers to visit the little auks. We also need more information regarding the age at which the young become independent of their parents and how old they are before they are able to breed themselves. Both these requirements will be very difficult to satisfy since the birds are so spread out along the ocean currents. The only chance will be *via* a really intensive ringing scheme which will be time-consuming because the nature of the habitat means that there is a very low rate of return.

Table 4   An Analysis of the Behaviour of the Little Auk (*Alle alle*)

Flight	Sea-Based Behaviour	Body-Based Behaviour		Vocalisations
		Antagonistic	Sexual	
Upflights: Mass movement in response to predator. *Mass Flights*: Many birds touring the colony making a great deal of noise. Typical of the period when eggs are being incubated. *Rushing Flight*: Few individuals involved. No vocalisation and birds return to starting position. '*Butterfly' Flight*:	Diving for food Diving to escape predator Rafting and sleeping	Head-vertical posture Landing posture Rolling walk	Head-bowing and billing Head-wagging Flashing Head-shaking Head-cocking Copulation	Alarm Warning 'Song' or trill Clucking Billing Snarling

Much more precise studies have been possible on the breeding grounds and both the sign language and the surprisingly varied vocabulary of the little auk is now much more clearly understood, although more studies are essential to unravel the finer details, and arrive at the correct sequence of some of the events. In Table 4, I have attempted to classify little auk behaviour and I am quite aware that some may find this approach too simplistic, and that other gestures and vocalisations await a translator.

FLIGHT BEHAVIOUR

Apart from its normal flight, which is typically auk-like, with whirring wings propelling it low over the water, other flight patterns in response to particular stimuli have been recognised in the little auk. *Upflights* involve a mass movement in response to a predator and there is nothing smooth or co-ordinated about the behaviour. In contrast, there are what have been termed *mass flights* when a large number of birds tour the colony and make a great deal of noise as they do so. This behaviour is much more frequent at the time the eggs are being incubated. It is always dangerous to speculate without an impressive mass of data as a back-up but it does seem that these mass flights may have the effect of acting as a deterrent to predators. Mass flights also often begin from rafts of birds which have been roosting on the sea and it might also be a method of stretching the wings prior to taking over for a stint of incubation. Most observers agree that little auks prefer to sleep on the sea and are usually very wary when perched on land. *Rushing flight* involves far fewer individuals, perhaps from their own little sub-colony, and is typified by an individual skimming through the colony and, apart from the winnowing of the wings, makes no sound. The bird always seems to return to its original position and it seems likely that this forms part of the display necessary to cement the pair bond. In 1950, Conder described a *butterfly-type flight* which was part of the display of the common guillemot and Evans first noted similar flight patterns in the razorbill and then in the little auk. The extravagant fluttering is very much a part of the display period and is usually of short duration with both partners often involved. Butterfly and rushing flights may well prove to be part of the same process of persuading all the females to lay their eggs at the same time, an essential part of the biology of a species which is as gregarious as the little auk.

SEA-BASED BEHAVIOUR

What I have referred to as sea-based behaviour is to a large extent self explanatory and the diving for food will be described in more detail below. The dilemma facing a bird confronted by a predator, such as the glaucous gull, is whether to dive or fly. Little auks rise from the surface of the sea much more easily than many of their larger and heavier relatives, but, during the long moult or in periods of high wind, diving is much the safer of the two. The idea that there is safety in numbers is carried to extremes by auks in general, but little auks in particular both feed and nest surrounded by a raft of companions. It does not take them long to stake out their own area of living space and this is where body-based movements and vocalisations come into play. These have mostly been observed on land, but some are also used for communication between birds at sea, although it does seem that little auks are not very noisy or demonstrative outside the breeding season.

BODY-BASED BEHAVIOUR

In the early period of the breeding season when territories are being established there is a lot of chest to chest pushing and jabbing, although it is doubtful if the small bill could cause much damage. Actual fighting does occur, with the combatants grappling with the bills interlocked. A bird laying claim to territory will advertise the fact by what has been termed the *head-vertical posture*. The response of a bird which accepts that it is intruding is to go into a hunch-backed pose which looks like, and is in fact termed, the *landing posture*. Both the bill and tail are pointing downwards as the unwelcome visitor picks its way through the territory owners. It is, I suppose, the human equivalent of keeping one's head down! Even when walking, the intruder endeavours to appease and this movement has become known as the *rolling walk*. At least the little auk can seek refuge in its own crevice and this accounts for its antagonistic displays being less spectacular than those of the common guillemot, which has to defend its own little patch of bare rock. It is really amusing to watch an unmated little auk late in the season, hopefully carrying a stone into a likely-looking burrow only to be ejected seconds later by an outraged occupant.

In the early period of their bond establishment the pair may engage in head-vertical postures and respond by the landing posture in an effort to appease but, once trust has been built up, the sexual display can commence and bring the female into breeding condition. One pair stimulates the next and ensures that the young are hatched around the same time. Important movements in the sequence include head-bowing and billing, wagging, flashing, shaking and cocking but these are not performed in any particular order. However, a combination of all will result in copulation which lasts for about 30 seconds and, if performed often enough, will ensure fertilisation of the egg. Butterfly flight (p. 52) is probably an important part in this ritual.

VOCALISATIONS

The interpretation of bird vocalisations in human terms has not been easy since the anatomy of birds' and mammals' sound-producing and ventilating organs are very different. In the early days, ornithologists had to write phrases such as 'ak aak ak-ak-ak' and it was impossible to find other workers who could produce the same sound or deliver it at the same speed. Modern technology has provided the ideal solution. Tape recordings can be made, but even then the bird's delivery may be too fast or the pitch too high to be fully appreciated by the human ear. The tape is therefore fed into an oscilloscope and recorded onto paper which records pitch and timing. The resultant line of paper packed with information is called a *sonogram* and is a very precise visual record of the sound a bird makes, the time it takes and its rhythm. In 1969, Ferdinand elucidated the calls of the little auk and noted two types of unit which he called 'glissando' and 'serrated' by which he referred to smooth sequences interspersed with harsher shorter noises.

The *alarm call*, as expected, is a harsh sound and, when used by a bird acting as the watcher outside the breeding hole, causes the sitting bird to push the egg or young deeper into the burrow, using its wing for the purpose. There is also a *whinnying call* which is used by a number of birds if an intruder approaches the colony. Apart from danger signals, the birds also need a love call and this is the function of the well-named *trilling call*, which is used both on water, land and in the air, presumably having a secondary function as a contact call. The *clucking call* is much more seductive and is often used by birds sitting close together and indulging in a little bit of head-wagging and 'butterfly' flights. After the egg has been laid, the mated pair use the rather harsh (to human ears at least) *billing call* as a duet at the same time as the head-wagging movement. The rapid rhythmic *snarling* sound seems to be restricted to the early period of the reproductive cycle whilst the birds are prospecting for nest sites.

Food and Feeding

In the *Handbook of British Birds*, published by Witherby in the 1940s, the work of W.E. Collinge (1924) was quoted. He examined the stomachs of 29 little auks and his analysis of the contents revealed 97.84% animal matter. Of this, 80% was crustaceans, 9.39% annelids, 7.28% molluscs and only 1.17% small fish. Work since this time has succeeded in identifying individual species, but the almost total dependence of little auks on planktonic crustaceans is beyond question. It is the plankton which is responsible for the distribution of the little auk. On land we recognise the four seasons of spring, summer, autumn and winter, but the sea also has its seasons, although they do not correspond in time to those on *terra firma*. During the winter many plants and animals die and as their bodies decay the basic nutrients in the water increase. As days begin to lengthen and temperatures rise, the population of phytoplankton (small plants) increases and this, in turn, provides food for the zooplankton, which is made up of small animals, including *Calanus finmarchicus*, the main item in the diet of the little auk. This is the sea spring, during which populations increase rapidly. In summer, as the nutrients are used up, there is a fall off in numbers but the autumn gales stir up nutrients which are brought to the surface. There is therefore another burst in the plankton population. With the onset of winter, the days become shorter and the reduced amount of light limits the amount of food which the phytoplankton can make. The populations therefore fall and the cycle is repeated. At the polar regions there is a short but sharp increase in growth during the spring but, towards the Equator, the winter season is lacking and there can be no build-up of nutrients. Plankton in the Tropics is therefore in comparatively short supply, except around river estuaries where flood waters increase the supply of nutrients.

In the polar regions the reverse is true. Currents developing as the ice melts, plus strong winds, give the nutrients a thorough shake-up and the short summers have almost constant sunlight. In these conditions the plankton is so thick in some places that it resembles a soup. This explains why little auks are found breeding so far to the north. Whilst zooplankton can swim, they cannot battle against currents and are carried along by them. They can, however, move up and down in the water and they migrate from deep water to the surface each day, and back again at night. The upward movement towards light is easily explained but why they descend at night still a mystery. A possible explanation might be that deeper ocean currents do not always move in the same direction as those on the surface. The plankton may therefore be carried in one direction by surface currents during the day, and then be carried back at night by deep-water currents. Thus they maintain a constant position over a 24-hour period. The up and down movement is called *vertical migration* and some of the larger crustaceans can travel from the surface to depths of 600 to 1,000 metres (1,970 to 3,280 feet). Even smaller species may reach depths of 150 metres (nearly 200 feet). Dawn finds the zooplankton at the surface, but by noon they have disappeared into the deep only to appear on the surface at dusk. During the night there seems to be a more random distribution, but it is quite clear that little auks feeding at dawn and dusk will find more to eat at these times.

Little auks are less gregarious when feeding, but large numbers will obviously gather where there are concentrations of plankton, although information on diet outside the breeding season is difficult to obtain. Apart from *Calanus finmarchicus*, other crustaceans in the diet include *Gammarus* sp., *Mysis* sp., *Atylus carinatus* and many other species, plus some molluscs, especially *Argonauta arctica*, with an occasional small fish or annelid. Most information has obviously been gleaned from material brought in in the gular pouches of the adults as food for the young.

Adults probably eat rather more fish but crustaceans caught by diving from the surface still make up around 90% of the diet. In 1983, Rees reported little auks feeding without diving on the waste thrown from a trawler. They were almost certainly feeding on the undigested crustaceans released from the fishes' stomachs during the gutting process. Bateson (1961) recorded diving times of around 30 seconds during which there was considerable lateral movement. This time is broadly in agreement with those made a year earlier by Kartashev (1960), who recorded periods of 25 to 40 seconds with rest periods of between 10 and 20 seconds between dives.

As more and more birdwatchers find the time to visit the Arctic and follow the little auk further north as the temperature continues its gradual rise, we can look forward to learning more of its life history. At the moment we have done little more than scratch the surface.

5

RAZORBILL

A late March wind raged throughout the night and icy rain rattled on my tent which was pitched in a sheltered hollow overlooking the cliffs of a tiny Hebridean island. Sleep was impossible, but it didn't seem to matter. Just before dawn the wind dropped and the rain first eased to a thin drizzle and then it became so quiet that I could hear the lap of the sea against the cliffs and the disputes of the birds on the narrow rock ledges below me. Opening the flap of my tent I saw that the razorbills had returned to the breeding ledges, their shining black plumage dripping with little pearls of water which gleamed in the shafts of weak sunlight. The long uncomfortable night had been worth it, as it invariably is for those naturalists who take lodgings in a sea-bird city.

Habitat

Unlike the little auk, razorbills do not like ice and this is clearly reflected in their distribution, which lies broadly within a belt of water whose temperature in August falls between 5°C and 20°C (41°F and 68°F). Some work has been done which indicates that they prefer areas which have a salt content in excess of 34 parts per thousand, although there are a few sites in the Baltic which would seem to below this limit. Shallow, brackish water is, however, always avoided and the favoured breeding sites are rocky islands surrounded by deep clear water. Razorbills require fairly broad ledges with cracks or crevices among rocks which make ideal breeding sites. Whilst some nests are sited in areas cushioned by vegetation, such as sea campion (*Silene maritima*), scurvy grasses (*Cochlearia officinalis* and *Cochlearia scotica*) and sea plantain (*Plantago maritima*), or even detritus deposited by a combination of spring tides and high winds, the majority of eggs are laid directly onto bare rock. The most unusual nest I have seen was on the Island of Canna, one of the Small Isles now owned by the National Trust for Scotland in the middle Hebrides. Looking through my binoculars I could see a bright red area under an overhanging rock on which was perched a very comfortable-looking razorbill. After watching in bewilderment for more than 2 hours, I

Five razorbills in the background but in the foreground is a common guillemot, the white around the eye being a feature of the bridled variety.

saw the bird rise to turn its egg and I could see the nest site was on top of a red woollen bobble cap which must have blown from the head of a climber and become lodged in the rock crevice. In contrast to the guillemot, razorbills never utilise the tops of cliffs or stacks, but will lay their egg on low-lying shores, providing there are enough rocks to provide cover.

Although the occasional bird may wander through estuaries and up rivers, usually as a result of high winds combined with exceptionally high tides, razorbills generally head out to sea following breeding. The species is, however, not so adventuresome as most other auks and usually remains either in, or close to, coastal waters.

Description

Once called the razorbilled auk, this species measures around 40 centimetres (16 inches) and has a short neck, squat body, short tail and, although the wings are narrow, the wing span of around 62 centimetres (25 inches) is sufficient to support the bird. In summer, the head, neck and back are a shiny black, which contrasts sharply with the narrow white line running from the bill to the eye; there are also white tips to the secondary feathers. The underparts are white apart from the coverts over the base of the primary and secondary feathers which are pale brown. The large black bill is flattened from side to side and accounts for its name of razorbill, which was obviously given in the days when cut-throat razors were in fashion. There is a broken white line running along the middle of the bill and down both upper and lower mandibles. The precise function of these white lines on the bill and also on the head is not yet fully understood. Some speculators believe that the lines play a vital, although not yet understood, role in courtship whilst others are of the opinion that the lines function rather like the sights on a rifle as the bird dives in pursuit of its prey. The lines can also be an indication of age. The inside of the mouth is yellow and this may play some role in sexual display. The irides are dark brown. The legs and feet are black and are placed so far back on the body that the bird stands very erect, even by auk standards. The central tail feathers are more pointed and the tail itself longer and therefore much more conspicuous than those of other auks.

The bulky bill and pointed tail enable the razorbill to be separated from the guillemot (*Uria aalge*), but these features are difficult to see when birds are in flight. The flying razorbill does have a very conspicuous wing bar which is easily seen either from above or below the bird and is much more obvious than that of the guillemot.

Adult birds moult in autumn and are completely flightless during this period when all the flight feathers are replaced together. Depending upon the breeding area, this can be any time between August and October. There is also often a partial moult, never involving the flight feathers, between January and April in preparation for breeding. This most often involves only the neck and head, but occasionally body feathers are also replaced.

Razorbills: in summer plumage (left) and winter plumage (right).

In the winter the white line on the face is not present, the darker areas on the back are dull brown rather than shiny black and the chin, throat and sides of the head are white.

Juveniles have dark brown upper surfaces, but they have large white areas on the throat and the rest of the undersurface is also white. By their first winter more adult features are apparent, but the bill is much less substantial and lacks the typical white marks. In northern areas where common guillemots tend to be much blacker than in the southern areas of the range there can be some confusion with young razorbills, although the latter do lack the dark streak behind the eye which is so typical of guillemots. The downy young are typified by very short greyish down on the head which is replaced by feathers round about the fifteenth day. There are white areas on the lores, crown, forehead and nape. The neck and throat and mantle are mottled with brown which contrasts pleasantly with the white of the breast and flanks and the greyer feathering on the head.

Distribution

The *Handbook of British Birds* (Witherby *et al.*, 1938–42) lists two subspecies of razorbill which are referred to as the Northern razorbill (*Alca*

Distribution of the razorbill (*Alca torda*).

torda torda) and the British razorbill (*Alca alca britannica*). Two sub-species are still recognised. The nominate *Alca torda torda* is found around North America, Greenland and Bear Island, Norway, Denmark and from Murmansk as far south as the White Sea. This is also the sub-species found in the Baltic. The nominate race is the larger of the two, with the wing being as much as 1.2 centimetres (½ inch) longer.

This conforms to the rule postulated by the nineteenth-century German zoologist, Bergmann. He noted that the overall body size tends to be greater in individuals of bird and mammal species living permanently in cooler climates than those living in warmer areas. The suggestion is that large bodies are able to retain heat more efficiently than smaller ones and therefore there is an adaptive size increase in populations which are constantly subjected to lower temperatures. The more southerly, and consequently smaller, sub-species is now more accurately named *Alca torda islandica*, the two being a perfect example of Bergmann's rule in action.

This sub-species is found in Iceland, the Faroes, the British Isles and Ireland but is found as far south as Brittany. Zoologists have always been fascinated by rules and Allen postulated that individuals of bird and mammal species living permanently in warmer climates tend to have larger appendages, birds' bills for example, than those individuals of the same species living permanently in cooler climates. This is clearly an advantage in cutting down heat loss from organs which are not covered by insulating feathers.

There are many exceptions to Allen's rule, the razorbill apparently being one, but before dismissing the rule altogether we ought to examine the statistics a little more closely. The *Handbook of the Birds of Europe, the Middle East and North Africa* gives average bill-length figures of 3.57 centimetres for *Alca torda torda* compared to 3.42 centimetres for *Alca torda atlantica*. [These figures clearly do not agree with Allen's rule, but Bergmann's rule has already told us to predict a larger body size for the northern race and we should not be surprised if the bill is correspondingly larger. What happens if we divide the size of the wing by the bill length. For *Alca torda torda* we have 20.97 centimetres divided by 3.57 centimetres and for *Alca torda islandica* 19.36 centimetres divided by 3.42 centimetres. This gives us figures of 5.87 and 5.67 centimetres respectively which takes us rather closer to an acceptance of both Allen's and Bergmann's rule.] A discussion of the sub-species of razorbill should not fail to mention Salomonsen's contention made in 1944 that a third sub-species should be recognised. He suggested that birds breeding around the Norwegian coast, Murmansk, western Greenland and eastern Canada should be separated on the presence of a third colourless furrow on the bill of a significant number of birds which he examined. This view is not considered valid these days and so only the two sub-species discussed above are accepted.

Like all the auks, razorbills are difficult to census but it is not a common species and the world population will probably not exceed 200,000 and almost 75% of these are concentrated around Great Britain and Ireland. 'Operation Seafarer' was a survey of British sea birds carried out during 1969–70 and workers found razorbills especially difficult because most colonies are small by auk standards and are interspersed with those of other species. Workers gave a minimum figure of 144,000 pairs breeding around the coast of the British Isles. Lloyd (1979) estimated that Britain supported 70%, Norway 12% and North America 9% of the razorbill population which is confined to the North Atlantic. In reporting on the sea-bird distribution in the North Sea up to 1984, the Nature Conservancy Council was able to provide more detailed statistics on the breeding of razorbills around the North Sea. Orkney and Shetland have around 19,000 pairs, eastern mainland Scotland 28,000 and eastern England 3,300. Large areas of eastern England lack any breeding guillemots because there are simply no suitable cliffs. The report notes that the only breeding razorbills on the continental side of the North Sea are some 2,920 pairs spread along the western coast of Norway as far north as 63°N according to the work of Brun (1979). This suggests a North Sea population of between 50,000 and 60,000 pairs with rather more pairs breeding along the more rocky areas of the west coast of Britain which is much richer in isolated islands. Most of these colonies are likely to be small and, as we have seen, difficult to census. A splendid exception is at Horn Head off Donegal in Ireland where as many as 45,000 razorbills may breed.

Lloyd (1976) suggested that 5,000 pairs may breed in Iceland although no complete count has yet been accomplished and this figure may well be too low. No thorough census has yet been taken of the Greenland population either but Evans (1984) puts the population at between 1,500 and 5,500 pairs concentrated on the rather warmer west coast and underlining the razorbills dislike of ice. Breeding still probably occurs in Spitzbergen but there is no recent evidence to confirm this whilst only small numbers breed on Bear Island. There seemed to be no birds breeding here between 1948 and 1958 according to Løvenskjold but, by 1970, razorbills had returned and Brun reported eight pairs. On Jan Mayen a population of between 100 and 200 pairs is suggested by Franeker and Camphuijsen. Denmark also has between 100 and 200 breeding pairs, Sweden around 2,000 and, in Finland, a population of up to 4,000 is thought to be present but is adversely affected by harsh winters. Once more we see how the distribution of the razorbill is affected by ice and this certainly accounts for the small Russian population, which is probably not more than 300 pairs.

Behaviour and Breeding

PRE-BREEDING BEHAVIOUR

Razorbills return to their colonies usually in February, but occasionally as early as January. On one occasion I visited the cliffs at Bempton in Yorkshire in the early morning of 27 December and watched some 30 birds going through the early stages of display on the breeding ledges. Initially these visits to the breeding sites are irregular and it is almost as if the birds are merely keeping an eye on the home area. Some workers have even noted individuals checking on the nest sites during October. During my stay on the Hebridean island described at the beginning of this chapter I noticed that, even during early March, the visits were not very long but, as the March winds gave way to April showers, the visits increased in length and the displays became more intense. It is difficult to establish a daily rhythm of activity typical of all razorbills since feeding patterns (see page 71) must vary with the distance the birds have to travel to the richest areas. Behaviour patterns must also vary according to the stage in the reproductive cycle.

In contrast to puffins (*Fratercula arctica*), razorbills spend little of their time in the pre-breeding phase loafing about in huge rafts, and Lloyd (1976) pointed out that the paired birds loaf around the nest site and that it is likely that each bird is faithful to the nest site and that pairs do meet up and breed together often for several years. Several pairs which nest in close proximity may also have a group loafing area, often a flat rock and thus it is possible to recognise sub-colonies within the main breeding population. Hudson (1979b) made a distinction between razorbills nesting on ledges and those

A pair of razorbills.

which lay their egg at the end of tunnel-like crevices. It is suggested that tunnel-nesters spend more time on the *loafing ground* than the cliff-nesters. This is probably due to the fact that cliff-nesters are more exposed to sunlight and sea breezes than those which site their nests in crevices and have less need to loaf around as they are able to do a little loafing whilst incubating. A behaviour pattern noted at the loafing areas has been named *foot-looking*, during which the bird stares down at its feet, occasionally picking at the area between its toes. Bedard (1969a) was of the opinion that the bird was ridding itself of parasites.

In the early stages of the breeding season, razorbills are very nervous and turn their heads and dive when at sea. They may raft together for safety but the numbers making up these groups are almost always less than 20, although some workers have recorded flocks of up to 50 birds. Birds will approach land in quite stiff breezes but gales cause desertion of the cliffs, especially when there are no eggs or young requiring protection. It is far safer for a bird which can dive so efficiently as a razorbill to ride out rough weather at sea rather than risk being blown into cliffs or off exposed ledges.

Those thinking of taking up synchronised swimming may do well to spend some time watching razorbills as they first move in line abreast, sometimes diving and eventually congregating in a frenzied group. Birds often raise themselves in the water and vigorously flap their wings in a manner very reminiscent of the behaviour of wildfowl. During what has been termed *swimming together*, the birds shake their heads from side to side, the males in particular holding their heads high in an effort to stimulate their mate. At this stage the pointed tail typical of razorbills is brought into play and, when it is cooked, the white area of the undertail coverts is revealed. The object of these communal displays is to bring the birds into breeding condition at around the same time, a great advantage in a busy sea-bird city. A displaying bird swims towards its partner in a hunch-backed posture with the tail held low and the neck and head stretched forward. The partners then follow a delightful greeting ceremony: the pair point their bills upwards and 'bill fence' with each other, displaying the yellow interior of the mandibles and even holding the bill of the mate. Conder (1950) was of the opinion that this behaviour was also contagious and served to co-ordinate breeding.

I have often watched this behaviour among my Hebridean razorbills and, on calm days, you can see the head feathers being erected during this ceremony, as well as the occasional display flight when one partner, presumably the male, rises from the water during the 'hunch-backed' stage and flutters for a short distance in a very delicate manner. Occasionally the female follows the male and, after landing, the pair go into a session of billing and mutual preening technically known as *allopreening*. This has so far been recorded in 20 of the 28 orders of birds and is usually performed by two birds of the same species, often a mated pair. It may occasionally involve a group of birds or even two birds of a different species.

I observed this over a period of an hour on the Bass Rock off the east coast of Scotland. A puffin and a razorbill both seemed to find a certain crevice close to an overhanging stone which was part of an old castle, an ideal nesting site. The pair bustled each other and then each began to preen the other.

Display movements of the razorbill.

A group of razorbills on the breeding grounds.

The generally accepted explanation of this behaviour seems to be that the aggressive urges of the birds are being redirected along a less dangerous channel. The razorbill eventually left the puffin in possession, but this does not mean that the puffin would always win these encounters. On this occasion the site looked to me to be much more suitable as a nest site for puffins than razorbills. A count of nesting pairs in the close vicinity revealed 12 pairs of puffins and no razorbills at all. The confrontation and subsequent allopreening was nevertheless a fascinating experience.

When compared to the common murre or guillemot (*Uria aalge*), razorbills spend more time displaying on the water and consequently less on the breeding cliffs where the former species seems to be far more aggressive. Razorbill nests are, however, much more widely separated. We must not draw the conclusion that razorbills are not aggressive and even a short period of watching birds on the water will show that males fiercely defend an area of water around their mate. No intruder is usually allowed within three body lengths of a paired female without invoking a growl from the male, during which he opens his bill wide and displays a wide expanse of threatening yellow. If this does not work then the head feathers are erected and the intruder is 'rushed'. If this fails to make him dive then a fight ensues during which the bills clash together and wing-fighting and growling can be heard over quite a long distance. Obviously the larger the colony the more displays of aggression there are likely to be, especially when rafts of immature birds almost ready to breed get in the way. Fighting is usually avoided by the potential loser displaying appeasement postures which have not yet been fully elucidated. 'Turning away' may well deter the aggressor but the 'landing posture', during which the intruder tilts the body and wings forward and raises the wings, may also help.

The behaviour so far can be seen to take place on water, but it is much easier to observe pairs in courtship on land. By the time they reach the ledges the razorbill pairs may be well established, but distinct courtship movements can still be recognised. The sequence of movements is not understood, but it may well be that there is no sequence and that any movement can be triggered by the appropriate signal depending upon times of day and the presence of external stimuli, especially other razorbills which may be potential rivals, predators or even the human observers. Billing and allopreening are both common, and therefore presumably important, and males often indulge in *ecstatic display* during which the head is held vertically, the body tilted backwards, the mandibles of the bill clicked rapidly together and a low growling noise produced. This movement does seem to be restricted to birds on land, but it would be difficult to go through these motions on water. There is, however, some neck-stretching by water-based birds which may be the aquatic equivalent to the ecstatic display. Birkhead (1976) noted that the ecstatic display was used by males as their mates approached the breeding ledge, but the aggression was soon abated, unlike his attitude when predators were about and the display was continued until the danger had gone. Bedard (1969a) pointed out that parents with young about to fledge also indulged in this type of display. The female often placates the aggression of the male by hunching her back and pointing her bill towards the ground, but keeping her wings by her side. This tucked posture in which the mouth is opened wide is often copied by the male as if to assure the female that her presence is accepted and that she is safe from further aggression.

Once the bond between a pair is established, but not before, copulation occurs. The act never occurs at sea but takes place on loafing areas or around the nest site, three or four times per day during the 2 or 3 weeks prior to egg-laying, but not usually thereafter. Mature birds which for some reason have failed to breed or have lost their eggs to a predators may continue to copulate throughout the season.

POST-COPULATORY BEHAVIOUR

NEST SITES

Just prior to egg-laying, the pair begin to prepare the nest site which they do by planting the foot nearest to the edge of the cliff on firm ground before scraping with the other. The birds will often push or even carry stones and push them into the space, although nest-building as a protracted action is not regular. There does appear to be some differences in observed behaviour in razorbills on either side of the Atlantic. Paludan (1947) and Plumb (1965) reported few instances of nesting material being accumulated around the site in Britain and, apart from the incident with the red bobble cap described at the beginning of this chapter, my observations of 197 razorbill sites show only nine with any nest material, including one egg laid on a mat of seaweed which had almost certainly been deposited before the nest site was selected. Bedard (1969a), working in Canada, found rather more evidence of deliberate nest-construction and, of 67 sites investigated, he found 41 contained grass roots, 55 contained evidence of deliberately accumulated gravel and only six eggs were laid directly onto bare rock. Clearly more research is needed around the razorbill colonies on both sides of the Atlantic if this apparent difference in behaviour is to be satisfactorily explained.

Razorbill resting beside its egg under the shelter of an overhanging cliff.

The average date of laying obviously depends upon climate and is earlier in those areas where spring comes early. British colonies can be incubating by mid April, although it is usually well into May, whilst it can be towards the end of June before the Greenland colonies are in full swing. Occasionally two eggs may be laid, but this is most unusual, the normal being just a single egg. Should the first egg be lost a replacement is often laid which is always smaller than the first. The shape is described as oval or sub-elliptical, the egg being finely granular, non-glossy and slightly rough to the touch. The colour varies a great deal in both ground colour and darker markings. A white egg is occasionally found in which case the greenish inner shell membrane is obvious. The occasional all-black egg is also on record. The ground colour however can be quite dark brown and the spots, speckles, bands and blotches of dark brown and black also show a great deal of variation. It seems that incubating birds are able to identify the unique patterning on their own egg, a most essential situation in the case of colonial birds. This also seems to be the case in the common guillemot. The size of the egg averages 7.31 by 4.69 centimetres ($2\frac{29}{32}$ by $1\frac{7}{8}$ inches). The egg of *Alca torda torda* tends to be slightly larger than that of *Alca torda islandica* although, rather strangely, the nominate race tends to produce a slightly lighter egg of around 90 grams (just over 3 ounces).

The period of incubation would seem to vary, Witherby's *Handbook* quoting 25 days in an incubator (F.G. Paynter), 26–30 days (O.A.T. Lee), 30 in an incubator (W. Evans) and at least 35 (E. Miller). This last figure seems more in line with the recent work of Lloyd (1979) who reported 35.1 days plus or minus 2.2 days. My work is much less precise than this, but I was able to record figures of 36, 38 and 38 days on three Hebridean nests watched from laying to hatching. It will be interesting to see whether the incubation periods are on average longer in the cooler north and also to discover whether the average ambient temperature and amount of rain and wind during the incubation period have any influence on the time taken. The female seems to remain with her newly laid egg for around 48 hours after which the chore is shared with changeovers taking place twice over a 24 hour period. It seems to make no difference which of the sexes incubates during the hours of darkness. Whilst watching my Hebridean colony, I noticed eggs to be predated mainly by herring gulls (*Larus argentatus*) which I saw take five eggs but two were also taken by a brown rat (*Rattus norvegicus*) and two by hooded crows (*Corvus corone*). On a colony under observation on the Island of Skokholm off Wales, Lloyd (1976) noted that jackdaws (*Corvus monedula*) were also a problem to breeding razorbills but, despite this and the attentions of gulls, 71% of the eggs laid hatched successfully. There is plenty of evidence to show that older birds are more successful in protecting their eggs and young than younger less experienced birds.

The availability of nesting sites must also be important. A colony laying on a wide cliff must be more vulnerable than one sited in an area where the eggs can be secreted in narrow cracks into which the larger predators are unable to squeeze.

THE YOUNG

Defined as nidicolous and semi-altricial, the young are around 15 centimetres (6 inches) long when first hatched, weigh between 50 and 80 grams ($1\frac{3}{4}$ to $2\frac{13}{16}$ ounces) and have huge feet out of all proportion to their size. These are useful for propulsion when they leave the nesting ledges about 2 or 3 weeks later. How long the youngsters are cared for by the parents is not known with any certainty, but the fledging period would seem to be about 3 months. Leaving the breeding area, often high above the sea, is a traumatic time for nervous chick and worried adult and is not achieved without problems. Eventually, after much calling and bobbing, the chick jumps with a whirring of its tiny and not yet functional wings and hits the sea below, to be followed a few seconds later by the adult which dives and calls until the two are united. They then move out to sea together away from the colony. Should any chick land on the beach rather than the water and survive, it makes contact with the adult and the two scramble over the rocks to the sea. Any injured chick is eventually abandoned. The male parent seems to take charge of the young during their early days at sea. The winter rafts are mainly small, the aggregations increasing in size as spring approaches prior to the whole cycle being repeated. Razorbills do not breed until they are 4 or even 5 years old but ringing returns suggest that the birds may survive for longer than 30 years, so a long adolescent period can be well afforded.

VOCALISATIONS

As in the case of the little auk a great deal of work remains to be done on the 'language' of the species and understanding will only come as recording techniques improve. It is possible to recognise four distinct types of adult calls and also the efforts of the young to communicate with their parents is now becoming clearer (see Table 5).

Table 5   An Analysis of the Vocalisations of the Razorbill (*Alca torda*)

Adult to Adult Calls	Adult to Young Calls	Young to Adult Calls
Defence: Alarm call *Offence*: Attack growl *Breeding*: Ecstatic growl Billing call Copulating call Settling call	Luring call	Brooding call Contact call Distress call Leap call

Most of these calls are self-explanatory and are all based upon a growling sound which Witherby described as a 'tremulous, whirring sound and a prolonged grating growling "caarrrr"' and the young were said to have a plaintive note. Since this was written in the 1940s, razorbill language has been studied and translated, although most of this research was carried out on the breeding grounds. The *alarm call* is a rhythmic series of short sharp growls. This is produced when the bird is alarmed, in sharp contrast to the attack call which lasts longer and occurs when the individual has decided that attack might be the best form of defence. The 'breeding vocabulary' is much more clearly understood and four separate calls have so far been identified. The *ecstatic growl* was recognised by Paludan in 1947 when he called it the nest song. Since this time, other workers, particularly Bedard (1969a), have split the ecstatic growl into three separate components. The same worker noted that one phase was associated with the head-forward posture and a longer growl was produced with the head-vertical position. During this phase, a mechanical sound was added and produced by vibrating the mandibles of the bill together. This had already been noted in 1940 by Perry who pointed out the similarity in sound to that produced by castanets. A much more low-key call is uttered by birds in the tucked-up posture; this is a growl of much reduced intensity possibly associated with submission.

The *billing call* is a growl lasting around 2 seconds followed by a more chattering growl and is associated with billing and allopreening, both aimed at successful copulation during which both the male and female have a recognisable call. In the male this has not been fully described but many males growl throughout the act whereas the female tosses her head whilst uttering short growls. Once the eggs have been laid and incubation has started a succession of growls becoming gradually shorter in duration are produced as the on-duty bird settles down on the egg or broods the young. This has been well-named the *settling call*. Once the chick has hatched, a *lure call* consisting of single growl notes is repeated every couple of seconds or disyllabic calls are repeated every 4 or 5 seconds. At this time the chick itself is able to respond by means of at least four calls. After the first 2 or 3 days, the whistling plaintive call described by Witherby is very obvious and is the chick's own *contact call*. It can be a quite loud 'dui dui dui' sound but, from the time of hatching, a softer 'du di dui di du du' call lets the parent know that its offspring is cold and wants to be brooded. This call increases in pitch and intensity when the chick is distressed. Workers, particularly Dunn and Sellar, have pointed out that the distress call varies from one individual chick to another. This is very important in colonial species and enables the adults to 'home in' on their own young which is particularly valuable at sea. Such individual calls are very likely to be a feature of the language of all auks. The chick also has what has been labelled the *leap call* which obviously registers the bird's anxiety at the prospect of having to jump and follow its father to sea in search of food.

Food and Feeding

All the food of razorbills is captured by diving from the surface. It consists mainly of fish, but a few invertebrates are also eaten. If a large shoal of fish is seen whilst the bird is in flight, it can 'crash dive' into them and emerge with several fish which can be held, puffin-like across the bill. F.W. Frowhawk recorded as many as 12 fish being carried, but Lloyd (1976) noted 20 sand-eels (*Ammodytes*) in the bill of one efficient razorbill. This is typical of birds which are feeding young on the breeding grounds. The more usual feeding technique is to swim around with the head dipping periodically into the water to spot prey. It is at this point that the white markings on the bill may be important in lining up prey.

Several workers have estimated both the time of dives and the depths reached by feeding razorbills. Witherby noted that the submerging bird kicks hard with its legs and flicks the partially-opened wings and that both legs and wings are used in the swift underwater propulsion. J.M. Dewar (1924) recorded diving times of 52 seconds and a maximum depth of nearly 8 metres (24 feet). Obviously the depth must to some extent be determined by the area over which the birds are fishing. Madsen (1957) reported a preferred depth of 2 to 3 metres (6 to 9 feet) whilst Kozlova (1957) noted a maximum depth of 5 to 7 metres (15 to 29 feet) and Bianki (1967) thought that some birds could reach depths of 10 metres (33 feet) on occasions, although the diving times seem to be under 1 minute.

In the breeding season the favoured feeding sites are usually less than 20 kilometres ($12\frac{1}{2}$ miles) from the nesting colony and several workers have noted that razorbills often kleptoparasitise puffins (*Fratercula arctica*). *Kleptoparasitism* is a technical term describing one animal stealing food from another and it seems that razorbills were experts in piracy on the high seas long before the days of Treasure Island! Razorbills have been seen to attack flying puffins until they drop the food which they are carrying to their young. The razorbill then retrieves the fish from the surface of the sea. The more usual approach, however, is to swim beneath the puffin and torpedo it from below or actually pursue the puffin under the water.

As we have already seen, the depth of dive is to some extent determined by habitat. What appear to be favourite items of diet are a reflection of availability as much as preference. Sand-eels of the family Ammodytidae are a vital part of the diet and Swennen and Duiven (1977) noted that length was not the limiting factor and fish of up to 2.3 centimetres (almost 1 inch) diameter could be coped with, but those larger than this could not be swallowed. The classic study was done by Collinge (1924) who examined the contents of 43 stomachs and found the material to be almost exclusively animal, although some workers, including myself, have noted young razorbills eating rose-root (*Sedum rosea*) but this must be regarded more as an example of youthful curiosity rather than a regular constituent of diet. Collinge (1924) calculated a diet of 46.91% fish, 42.23% crustaceans and annelids and 10.45% marine molluscs. It may well be that many of the

Razorbills are heavy birds and may often struggle to take off in calm water.

crustaceans and molluscs are actually derived from the contents of the guts of the fish rather than from the razorbill's own feeding. Apart from sand-eels, many other species of fish are also eaten, including sprats (*Sprattus sprattus*), sardines (*Sardina pilchardus*), cod (*Gadus morhua*) and herring (*Clupea harengus*). It is interesting to note that the herring is related to the sand-eels, which are not eels at all but are so-named because of their long thin bodies.

Regional studies in recent years have done much to demonstrate how the diet of the razorbill depends upon the availability of prey, although the dependence upon fish is everywhere apparent. Madsen (1957) found that razorbills around the Faroes fed almost entirely on sand-eels and work in the Russian Barents Sea by Belopol'ski (1957) produced a figure of 92% fish in the diet of this species. In Greenland, Madsen (1957) reported that razor-bills fed mainly upon capelin (*Mallotus villosus*) with a small number of crustaceans and polychaete annelids.

All these studies were carried out on birds feeding around the breeding sites but the few studies carried out in winter indicate that 83% of bird stomachs examined contained only fish whilst less than 3% showed no evidence of fish, although this does not mean that the birds in question did not eat fish.

6

GUILLEMOTS OR MURRES

The common guillemot (*Uria aalge*) and Brunnich's guillemot (*Uria lomvia*), which both measure 41 centimetres (16½ inches) from head to tail tip, are very similar species but, providing they can be observed close at hand, clear differences can be detected at all seasons of the year. The bill of Brunnich's guillemot is shorter and thicker and is also distinguished by a pale narrow line running along the sides of the bill. It is, however, much narrower than that of the razorbill (*Alca torda*). It is surprising that two such similar species of guillemot have evolved, but they are separated by the fact that they occupy different geographical ranges, Brunnich's being a much more northerly-based bird. The area of breeding overlap is relatively small and thus both have their own ecological niche. The name 'guillemot' is fascinating as the entry in the *Oxford Book of British Bird Names* amply shows.

"Guillemot. A name of French provenance, known since Belon 1555, who stated that the name denoted the immature bird. It was introduced into English to name the Common Guillemot by Ray 1678. Pennant 1768 took up the word, using it both specifically and generically (see Black Guillemot) and de facto established it as a standard name. Presumably the exotic term was felt to stand above the various regional names, but only during the last hundred years or so has it actually been replacing these synonyms locally. The bird name, as we have it, is the same as the French personal name Guillemot, *a pet form of* Guillaume, *which goes back to Old French (11th cent.)* Willelm.*

The commonest native name for the Guillemot is Willock, first attested in 1631, in Scotland also Willick, further Sussex Willy, Will, Scottish Wilkie (see-kie) all sometimes transferred to the Razorbill.

All the above names are ultimately echoic in origin, the clear high-pitched call of the juvenile bird being reproduced as will, *and used to denote the species as a whole. Such a base could hardly fail to be brought into association with pet forms of Old French* Willelm, *William, an everyday Christian name in this country after 1066. And, of course, the same thing happened on the French side of the Channel. Guillemot, too is ultimately the product of the same onomatopoeia.*

With around 600,000 breeding pairs in the British Isles the guillemot is the most common sea bird in Britain and, because of its gregarious nature,

The razorbill (left) is easily distinguished from the common guillemot (right) by the shape and size of the bills.

it is an easy bird to observe. Whilst out on a fishing trip in the Hebrides during early December, I observed guillemots keeping an eye on their breeding ledges, apparently oblivious of wing and wave.

COMMON GUILLEMOT (*Uria aalge*)

Habitat

The guillemot prefers areas around the coast and islands south of the low Arctic, putting up with rain and high wind but showing a marked aversion to ice. The main demand appears to be an August temperature between 5°C and 20°C (41°F and 68°F). Like the razorbill, guillemots appear, with a few exceptions based in the Baltic, to be centred in areas with a salinity above 34 parts per thousand. (Brunnich's guillemot, on the other hand is found in waters with salinity levels below this figure.) Shallow and brackish waters are avoided. Only Brunnich's and the common guillemot appear able to rear their young successfully on rock ledges which are so open to the elements. Stacks, cliff ledges and the sloping summit of islands often seem to overflow with jostling birds. Once the breeding season is over, common guillemots seldom move very far away from the colony, and this seems to contrast with the behaviour of Brunnich's guillemot. This is hardly surprising, however, when the more northerly distribution of the latter species, with the tendency to encounter frozen seas, is considered.

A group of densely-packed guillemots on the Elegug stacks, south Wales. *Elegug* is the local name for the guillemot and is derived from the noise made by the birds.

Common guillemots seldom fly higher than 200 metres (650 feet), and usually much lower, and they do most of their feeding by diving into the first 20 metres (65 feet) of sea. This, coupled with their reluctance to fly, as with the rest of the auks, means that guillemots are particularly vulnerable to oil pollution and poisons such as the polychlorinated biphenyls which are carried from industries on the ocean currents (see Chapter 11). The threat once posed by protein- and fat-starved human populations has now disappeared, as has the so-called sport of 'auk potting' by holidaymakers.

Description

The common guillemot is just a little larger than the razorbill (*Alca torda*) and somewhat slimmer in build. The head, neck, back and wings are brownish black and contrast sharply with the clean white of the undersurface. When the birds are perched on the breeding rocks they seem to be wearing white sweaters. It does seem that the shape of these 'sweater necks'

The common guillemot can be distinguished from Brunnich's guillemot by the slightly narrower bill and the lack of white on the bill. Brunnich's guillemot (above): adult in summer plumage (left), adult in winter plumage (right) and downy young (bottom). Common guillemot (bottom): adult in summer plumage (top), adult in winter plumage (right) and downy young (bottom).

varies with the individual but more work must be done to see if the pattern is maintained through the moult into subsequent years. Although there is some overlap, Brunnich's guillemot does seem to have a slightly larger body which would appear to satisfy Bergmann's rule (page 60). The longer, more tapered, bill of the common guillemot means that more heat would be lost in cold climates and neatly supports Allen's rule.

A feature typical of the species is a dark furrow running behind the eye, a feature obvious in all birds but particularly easy to see in the adult's winter plumage and also clearly seen in immature birds. At this point, mention should be made of the bridled guillemot which, contrary to the belief of early naturalists, is a variety of *Uria aalge* and is neither a separate species nor a sub-species. In 1846 the species was described by William Macgillivray under the title of *Uria troile*, the foolish guillemot. He noted that there was 'a line of white encircling the eye and extending behind it.... Some individuals want the white lines on the head'.

When Howard Saunders revised Yarrell's *History of British Birds* in 1885 he noted that:

In former editions of this work the Ringed or Bridled Guillemot was figured and described with the concluding remark by the author that 'opinions seemed fairly balanced as to whether this bird is a species or a variety'. Since those lines were written the general opinion of ornithologists has inclined to consider it merely as a race with a tendency to develop an unusual amount of white encircling the eye and running along the crease or furrow which passes thence down the sides of the head. It inhabits the same localities and it is always found in company with the common species but in far inferior numbers. At Lundy island it is rare, so it is at Flamborough on the Farne Islands, where the Editor had an opportunity of watching breeding guillemots at very short distance, he observed several birds with well-developed eye-rings and streaks, sitting on the eggs, whilst others exhibited gradations from the above to the usual furrow with only a few white feathers at its junction with the eye .... On Handa, off the coast of Sutherland, the Ringed variety is said by Mr Harvie-Brown to be abundant as compared with other bird stations in Scotland, being in the proportion, of about one in ten or twelve, and he has many times seen the Common and Ringed birds paired .... At Grimsey, to the North of Iceland, according to Mr Procter there is a considerable proportion of the Ringed variety; and there appears to be a general although not invariable increase in the number of this form towards the north. From Baird's 'Birds of North America' (p. 914) it would seem that this variation is equally found in the Pacific Uria californica*: a strong argument against the specific value of the white markings.*

Later workers refute the presence of the bridled form in the Pacific population and it now seems clearly established that the bridled form is a variety of which the proportion increases from north to south, but it is still not at all clear what the function of the bridling might be. The bridled

A colony of common guillemots with a bridled bird on the far left of the group in the foreground.

morph, as it is now called, has been investigated statistically in the Atlantic and Arctic populations. In western Iberia the bridled morph is totally absent whilst on Bear Island the proportion in the population is 57.3% (J.A. van Franeker). In England the figure varies from 1 to 5% whilst in Scotland this rises as high as 17%. Brun (1970) found the southern Norway populations to have 12.5% bridled individuals whilst in the north this figure was as high as 24.6%. Southern (1962) obtained figures for Iceland of between 50% and 70%. All workers agree that the proportion of the morph increases as we move north, but the question remains – why? Could the white eye pattern be important in the darker northern springs when breeding pairs are being established in low light intensities? During 'bill fencing' in the early stages of breeding it might help to know where your partner's eyes might be. Could the markers be useful during feeding in the poor lighting conditions beneath the waves and act as a sighting mechanism? We may never know for certain but all scientists love to speculate. Southern's work (1962) suggested that bridled birds become more common as one moves from south-west to north-east and show some correlation with the temperature of the surface water.

In his book *Inheritance and Natural History* (published in 1977), Professor R.J. Berry summarised some of Southern's findings and offered some ideas of his own.

'At one time these spectacled birds were thought to be a distinct species, but recently it has been possible to raise a family in captivity and show that bridling is a recessive inherited condition, produced by alleles at a single locus (Jefferies and Parslow).

In 1938 and 1939 members of the BTO were enlisted by H.N. Southern to count the numbers of bridled and non-bridled Guillemots in as many colonies as possible. With a few irregularities the frequency of bridled birds increased with latitude: at the southern edge of the race in Portugal not a single bridled bird was seen, but northwards the proportion of bridled birds increased until it reached over 50% in Southern Iceland. Bridling does not occur in Pacific populations of the species. In Iceland the common guillemot is replaced by Brunnich's Guillemot (Uria lomvia) and the frequency of bridling apparently falls with the species density so that only 10% of Guillemots are bridled on the Island of Grimsey, north of Iceland.

The counts were repeated in 1948–50 and the proportion of bridled guillemots were found to have fallen by up to 10% in quite a few colonies (although it was the same as before in over half) but in a third count ten years later (in 1959–60) the frequencies were the same as in the first count position (Southern, 1962).

Now it is difficult to collect information about the population structure and amount of movement of individuals between colonies of Guillemots, never mind about the relative fertility and survival of different morphs. Southern, Carrick and Potter (1965) made an intensive study with colour ringed birds of a Guillemot colony near Aberdeen. They found that the generation time was about 9 years, and that the rate of population turn over was normally very low. This *meant that the change in bridling frequencies in the two ten year periods between surveys could not be due to selection, and must be due either to a mass movement of birds which has sometimes been recorded for Guillemots – they spread, for example, rapidly up Labrador to West Greenland, and the highest recorded frequency of bridling (71%) occurs at Nunarsuk, Labrador (Tuck, 1960) or that the counts were inaccurate because of patchy distribution of bridled birds.*

Whatever the true explanation for the frequency changes in time, the reasons for the cline in space is completely unknown. Southern (1962) showed that bridling frequencies increase as water temperatures fall, while Jefferies and Parslow (1976) found slight evidence that bridled birds had a higher basic metabolic rate than non-bridled ones. If so, this could be the explanation for the northern extension of the species (mainly bridled birds) in this century (Southern, 1962). Certainly, the increase in proportion of bridled birds with latitude is so consistent that it must have some causal explanation, and presumably this will be similar to that in the Arctic Skua, where the proportions of colour phases merely act as indicators for a behavioural adaptation. It is easy to speculate about bridled Guillemots, but very difficult to find out why they occur.

A parallel cline to that in Common Guillemots is found in the Fulmar (Fulmarus glacialis), where high frequencies of a dark or 'blue' colour phase occur in the 'high arctic', i.e. northern latitudes where the sea temperature is at or near freezing point even during mid-summer. Nothing whatsoever seems to be known about the inheritance, characteristics, or stability with time of this northern morph (Fisher 1952).

The black bill has a yellow gape and the eyes are dark brown which makes them difficult to see against the head feathering, except at close quarters. Guillemots do allow quiet and slow-moving observers to approach closely and the eye colour can then be appreciated, as can the yellowish legs and brownish webbing between the toes.

Whilst the bridled morph is not now regarded as a sub-species, at least five such groupings are now recognised. The nominate *Uria aalge aalge* occurs in eastern Canada (where it is known as the common murre), Greenland, Iceland, the Faroes, Norway south of 69°N, the Baltic and in Scotland north of 55°38′N. *Uria aalge albionis* occurs in Britain, south of 55°38′N, as well as in Ireland, Brittany and Western Iberia. Witherby *et al.* (1944) noted the differences from the nominate form by pointing out that: '... Northern form may have a body as dark as a razorbill'. Breeding guillemots on the islands and stacks of St Kilda are certainly much darker than those inhabiting the cliffs at Bempton in Yorkshire or St Bees in Cumbria. *Uria aalge hyperborea* is a larger sub-species found in Norway to the north of 69°N, as well as along the coast of Murmansk, Bear Island, Spitzbergen and Novaya Zemlya. Measurements show that this sub-species is significantly larger than the nominate type and is thus yet another example of the truth of Bergmann's rule. A consideration of the average wing length of males shows that of *Uria aalge albionis* to be 19.6 centimetres ($7\frac{23}{32}$ inches), *Uria aalge aalge* 20.4 centimetres ($8\frac{1}{32}$ inches) and *Uria aalge hyperborea* 21.2 centimetres ($8\frac{11}{32}$ inches), a clear, confirmation that the species is increasing in size as we move north. The weights of the birds show a similar increase which will allow those in the colder areas to hold their body-core temperature steady by losing less vital energy. The sub-species *hyperborea*, like the nominate race, has significantly darker dorsal plumage than the southern race. *U.a. spiloptera*, restricted to the Faroe Islands, and the Baltic-based *U.a. intermedia* are rather lighter in plumage but are impossible, in the present author's view, to separate in the field.

There are also two American sub-species to consider: *Uria aalge inornata* found in the North Pacific and the slightly smaller *Uria aalge californica* found, as its name implies in the more southerly areas around California.

In winter the adult guillemots of all sub-species undergo a marked change, especially around the head and neck. The furrow around the eye is maintained, but an initial light mottling of white on the chin, throat, cheeks and crown is eventually replaced by larger areas of white which give the bird the appearance of having a collar.

Distribution and Populations

Anyone who has sailed around or sat among the vast sea-bird cities will know just how difficult it is to conduct an accurate census of the inhabitants. All estimates should therefore be regarded as tentative and certainly the reports of the naturalists in former times which tell us of 'millions upon millions' of birds must be treated with caution, although there is little doubt that some populations have shown dramatic declines. The methods described by Cramp *et al.* (1974), which were operated during 'Operation Seafarer', have proved, as one would expect of such skilled ornithologists, to be as reliable as any. It is pointed out that counting individual birds is one thing, but arriving at an accurate figure for the number of breeding birds is quite another. Gibson (1950) had already pointed out that birds which were either incubating an egg or brooding a very young chick could be identified by their very crouched stance. Observers who approach too close are likely to disturb the incubating bird and the eggs or young will fall victim to predators, especially the larger gulls. Brun (1979) tried a method of sample counts, but this too had drawbacks in the sense that breeding density is bound to vary from one part of the colony to another. There are sub-colonies within the main colony which are equivalent to the street communities in highly-populated towns. Careful observations by Joensen (1963), Southern *et al.*(1965) and others has suggested that between 50% and 60% of incubating pairs are present on the colony at any one time and direct counts adjusted with these statistics in mind might be the best available method of estimation providing they

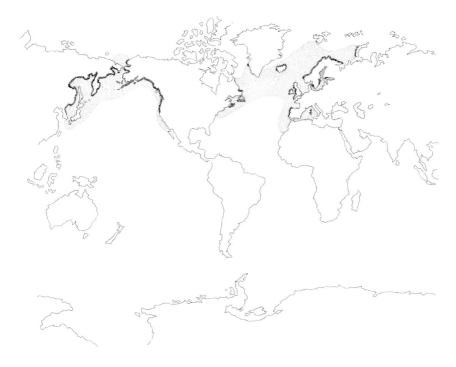

Distribution of the common guillemot (*Uria aalge*).

are done at the peak of the breeding season. This time will also vary with latitude.

In Greenland the total population is probably between 300 and 500 pairs, concentrated in two colonies around the southerly areas at Sermilinguaq Fjord and at Ydrekitsigsut, but very much swamped by huge colonies of Brunnich's guillemots. As the climate of Greenland seems to be ameliorating it will be interesting to see whether the common guillemot is able to extend its range and what inter-reaction develops, if any, with the well-established rival species. In Spitzbergen, where Brunnich's guillemot is also the dominant species, Norderhaug (1974) reported only one colony of common guillemots and this did not exceed 100 birds. The same situation applies on Jan Mayen Island where as many as 300 pairs of common guillemots may breed among the host of Brunnich's. On Bear Island and Iceland, huge numbers of both species breed and either of these two stations would be ideal areas to study the inter-reaction between the two. Belopol'ski (1957) noted that, where the two species occur together, the birds become thoroughly mixed in the colonies, but the common guillemot is always the more dominant and often usurps the nest site originally claimed by a pair of Brunnich's guillemots. Luttik reported around 1 million breeding pairs on Bear Island and Einarsson estimated $1\frac{1}{2}$ million pairs around the coast of

Iceland, a figure which seems to have remained stable during the twentieth century. Dyck and Meltofte (1975) thought that the population on the Faroes was declining and was around 390,000 pairs, a drop of around 20% between 1961 and 1972.

In the British Isles, there has been an often dramatic decline in breeding populations in the south. On Lundy for example the population fell from around 19,000 pairs in 1939 to less than 2,000 in 1969–70. Colonies which once thrived in the Isle of Wight, Devon, Cornwall, Dorset and Wales have also declined markedly since 1950. These colonies, however, have always formed a relatively small proportion of the total British population. Despite some heart-breaking losses due to oil pollution, the population of guillemots is at least stable and has probably increased since 'Operation Seafarer' estimated that, at 577,000 breeding pairs, *Uria aalge* was Britain's most numerous sea bird. 78,000 pairs occur in Ireland. The numbers have certainly risen in the more northerly colonies especially on St Kilda, Fair Isle, Canna, Mingulay, St Abb's Head, Bass Rock and the Isle of May.

It has been suggested that the losses in the south are counterbalanced by gains in the north and that the British need not worry about their guillemot populations. We should remember, however, that the northern birds belong to the race *Uria aalge aalge* whilst those of the declining southern colonies are of the sub-species *Uria aalge albionis*, which has a very restricted range outside the British Isles. Reasons for any declines should certainly be investigated and, if possible, protective measures taken. There have been significant declines in Portugal, Spain and France. The Portuguese population was estimated at around 6,000 pairs by Lockley in 1942, and in 1982, Barcena estimated the population to be as low as 75 pairs. This represents a decline almost to the point of extinction and the Spanish situation is even worse, the 1982 estimate being only 38 pairs compared with just over 2,000 pairs around 1960. The French populations, according to Guermeur and Monnat (1980), have also shown a sharp decline since 1940 and there are now probably less than 300 pairs. The West German population appears to have survived its crisis. In the area around Heligoland, there were an estimated 3,500 pairs in 1880 but these had decreased to around 1,000 pairs by 1950. However, by 1981, Vauk-Henzelt thought that the population had at least doubled. There also appears to have been an increase in Denmark's only colony to something approaching 2,000 pairs.

In Norway and Sweden, populations have declined, sometimes dramatically due to birds becoming entangled in fishing nets, pollution (mainly by oil) and human predation of the nutritious eggs and fat-rich adults. The population of around 160,000 pairs estimated by Brun in the 1960s had been halved by 1982. In Sweden, however, there is cause for some optimism following protective measures and the population of 8,000 pairs now appears to be rising steadily. In the USSR, the common guillemot is found around the coast of Murmansk with a population estimated by Gerasimova at around 16,000 pairs in 1962. Finland has only one colony, which was

Guillemots (*Uria aalge*) on the Pinnacles, Farne Islands, Northumberland, England, with kittiwakes (*Rissa tridactyla*) on the ledges.

established in 1957, and had only 14 pairs in 1974 but, by the mid 1980s, this figure had risen to almost 50 pairs.

In conclusion it would seem that the nominate race of the common guillemot is thriving over most of its range, but the sub-species *albionis* and *hyperborea* have been less successful of late and are in need of a more careful study and we should perhaps be thinking of some extra degree of protection.

Behaviour and Breeding

Common guillemots usually return to the breeding areas before Christmas, although this does depend upon the latitude of the colony. The timing of the forging of the pair bonds may well be the reason why they show an aversion to ice floes. They do not stay on the breeding cliffs, but make visits usually early in the morning. During these initial scouting trips the birds seem very nervous and it is not usually possible for a boat to approach close to the cliffs without the birds rising in a protesting cloud and, after circling the site, heading out to the open sea. Should the boat continue on its way, the birds loop round and return to their positions. At this stage, they are, of course, in winter plumage and there are no serious pretentions to holding territory, nor are there any eggs or young to protect, and thus there is no real incentive to remain in the danger area. Once the breeding season is in full swing the birds will usually allow a very close approach.

The density of the breeding pairs on even the narrowest of ledges is almost unbelievable and the birds landing to attend to the nests have sometimes to crash into the throng and force their way to their own tiny territory. Trumpeting calls echo along the ledges and birds bow continually to each other, the whole bobbing community resembling a convention of old-time Chinese mandarins. Tuck (1960) reported that copulation rarely occurs at sea but the pair find time to mate even in the midst of such a busy throng. The ritualised courtship movements will obviously serve to bring the females into breeding condition at the same time and this is an essential feature in the breeding of colonial species. These ritualised movements have been studied by many workers but in particular by Tschanz (1968), Williams (1972) and Birkhead from 1976 onwards.

Let us follow the courtship of a pair of guillemots on a typical sea cliff. Imagine you have a notebook and pencil, a pair of binoculars and a flask of coffee. (You can have a hip flask if you like!) A stiff breeze blows from off the grey sea and you are glad of your gloves. Even early June can be chilly as dawn breaks and you prepare for a full day of guillemot-watching.

In the lives of all birds, body language is of vital importance, not just for the purpose of attracting a mate and the successful raising of offspring. Guillemots have recognisable movements to register alarm, keep flocks in contact, antagonism, appeasement, a desire for sexual bonding and for contact within the family.

The initial reaction to any unusual or potentially dangerous event is for the bird to open its eyes wide enough to assume a distinctly startled expression, during which the neck is extended, the feathers sleeked down and the carpal joints spread wide. This is called the *alert posture* and it is invariably followed by *alarm-bowing* and an accompanying call. This behav-

Table 6   An Analysis of Guillemot (*Uria aalge*) Language

Adult to Adult Calls	Adult to Young Calls	Young to Adult Calls
Alarm bowing call	Stopping brooding call	Pecking call
Distress	Alarm-contact call	Contact call when brooding
Growling call	Lure call	required
Barking call	Leap call	Contact distress call
Copulation call		Distress call
(male and female)		Threat call
		Pain call
		Water call in response to
		parents' leap call

Compiled with reference to the works of Hall-Craggs (1984), Tschanz (1968), Birkhead (1976), Witherby (1941), Nørrevang (1958) and Dunn (1984).

iour occurs more commonly in clubs of birds which are not very densely congregated and this serves to underline the guillemot philosophy that there is safety in numbers. The alarmed birds may raise themselves on their tarsi and engage in a very vigorous bout of wing-flapping. If the danger continues the birds take flight and plunge into the sea before quickly submerging.

Common guillemots show a tendency to form flocks both on the breeding ground and on the sea, although in the latter behaviour pattern they are less gregarious than Brunnich's guillemot. Having said this, we should bear in mind that all things are comparative. There are feeding, migratory and pre-breeding flocks, but these play no part in pair formation. Once a pair is formed, however, the male may prevent rivals approaching within around two body lengths of his female, although the pair may join in the group activities outside this one restraint. In the pre-breeding flocks, other species are often involved especially, in Britain, puffins (*Fratercula arctica*). The birds seem to chase over the water looking like a living game of 'ducks and drakes' as they patter over the waves before either taking off for a brief aerial ballet or plunging beneath the waves in a brief mist of spray. They may even 'bump' each other, thus forcing a dive, and, when they emerge, the birds stretch their heads and open their bills wide. Having watched this behaviour on many occasions it is difficult not to become too anthropomorphic and to suggest that the auks are just enjoying their playtime. Once off the Farne Islands I almost fell out of my boat whilst laughing at a flock of guillemots. They kept swimming beneath others in the flock before emerging, bill uppermost, to stab the startled-looking birds which had been thus 'torpedoed'. This cartoon-like entertainment is just one of the rewards reserved for the field naturalist. It quickly warms cramped and shivering limbs. Even this is a more 'friendly' performance than the antagonistic movements which are really quite vicious, especially amongst the noisy densely packed colonies in which individuals find themselves really pressed for space.

As usual in the avian world, threat always comes before any actual fighting. The alert posture is usually followed by feinting stabbing motions and the owner of the ground points its bill at the intruder. If the latter stands its ground a fight may result, during which wings are used to batter the adversary, bills are interlocked and fierce growls are generated.

The number from the musical *The King and I* in which it is suggested that 'Whenever I feel afraid, I whistle a happy tune' is a perfect example of what biologists call displacement behaviour. The *Oxford Dictionary of Natural History* (1985) defines this as:

Behaviour of an animal which tends to be irrelevant to the situation in which it occurs and that may interrupt other activity. It may reduce conflict; or it may arise because the animal is prevented from attaining a goal, and the consequent frustration causes the attention to be switched to another stimulus to which it responds.

In the guillemot, an intruder wishing to 'back off' may engage in wing-flapping, bend forward to look at its feet (foot-looking) or pick up stones before dropping them and shaking its head. If this *displacement behaviour* fails to reduce the aggression then it may be necessary to indulge in a more direct form of appeasement behaviour. This takes the form of turning away, stretching away and side-preening. The *turning-away* movement is a very obvious effort to divert aggression and usually succeeds, especially when accompanied by a shaking of the head. The victorious bird often joins in by also turning away and the conflict is at an end. When a bird is incubating and disturbed by its neighbours fighting or a potential competitor flying too close, it may produce its *stretching-away* behaviour. It may also be used at the end of a fight when the birds are signalling that they would like to stay where they are, but would prefer not to fight. Birds moving through the colony on their way to their own nest site, but with no aggressive intention, hold the landing posture or even hold their wings high during walking. These signals do seem very effective in placating aggression. *Side-preening* is a form of displacement behaviour and the bird may actually preen or merely pretend to until the aggression aimed at it is dissipated.

Apart from reacting to the aggression of rival pairs, the male guillemot must also attract a mate and successfully breed with her. Guillemots do not usually breed until they are 5 years old and tend to return to the same site and almost invariably to the same mate in each subsequent year. In a surprising parallel to human behaviour, the adolescent bird tends to find its mate in clubs within the colony where initial pair-bonding occurs. Once mated, adults seldom return to the 'courting clubs' unless they lose their mate or breeding fails. Hudson (1979a) working on the Welsh island of Skomer estimated that 63.5% of club members were 3-year-olds, 18.7% were 4-year-olds and only a small proportion were of efficient breeding age. Several display patterns have been observed, but they do not seem to be part of any

Common guillemot showing display movements.

ritualised sequence, and futile attempts at copulation and many displace-ment activities are all commonly observed. The head-vertical posture, sometimes called *sky pointing*, is accompanied by bill-fencing and bowing but the birds tend to remain stationary.

Birds laying claim to a nest site are much more mobile and the bowing actions are much more frequent, the birds in territory often grasping one another's bills. Williams (1972) reported birds exchanging stones, and even fish, although the latter play no part in courtship feeding, which is so much a part of the breeding biology of some species. Once pairs are well established, the pair greet each other with bill-fencing, grasping and allo-preening. Williams reported allopreening between *Uria aalge* and *Uria lomvia* but this is not usual. It is usually the female who initiates copulation, uttering a copulation call before tossing her head from side to side. The male mounts from the side and flaps his wings in a noisy exchange of emotions. Copula-tion occurs frequently and almost always at the nest site. Although there is occasionally promiscuous behaviour, the pair bond usually holds steady.

NEST SITE

Normally no nest material is used although Johnson (1941), working in Canada, suggested that small piles of stones were constructed, especially where the nests were sited in crevices subjected to splashing by waves and liable to fill with water. The pear-shaped eggs have been said to rotate on the nest site in response to a strong wind and thus spin around like a top rather than blow off the cliffs and be lost. Many workers are sceptical of this but the fact remains that very few eggs do seem to be blown off the breeding cliffs. I was aware of the work of Nørrevang (1958) which suggests that guano may be used to stick the eggs to the rock before I observed the phenomenon for myself whilst photographing guillemots on the Island of Canna in the Hebrides during July 1979. I unexpectedly came upon an unattended guil-lemot egg on a fairly wide ledge. I blew hard upon the egg in order to find out whether it rotated, but I could not make it move. I pushed it with my finger and found it stuck fast with guano. Perhaps Nørrevang was right, but it is surprising how often Victorian naturalists were correct, and it would be a shame to abandon the spinning-top theory without further experiments.

EGG-LAYING

Only one egg is laid, but if this is lost than a replacement egg is laid often about a fortnight later, especially by well-established pairs. Each egg is huge compared to the body size of the female and weighs between 100 and 110 grams ($3\frac{1}{2}$ and $3\frac{7}{8}$ ounces) compared with the female body weight of around between 600 and 1,000 grams ($21\frac{3}{16}$ and $35\frac{1}{4}$ ounces). The size averages 8 by 4.5 centimetres ($3\frac{3}{16}$ by $1\frac{13}{16}$ inches) and they show a very great variation in colour. The ground colour can be almost white to brown, markings can be altogether absent, faint scribbles or deep blotches of red, brown or black. There is some evidence to suggest that each pair may distinguish its own egg

Guillemot (*Uria aalge*) with its pear-shaped egg which rotates rather than blowing off the cliff.

from those of surrounding pairs. This would certainly be very useful in a crowded colony. The birds could then home-in on a known topographical feature, such as a cliff overhang, and then find their own egg by sight. Obviously the date of egg-laying varies with latitude; British guillemots often begin the incubation early in May whilst it may be well into June before Icelandic birds are ready to start laying.

Both sexes share the incubation in shifts of between 16 and 24 hours. The egg is incubated by resting it upon the feet with the pointed end directed tailwards and warming it with the belly feathers. The actual period of incubation was given in Witherby as between 28 and 37 days whilst Perry, writing in 1940, thought it might be somewhat longer and varied from 34 to 49 days. Recent work by Hedgren and Linnman, published in 1979, postulated an average of 32.4 days. In four guillemot nests which I fully documented on St Bee's Head during 1985, the times were 36, 36, 37 and 39 days. This is a very small sample but suggests a rather longer period of incubation, although the weather was very cold and wet. It is almost certain that average weather conditions over the incubation period must have some effect upon development times.

THE YOUNG

The youngster emerging from the egg is defined as semi-altricial and nidi-colous. The down is thick all over the body, that on the head and neck being longer and coarser. On the head black is the dominant colour but several feather filaments are streaked with white. The body down is a sooty brown but with a delicate mottling of grey and, if ruffled by the breeze, the buffish white on the underfeathering can be seen. Within a few days the feathers begin to push through the down, giving the chick a somewhat dishevelled appearance. The eyes are almost as brown as their parents, the bill is blue-grey and the legs and huge feet are yellow with black on the back of the legs and the webs. The young are fed by both parents and are brooded until ready to leave the breeding ledges. The young seem able to control their own body temperature by the time they are about 10 days old.

Language is very important from a very early stage and this is probably the best place to discuss guillemot vocabulary, which is summarised in Table 6. This table is certainly not complete but gives some idea of the importance of language in the life of guillemots. There is even what Tschanz described as the 'small chick sound' which is produced whilst the young is chipping and the incubating parent reacts to this by turning the egg more often than usual and even occasionally attempting to feed the egg. I have observed eiders (*Somateria mollissima*) also reacting to young chipping out of the egg by turning the clutch. Writing in *Bird Study* in 1976, Joan Fairhurst documented gannets brooding guillemot chicks. She wrote:

During four Seasons' watching at the Bempton Cliffs gannetry, Yorkshire, I have recorded four cases of Gannets Sula bassana *adopting Guillemot* Uria aalge *chicks.*

Guillemots bred on these cliffs long before the Gannets arrived, and they occupy the larger, flatter ledges along the cliff-face. These are the ledges most suitable for breeding Gannets, and as the colony expands, old-established Guillemot sites are taken over each year and there is much aggression between the two species. This can result in parent Guillemots being forced off the ledges and separated from their chicks, and in these circumstances a lone chick can be taken over by a Gannet.

Guillemot chicks seem to adapt readily to a Gannet foster-parent, and the ones I watched all behaved similarly. Between long spells of being brooded, they would come out to preen and exercise their wings, and they were also preened by the Gannet. If they wandered too far away they would be gently guided back by the Gannet's bill and tucked underneath it again. During the period of adoption they were sometimes able to rejoin their parents or other Guillemots along the ledge, but if this happened it was surprising to see that after a while they returned of their own accord to the Gannet foster-parent.

All my watching was done at a range of 150 m with a × 35 telescope, as a closer approach was impossible. The first case of adoption I saw was on a Guillemots' ledge where a Gannet, sitting on the bare rock, was brooding a week-old

Guillemot chick. The Gannet displayed normal chick-care behaviour, and though there was no nest, it picked up minute particles of wind-blown material and placed them carefully around itself. The chick was well underneath out of sight, sitting on the Gannet's webs. Several times the Gannet was seen to offer food in the normal way by opening its bill over the chick. The latter mostly took no particular interest in this action, but it is possible that sometimes attempts were made to get food from the back of the Gannet's throat. As the tiny chick was completely hidden inside the open bill at the time, it was difficult to see exactly what happened.

This adoption lasted about 17 days and during this time the parent Guillemots continually tried to bring food on to the ledge for their chick, but more often than not they were chivvied off by the Gannet. At times they did manage to feed it, and once brought in a fish that was so large that the chick could not at first swallow it. After several attempts, it picked the fish up and took it underneath the Gannet. The Gannet got hold of one end of the fish and the chick tugged at the other end. The Gannet let go, and the chick, after further efforts, finally swallowed it.

The amount of food the chick managed to get from its parents during the adoption period was evidently not sufficient to sustain normal growth, and all the time it was gradually getting weaker and less active, and could not have lived much longer. When I arrived at the gannetry on day 17, a prolonged skirmish was taking place between two Gannets on the ledge. All the Guillemots had gone, and there was no sign of the chick. (Guillemot chicks normally fledge after about 18 days.)

Another tiny week-old chick was adopted by a pair of Gannets, which for two seasons had built a nest on their site but had failed to lay. Guillemots were using a ledge just above them, and it seems likely that a chick from this ledge either fell into their nest or was deliberately guided down to it by one of the Gannets. Again normal chick-care was seen, only this time both birds were involved. The chick was brooded in the nest and the relief ceremony was performed when the birds changed duty. After long brooding spells the chick would climb on to the rim of the nest, where it would preen and exercise its wings, the time spent out there depending on the temperature and general weather conditions. It begged for food from the Gannet by climbing out and tapping vigorously at the base of its bill. This always met with an immediate response, and the chick, on gaining entry, could be seen trying hard to reach up into the back of the Gannet's throat for food. Usually it seemed unable to get anything, and one day I watched it make seven entries in quick succession following the bill-tapping behaviour. Once the Gannet regurgitated fish on to the nest and the chick was then able to eat it. Had this happened more often it might have done better, for unlike the first chick, this one had no access to its parents and was dependent on what it could get from the Gannets. This adoption also lasted about 17 days with the chick growing weaker, and when brooding behaviour ended suddenly, it was assumed that it had died in the nest.

The other two adoptions occurred on ledges that were too narrow for the

Gannets to brood the chicks properly, and the attempts were soon given up.

This random adoption of Guillemot chicks on bare ledges is all the more surprising in view of Gannet behaviour towards chicks of their own species in similar circumstances. When Gannet chicks are left alone (which only happens in unusual conditions), they incite aggression from surrounding adult Gannets to such an extent that they may be killed by the prolonged and vicious attacks made on them; yet there was no sign at all of aggression towards these lone Guillemot chicks.

There is a considerable difference in both behaviour and appearance between the chicks of the two species. At the time the Guillemot chicks were adopted they were small editions of their parents, moving actively about the ledges, whereas Gannet chicks of the same size are all white, and still helpless in the nest. It is probably this difference in appearance that saves Guillemot chicks from aggression, their black and white plumage pattern being the releaser for chick-care response in Gannets. Small Herring Gull Larus argentatus chicks, being all brown, would be attacked and killed (Dr B. Nelson, pers. comm.).

It might be supposed that Gannets attracted to Guillemot chicks would be more likely to be breeding birds that had lost their own eggs or chicks. But the pair with the nest demonstrated the ability of Gannets to switch to chick-care behaviour without having had the external stimulus of a hatching chick, or even an egg.

I must admit that I had seen guillemot chicks in gannets' nests on both the Bass Rock and at Bempton without ever realising that the gannets may have welcomed them.

It is hard to see how the chicks are able to survive if the gannet prevents them reacting to the parents' so-called shrill crowing 'leap call', inviting the young flightless offspring to jump into the void down onto the sea to begin their first journey. The young reply with their own plaintive water call which sounds as if the young bird is asking for reassurance. Witherby *et al.* thought that the young left the ledges at about 14 days but Birkhead's work (1976) on the guillemots of Skomer suggests that most are around 3 weeks old before they make their perilous leap. My own Hebridean watchings suggest a period of between 23 and 26 days, but the youngsters are still a long way from being able to fly, a feat first accomplished, according to Belopol'ski (1957), between 50 and 70 days after hatching. The chick is very dependent upon the parents, usually the male, for several weeks but when it finally becomes completely independent is not yet known. The majority of guillemots do not breed until they are 5 years old but ringing returns are beginning to suggest a possible life-span of over 20 years, although life is tough for a species surrounded by many hungry predators. Guillemots are good careful parents and although some eggs and chicks are lost either to gulls – mainly herring gulls (*Larus argentatus*) in Britain – or by rolling or falling off the ledges, over 80% of the eggs laid hatch successfully and, of these, almost 90% can survive to take their chance on the open sea, where the food supply can be quite crucial. Rydzewski's work (1978) reports a ringed bird which was 32 years and 1 month old.

The majority of adult birds stay quite close to the native colony and the fact the species is sometimes described as dispersive is due to juvenile and adolescent birds having something of a wanderlust. Deep oceanic waters are almost always avoided and inland records are equally rare, which means that guillemots are usually found in waters over continental shelves. Some stragglers from Atlantic colonies may be found as far south as Portugal whilst Pacific-bred adolescents have been known to reach Japan and are quite commonly seen in southern California.

Food and Feeding

Guillemots can feed alone but seem to prefer to hunt together in rather loose flocks. The usual method is to locate prey visually by head-dipping into surface waters prior to diving in pursuit of the fish which form the staple diet, or larger invertebrates. Occasionally the birds show a well coordinated hunting pattern and a line of guillemots will swim around the shoal, eventually encircling it before moving in to 'draw the net' and feed together. There are occasional sightings of guillemots gliding just above the surface, especially on calm days when the sea is clear, before crash-diving into a shoal of fish. The prey is usually swallowed prior to surfacing, a very useful precaution should there be any predatory gulls around hell-bent on kleptoparasitism. When the guillemots are feeding young, however, they must run the gauntlet of the gulls and the fish intended for the chick is carried and presented to the chick head first. The actual diving times and the depths reached obviously depend upon both the levels at which the fish are swimming and how deep the water is over the feeding grounds. Belopol'ski (1957) thought the maximum depth to be in the order of 20 metres (66 feet) but, as early as 1913, Gurney was suggesting depths of up to 55 metres (180 feet) and Scott (1973) reported guillemots taking fish from a depth of 60 metres (197 feet), the same worker noting a diving time of just over $2\frac{1}{2}$ minutes! Dewar (1924) estimated a maximum submersion time of 68 seconds with most dives being around 45 seconds, figures broadly in line with the figures calculated by the majority of workers in this field. As already stated, the depths and times must vary with geographical position, depth of water and prevailing weather conditions. Many more measurements must be taken and it is here that the amateur naturalist as well as 'more serious' students have the chance to enjoy many a happy day with a stopwatch, bobbing around in a small boat among the flocks of diving guillemots. I timed 100 dives in three separate areas during 1981. Off the Farne Islands in Northumberland the average was 42.9 seconds, off Canna in the Hebrides the figure was 58.6 seconds and between Harris and St Kilda the average length of dive was 41.7 seconds. The distance between the breeding grounds can be quite short and Birkhead (1976) expressed the opinion that, if an island holds more than one colony, each may have its own feeding grounds. Many birds may not have very far to travel in search of suitable prey and the Fair Isle birds, according to Hope-Jones (1980), only have to move about 6 kilometres (3¾ miles). In the period before the eggs have been laid, the distances may be much greater, occasionally up to 200 kilometres (125 miles) but more usually around 60 kilometres (37½ miles).

With regard to the nature of the food itself, the early work was carried out by Collinge between 1924 and 1927 who analysed stomach contents. The 98 birds killed for this purpose revealed that the diet consisted of 97.37% animal and 2.63% seaweed but the latter could well have been accidental, or even part of the diet of the animals eaten. A further analysis revealed 51.6% fish, 35.52% crustaceans and annelids and 10.19% marine molluscs. Later workers have suggested that the marine molluscs, especially the bivalves, may not have been taken directly, but were already present in the stomachs of the fish eaten by the guillemots. This almost certainly means that the proportion of fish in the diet is substantially higher than the figure quoted by Collinge. Many species are eaten by guillemots, but of particular importance are sand-eels (*Ammodytes marinus* and *Ammodytes tobianus*), as well as the sprat (*Sprattus sprattus*), capelin (*Mallotus villosus*) and the herring (*Clupea harengus*). Other species taken include both cod (*Gadus morhua*) and Arctic cod (*Boreogadus saida*), haddock (*Melanogrammus aeglefinus*) and the pollack (*Pollachius pollachius*). Some shallow-water species are also taken including the butterfish (*Centronotus gunnellus*), viviparous blenny (*Zoarces viviparus*), three-spined stickleback (*Gasterosteus aculeatus*), five-bearded rockling (*Ciliata mustela*), two-spot goby (*Gobiusculus flavescens*) and mackerel (*Scomber scombrus*).

The crustaceans which appear in the diet include crabs, copepods, amphipods and isopods. Polychaete worms include the ragworm (*Nereis diversicolor*) but once more it is difficult to be sure whether these creatures are the result of 'direct feeding' or already present in the guts of the fish eaten by the guillemot.

Who cares if we need to study the guillemots more carefully? What a lovely excuse to sit among them on the breeze-kissed cliffs and stacks or to bob about in a small boat on a tranquil sea! Perhaps we also ought to sail northwards and pay some attention to Brunnich's guillemot.

BRUNNICH'S GUILLEMOT (*Uria lomvia*)

Habitat

This species is restricted to the North Atlantic and is not found in the North Pacific. It is known in North America as the thick-billed murre.

The physical differences between *Uria lomvia* and *Uria aalge* and their climatic preferences have already been discussed (p. 74). For *U. lomvia*, it would seem that salinity is every bit as important as temperature in dictating distribution. Although it prefers August sea temperatures of between 5° and 10°C (41°F and 50°F) – in the Gulf of St Lawrence it will tolerate 15°C (59°F) – it is the salinity which is the crucial factor. The species insists on salinities below 34 parts per thousand, a dilution reached due to melting ice. Brunnich's guillemot avoids areas of permanent ice, but stays very close to ice floes where upwellings in the open water produce vast masses of plankton on which shoals of fish grow fat. Steep craggy islands are chosen as breeding sites and these usually provide a good measure of protection against predators, especially the Arctic fox (*Alopex lagopus*).

There also seems to be some difference between the two species of guillemot with regard to the choice of nest site. *Uria aalge* nests much more densely, but as a rule *Uria lomvia* selects steeper and narrower ledges, since it is a heavier bird and able to push into more confined spaces, its weight providing the essential stability. Although there are mixed colonies, this physical difference leads to some degree of segregation and most nests of Brunnich's guillemot fall away directly towards the sea and the youngsters are sure of a relatively easy glide down to the water.

The heavier pectoral muscles enable this species to reach depths of up to 75 metres (206 feet) in pursuit of fish, a feat which these days often gets them into trouble. As we shall see in Chapter 11 many feeding birds become entangled in the nets of salmon-fishers. The species is much more pelagic than the common guillemot.

Description

The size varies from 39 to 43 centimetres ($15\frac{13}{32}$ to $16\frac{29}{32}$ inches) with a wing span of between 65 and 73 centimetres ($25\frac{19}{32}$ to $28\frac{13}{16}$ inches), figures which are greater, but not significantly so, than those of the common guillemot. The weight, which varies between 700 and 1,100 grams ($24\frac{11}{16}$ and $38\frac{13}{16}$ ounces) is, however, greater and no doubt plays an important part in keeping the body temperature constant.

The head, neck and dorsal surface are dark grey, but in winter the throat and foreneck become white. The tips of the secondary feathers and the breast and belly are always pale, almost white. The stubby bill is the main distinguishing feature, being mainly black but there is a blue-green patch at the base of the upper mandible which also bears a pale line. The front of the legs and feet are yellow whilst behind they are quite dark, almost black.

The nominate sub-species, *Uria lomvia lomvia*, is the one most likely to be encountered but three other sub-species have been described. *Uria lomvia eleonorae* is found from the eastern end of the Taimyr peninsula as far east as east Novosibirsk. This was first described by Portenko in 1937 and the same ornithologist also described *Uria lomvia heckeri* in 1944, which he noted was found among the Wrangel and Herald Islands and along the northern coast

Brunnich's guillemots.

of the Chakotskiy peninsula. Writing in 1885, Howard Saunders described the distribution of Brunnich's guillemot and reports that it was:

... breeding in abundance on Bennett Island; but in the Bering Sea and in the North Pacific, down to Japan on the one side and California on the other it appears to be replaced by a closely allied form to which American naturalists apply the name of Uria arra.

This had been described by the ornithologist Pallas as early as 1911 but it is now reduced to the rank of a sub-species, *Uria lomvia arra*, restricted to the North Pacific. The differentiation between the various sub-species is made mainly on colour, but not all ornithologists are in agreement about the necessity to split them at all. The 'lumpers' would settle for two sub-species, namely *Uria lomvia lomvia* and *Uria lomvia arra*. Both *Uria lomvia eleonorae* and *Uria lomvia heckeri* are said to be lighter in colour than the nominate race whilst *Uria lomvia arra* is actually darker than *Uria lomvia lomvia*. As there is a degree of variation within any population, and given that not many skins have been examined, I am inclined, although not an expert in this area, to be a lumper rather than a splitter. Glutz and Bauer suggested in 1982 that the length of wing, culmen, tarsus and also the depth of bill tended to increase gradually as one moved from west to east. The distinction between the two questionable sub-species, *eleanorae* and *heckeri*, is so slight that it would seem preferable to place them within the Pacific sub-species and settle for two rather than four types.

Distribution

The range of the nominate sub-species ranges from the Gulf of St Lawrence, Labrador and Hudson's Bay to beyond Greenland where it breeds even in the north of this Arctic island. Novaya Zemlya, Jan Mayen Island, Iceland, Spitzbergen, Franz Josef Land and the Taimyr peninsula all have extensive colonies. *Uria lomvia arra* ranges from the Bering Sea to the North Pacific and winters as far south as California. Breeding occurs on Koliutschin Island, eastern Siberia and Alaska. Colonies are also found on the Commander, Kuril, Aleutian and Pribilof Islands and at points down the North American coast to California.

In Greenland, where the colonies were once among the largest in the world, there has been an alarming fall in population and, over the last 50 years, some have been reduced to a level of around 10% of their former numbers. This reduction is certainly a result of human hunting. Salomon-

Distribution of Brunnich's guillemot (*Uria lomvia*).

sen in the late 1960s reported an increase in the Eskimo population to almost 50,000 people , all with a strong and often essential hunting instinct. Whaling, sealing and fox-hunting are vital to their economy but the meat of Brunnich's guillemot is also still important. There was a cannery at Upernavik and this processed an estimated 825 tonnes of guillemot meat which meant an annual cull of 750,000 birds, apart from eggs which are also an important food source. The siting of the cannery was no accident since the largest colonies are close by, notably at Kap Shackleton.

The colonies are mainly on the west coast and on the east coast the guillemot is more or less restricted to the Scoresby Sund District and along the coast towards Stewart Island. Although Salomonsen (1950 & 1967), Joensen & Preuss (1972), Korte (1973), Evans (1974), Evans & Waterston (1976), Meltofte (1976 a & b) and Kampp (1982) have all studied the colonies in recent years, the majority of the Greenland colonies have not been subjected to accurate census very often. In 1965 there were reckoned to be 13 colonies with a total population of just over 1 million pairs and Kap Shackleton accounted for 970,000 of these. When the census was repeated by Kampp in 1983 he found that the Kap Shackleton colony had been reduced to 112,000 pairs. Allowing for over-estimation in the 1965 count, this decline is clearly alarming and, if continued, the future of the species in Greenland must be brought into question. The canning plant will certainly fail from lack of birds. The present Greenland breeding population is already below 250,000 pairs and, even allowing for fewer adolescent birds being taken by hunters, the effects are still significant, although recently passed laws are likely to have a beneficial effect, providing, and this is the difficult part, they can be enforced. Many would say that the laws are not tight enough but this is difficult to explain to a hungry Eskimo with a family to feed. It is now illegal to shoot birds within 2 kilometres ($1\frac{1}{4}$ miles) of the colonies and even by having a closed season between 15 June and 15 August, with the exception of the Upernavik District where the birds can be shot away from the colonies, there is still an annual kill of around 100,000 birds, which is much lower than Salomonsen's 1967 estimate of 750,000. Expressed in a percentage of the total population, however, the kills continue at the same rate and the population is bound to continue to fall. We must also add to this the fact that many Brunnich's guillemots, especially immature birds, become entangled in the salmon-fishermen's gill nets off Newfoundland where they winter, a fate which also affects birds from the eastern Canadian Arctic colonies.

In the USSR, human predation has also substantially reduced populations, but protection measures introduced in 1947 have reversed the alarming trend to some extent. In Franz Josef Land no accurate counts have been carried out but the population is still huge, as it is in Novaya Zemlya where Uspenski (1956) estimated it to be around 2 million birds and pointed out that numbers were recovering. This recovery was emphasised in 1961 by Tuck and it continues to the present time.

Brunnich's guillemots (white on bill edges) and common guillemots, with two bridled guillemots at the top and middle left. Taken in northern Norway.

No counts have been made on Spitzbergen, a sure sign that the birds are still so plentiful that accurate censusing has not been possible. Luttik estimated almost 2 million pairs on Bear Island in 1980 and in Iceland, where there are nearly 2 million pairs in only 19 colonies, the population appears to be holding steady. Smaller numbers (about 5,000 pairs) are found on Jan Mayen Island and Norway still has almost 1,000 pairs although populations appear to be falling.

Behaviour and Breeding

Behaviourists studying the postures of Brunnich's guillemot include Williams (1972) whilst Gaston and Nettleship (1981) worked on colonies around Arctic Canada.

It is perhaps too tempting to assume that because *Uria lomvia* is so closely related to *Uria aalge*, the two will have almost identical courtship behaviour. The fact that evidence of 'cross breeding' is rare indicates that the two species have displays which are sufficiently different to prevent this happening very often. Brunnich's guillemots seldom indulge in sky-pointing and bill-fencing but the signals must be clear enough since copulation is a much more frequent event than in the common guillemot. The adolescent clubs are not important, immature Brunnich's preferring to fly along the breeding ledges. Foot-looking, however, is very common, as are mutual exchanges of pebbles and seaweeds, whilst a 'hawing' display is frequently used which is not part of the common guillemot's pair-bonding repertoire. The bird arches its neck to one side and produces a cawing 'haw-haw-haw' call which is of such force that the whole body shakes. Only one bird of the pair calls, its mate remaining passive and silent. Once again this contrasts sharply with the behaviour of the common guillemot when both birds call. It is also most unusual for Brunnich's guillemots to present a fish to the mate and these variations certainly prevent interbreeding. The male also has a distinctive copulation call which results in the female squatting to allow mounting.

EGGS AND INCUBATION

A single egg is laid and, if lost within a couple of weeks, a second egg may replace it. The measurements average 8.0 by 5.0 centimetres ($3\frac{5}{32}$ by 2 inches) and it weighs around 100 grams ($3\frac{1}{2}$ ounces). The colour, like those of the common guillemot's eggs, varies a great deal but Witherby (1941) noted that fewer eggs had red markings. I am of the opinion that pairs are able to recognise the pattern on their own eggs and are able to use this to 'home in' on the nest site.

Tuck (1960) thought that the incubation period was around 33.5 days. Both sexes incubate by resting the egg on their tarsi and many observers have made the point that this species sits more closely than the common guillemot and is brave enough to grapple with insistent and hungry gulls of which the most formidable is the glaucous gull (*Larus hyperboreus*). In some colonies, as many as 40% of the first eggs may be lost due to the collapse of frost-shattered rocks and inexperienced young parents as well as predators.

THE YOUNG

Cared for by both parents, young Brunnich's guillemots are semi-altricial and nidicolous. The down is quite thick on the head and neck whilst shorter feathers occur on the back and especially on the undersurface. The head and neck feathers are also much darker – indeed they are almost black, apart from the sheaths which are white especially when ruffled by the wind, these can give the bird a strange piebald appearance. The back is sooty brown whilst the feathers on the breast and abdomen are buff white. The bill is blue-grey and the legs and feet are mainly yellow but dark brown on the back of the legs and on the webs. At this stage the chick is difficult to distinguish from that of the common guillemot but the white sheaths on the head and neck are certainly much more distinctive.

The youngsters are brooded carefully by the parents but they are then obliged to follow the guillemot pattern of leaving the breeding ledges before they can fly. This may be accomplished at any time between the 16th and 31st day following hatching. Roelke and Hunt (1978) and Gaston and Nettleship (1981) all postulated that the young bird is looked after by the male during this crucial period but other workers, particularly M.A. Ogilvie, have suggested that a sort of crèche arrangement may be carried out by as many as ten adults.

Post-Breeding Dispersion

The period between leaving the breeding ledge and reaching maturity is difficult to study in any auk, but with a species such as Brunnich's guillemot, which stays so close to the ice, it is much more of a problem than usual. This is reflected in the lack of data. Neither is the precise period between egg-laying and maiden flight known, nor the age when the species first breeds. Both these times are likely to be similar to those for *Uria aalge* but all scientists know only too well how foolish it is to make predictions based upon insufficient data.

A little information is available on moulting. The flight feathers appear to be replaced during August and September. The replacement of body feathers is at its most efficient during the winter but there is also a partial moult of the head and neck feathers during April and May in preparation for breeding.

Because of the adverse weather conditions often encountered, especially in Siberia, the north of the Bering Sea, Arctic Canada and Baffin Bay, there have to be regular and predictable migrations away from the ice packs whilst in comparatively warmer areas the movements are best described as dispersive. In unusually cold conditions, Brunnich's guillemots may be found well to the south of their normal range, as far as the British Isles and countries bordering the North Sea. If strong winds also occur then wrecks may occur in inland areas including the North American Great Lakes as reported by Snyder in 1957 and Tuck in 1961. A welcome increase in the number of ringing programmes has resulted in some information about the movements of birds from the colonies of the USSR, Greenland, Spitzbergen and Canadian populations.

Russian birds appear to winter among the pack ice of the Barents Sea and many also drift westwards to join the small Norwegian populations. A few birds may winter in the area towards Greenland. Birds from Spitzbergen drift south-westwards alongside the fringing pack ice until they reach the open waters off south-west Greenland. They arrive in this area during November and depart in February. This population seldom ventures far into the Davis Strait and so does not come into contact with the birds which have bred on Bylot Island of eastern Canada. To understand the movements of Canadian birds fully, much more ringing is required but birds breeding within Hudson's Bay and the Strait may wait until driven out by the ice and then drift gently on the currents down to Newfoundland. The timing of this movement seems to be very much dependent upon the weather. A number of Canadian birds do, however, reach the seas around Greenland, but appear to remain separated from both the Spitzbergen and Greenland populations. Some Greenland breeders winter in the southern reaches of the Davis Strait but the majority follow the Labrador current to the Newfoundland Grand Banks where the fishing is rich and the living comparatively easy.

Food and Feeding

As in most of the auks, the diet consists mainly of fish, especially the sand-eel (*Ammodytes tobianus*), capelin (*Mallotus villosus*), cod (*Gadus morhua*), Arctic cod (*Boreogadus saida*), herring (*Clupea harengus*) and the haddock (*Melanogrammus aeglefinus*). Many other species appear in the diet but this is not surprising as the birds must be opportunists. Prey is caught by diving from the surface and individuals can often be seen swimming around with the head partially submerged and looking for prey. These are then chased by the bird which propels itself surprisingly quickly by using half-open wings. Occasionally as many as 150 birds may surround a shoal of fish but the majority of birds feed either alone or in very loose groups. Many birds are caught in nets, especially in the fishing grounds around Newfoundland, and have become entangled at depths of almost 80 metres (220 feet) but normally the prey is captured at depths of less than half this, especially during the breeding season, a time when most of the information has been obtained. The average diving time is around 50 seconds but there are a few times in excess of $2\frac{1}{2}$ minutes reliably recorded. Kartashev (1960) calculated that between 90 and 95% of the diet was fish whilst, in 1957, Belopol'ski reported on his analysis of the stomach contents of 364 stomachs of Brunnich's guillemots shot in the Barents Sea. He found the stomach contents to comprise 95.6% fish, 2.0% crustaceans, 0.8% annelids (segmented worms) and 0.5% shellfish (molluscs) with the tiny balance made up of insects, which are not a normal part of the marine environment, and vegetable matter. As with other species of auk one is left with the suspicion that the diet is exclusively fish and that the other organisms appearing in the stomachs of the auks are there because they had originally been eaten by the fish.

Apart from stomach analysis, the only way to investigate the diet is by examination of food delivered to the young. Once more we find an almost total reliance upon fish, the young receiving one meal a day for their 1st week and thereafter they may be fed up to six times a day. It has been noted by many workers that the adults feed the young on fish larger than they consume themselves. This makes a great deal of sense since the breeding colonies can be some distance from the feeding grounds and adults do need to conserve their energy. Only one fish is delivered at a time and this is carried head-first in line with the bill. Although the majority of young are fed by this method, P.G.H. Evans (1984) did record the occasional youngster being fed on regurgitated food, but this must be regarded as the exception rather than the rule.

7

BLACK, PIGEON AND SPECTACLED GUILLEMOTS

There are three representatives of the genus *Cepphus* which are usually separated geographically although they resemble each other very closely. This indicates a relatively recent common ancestor which was almost certainly a species based in the North Pacific. The pigeon guillemot (*Cepphus columba*) still occupies the original niche whilst the spectacled guillemot (*Cepphus carbo*) is also found in the Pacific, penetrating as far south as Japan. The black guillemot (*Cepphus grylle*), however, is an Atlantic-based species which is found also in the cold Arctic seas. In various parts of its range it is known as the tystie and also as Mandt's guillemot, and the sea pigeon.

BLACK GUILLEMOT OR TYSTIE (*Cepphus grylle*)

Habitat

There are not many birds which are tough enough to survive the extreme conditions of the high Arctic in the depths of winter. The black guillemot is adept at finding gaps in the pack ice which are kept open by strong currents, high tides or perhaps by a combination of both. As it dives for its food, which, as we shall see later, consists of crustaceans and fish, it has few competitors in this specialised niche. Although Dementiev and Gladkov (1951) reported a few black guillemots around the Baltic where the waters are quite brackish, the species is almost totally marine but prefers to feed in shallow water rather than in the depths of the open ocean. The main demand appears to be an August temperature of between 0°C and 15°C (32°F and 59°F)

The site chosen for the nest also varies but the majority are close to sea level, although in 1910 Birulya reported nests on Spitzbergen at heights of up to 600 metres (1,950 feet) and some 3 kilometres ($1\frac{7}{8}$ miles) from the sea. This must, however, be regarded as exceptional, the majority of nests being set in crevices, blow-holes, among the talus on storm beaches and at the end of tiny inlets in the rock. Black guillemots are said to be colonial, but the nests are nowhere nearly so crowded as those of guillemots, puffins and even razorbills. The nests are also more concealed than guillemots' and the species has consequently suffered less from human exploitation. Human activities, especially in recent years, have caused a decline in some areas. Mink (*Mustela vison*) introduced by fur-farmers have escaped in some areas and have played havoc with eggs, chicks and incubating birds. It is not unusual for black guillemots to become entangled in the nets of fishermen and they have also proved vulnerable to oil spills.

Description

No student of sea birds can fail to be thrilled by the appearance of *Cepphus grylle*. My first experience of black guillemots was on and around the Slate Islands off the west coast of Scotland near Oban. We had just run the gauntlet across a stormy minch in a small boat battered by a combination of wind, rain, wave, swell and cross-current and the green of the sea matched my feeling of sea-sickness. After anchoring for the night at Oban, the following day dawned clear with bright sunshine, blue sky and a flat sea. Our dinghy carried us onto the flat islands, once an important source of roofing slate, the old quarries forming ideal nest sites for the black guillemots. Their sooty-black plumage set off the large white wing patches to perfection and, as they opened their mouths, the vivid red interior could clearly be seen. Birds preening on the sea revealed their equally scarlet legs and feet. All these features could clearly be seen once we had landed and began to watch

Black guillemot: adult in winter plumage (left), adult in summer plumage (centre) and downy young (right).

the birds, which measure around 30 centimetres (12 inches) in length. The black narrow bill is relatively small compared to other auks, a feature which is yet another example of a species with a northerly distribution having smaller appendages to cut down heat loss (Allen's rule, see p. 61).

Auks usually display seasonal differences in plumage but in two species the contrast is particularly striking. These are the tufted puffin (*Lunda cirrhata*) and the black guillemot. Doubtless in response to their life in the extreme cold, the winter plumage is almost entirely grey and white with just a few black feathers and even these are edged with white. The white wing patch, so much a part of the breeding dress, can still be detected against the grey colour of the rest of the wing. Some workers have suggested that the white wing patch becomes gradually larger in birds which breed further north. If the patch is important in display then it will be more essential in the shorter northern days of early spring when the birds prepare for breeding. Very occasionally individuals are found with no wing patch. These birds were at one time assigned to a separate species called *Cepphus motzfeldi*.

Distribution and Populations

The black guillemot has a circumpolar distribution. At the present time as many as five sub-species are recognised, but some would feel that they are separated on rather flimsy evidence. The nominate race, *Cepphus grylle grylle*, is confined to the Baltic Sea while *Cepphus grylle arcticus* occurs in North America, western Sweden, Denmark, Norway, Murmansk and the North Sea as well as Britain and Ireland. This sub-species is also found in Greenland but to the south of the third sub-species, *Cepphus grylle mandtii*. This is found in the Arctic areas of North America, Hudson Bay, James Bay and northern Newfoundland where winter conditions can be extremely cold. It also occurs in Labrador south as far as 58°N, in western Greenland south to 72°N and in eastern Greenland south as far as 69°N. The sub-species also extends its range into Jan Mayen Island, Bear Island, Spitzbergen and then into eastern Siberia and north Alaska. The last two sub-species are *Cepphus grylle faeroensis* restricted to the Faroes and *Cepphus grylle islandica* which is confined to Iceland. On what basis are these sub-species separated? Many authorities, including the author, would consider them too flimsy, and prefer to list only three sub-species. The birds from Iceland and the Faroes are very short-winged compared with Baltic-based birds, the respective wing spans being 16 centimetres ($6\frac{5}{16}$ inches) and 17.5 centimetres ($6\frac{29}{32}$ inches). There is however a degree of overlap which gives some fuel to opinion that we may do better to be 'lumpers' rather than 'splitters'. It would seem fairly certain, however, that both the nominate sub-species *grylle* and *arcticus* have less white in the winter plumage than *mandtii*. Much more work is needed if these five sub-species are to be confirmed or re-classified and there are also few reliable censuses of populations so that it is difficult to know what the trends are.

Distribution of the black guillemot (*Cepphus grylle*).

As many nests are hidden in crevices, accurate censusing is difficult and counts of visible birds are the only possible method. The best time to count is early in the season when displaying birds give the observer a chance to establish the number of pairs. Birds nesting on rocks or drifting around the sea can provide some evidence of numbers and, of course, distribution.

In the USSR, ornithologists list the black guillemot as being common but what this means in the light of no accurate counts it is impossible to say. Neither have there been any accurate counts around the coastline of Spitzbergen but, in 1964, Løvenskjold did point out that black guillemots were less common than other auks. Luttik (1982) suggested that at least 300 pairs were breeding on Bear Island and the Icelandic population may exceed 100,000 birds. Even in Britain and Ireland, where there is no shortage of competent field workers, there have been no counts which can be regarded as absolutely reliable.

'Operation Seafarer', the results of which were published in *The Seabirds of Britain and Ireland* by Collins in 1974, made the following points:

The number of Black Guillemots recorded nesting in Britain and Ireland, 8,340 pairs, is a great deal smaller than those of the other auks and could be an underestimate, though it would not be surprising in view of the species' more restricted range, confined to a narrow belt offshore in the north and its smaller, more widely scattered colonies. There has been no previous full survey in Britain and Ireland; indeed, the Black Guillemot has attracted little attention in the past. Some extensions or recolonisations seem to be taking place around the Irish Sea while in Scotland, where the bulk of the population nests, decreases have been recorded in west Ross and northern parts of west Inverness, and increases farther south in the latter county and in the Firth of Clyde. Further censuses are required before population trends can be adequately assessed.

The Black Guillemot has a predominantly northern and western distribution in Britain and Ireland, and its complete absence from the east coast of Britain south of Caithness, except for a single pair in Banffshire, is surprising. According to Nelson (1907), it once nested as far south as Bempton Cliffs (Yorkshire), where a pair was present in 1938 (Chislett 1952). In south-east Scotland it disappeared as a breeding species during the last century, and Baxter and Rintoul (1953) knew of none nesting south of Caithness except for a pair in Kincardineshire.

There is very little information on past numbers in the main breeding areas. North Ronaldsay (Orkney) was colonised in 1938–40 (Lack 1942–3) and 45 pairs nested there in 1969. On Handa (Sutherland) the species ceased to breed in 1891 (Baxter and Rintoul 1953) and, though four pairs nested again in 1962 (R.H. Dennis in litt.), none did so in 1970. Between 70 and 100 pairs bred on Priest Island (West Ross) in 1938 (Darling 1940) but there were only ten pairs in 1969; while on Raasay (west Inverness), where the Black Guillemot was described as numerous in 1936–7 (Temperley 1938), only a single pair was reported in 1970. Farther south, however, the increases reported on the Small Isles by Evans and Flower (1967) seem to be continuing, the number on Muck having risen from eight pairs in 1963 to 40 in 1969 and on Canna from 17 pairs in 1961 to 40 in 1969. Similarly, in the Firth of Clyde, where the Black Guillemot was first discovered nesting in 1898, the total population rose from 40 pairs in 1951 to 100 in 1969 (Gibson 1969).

On the shores of the Irish Sea there are signs that an expansion of range has occurred in recent years, though some of this could be the recovery of lost ground. In 1940 breeding was proved in Cumberland at St Bees Head, where birds had been observed previously and may have nested undetected (Stokoe 1962); in 1969 there were two pairs. In north Wales Thomas Pennant, the great 18th century naturalist, knew of Black Guillemots nesting on the Great and Little Orme Heads (Caernarvonshire) and in Anglesey. They recommenced nesting in Anglesey in 1962 and at least eight pairs were present in 1969, but despite recent sightings off the Caernarvonshire coast there are as yet no modern breeding records for that county. In Pembrokeshire, where Montagu (1802) recorded a few pairs breeding near Tenby, there have been recent sight records and a pair has summered.

On the north-west coast of Ireland Ruttledge (1966) noted that an increase had taken place in Co. Donegal. In the far south-west, the population on Cape Clear Island (Co. Cork) fell from 44 pairs in 1973 to 16 in 1967 (Sharrock and

Wright 1968) but rose again to 39 pairs in 1969. In Ulster the Black Guillemot bred for the first time on the Copeland Islands (Co. Down). Five pairs were recorded there in 1961.

The population in Denmark was estimated by Asbirk (1978) to have increased from around only 100 pairs in 1928 to around 450 pairs in 1978, and the population in Norway seems to be around 12,000 pairs according to Johnsson (1983). In Sweden 11,000 pairs still breed despite substantial losses between 1958 and 1972 as a result of introduced predatory mink (*Mustela vison*). In Finland there has been a decline during the twentieth century from 4,000 pairs to a mere 1,500, which Merckallio (1958) thought was due to a combination of human predation and cold winters. Both the eggs and the birds themselves have been part of the human diet.

When the International Council for Bird Preservation produced *The Status and Conservation of the World's Seabirds* in 1984 there was a detailed analysis of the distribution of the black guillemot in Greenland and North America. The following accounts are based upon this publication. P.G.H. Evans, the author of the Greenland account (1984), noted that the black guillemot is widely distributed around the coast and breeding occurs wherever there is open water. The west coast is warmer than the east and therefore the breeding birds penetrate further to the north-west, although Evans did not feel able to give a precise figure of the breeding population and

Black guillemots are easily recognised by the white wing patch.

thought that his estimates of the number of birds might require revision. He divided Greenland into regions and thought that the north-west may have had between 7,650 and 23,750 pairs, the south-west population between 7,225 and 18,875 pairs and the south-east between 8,075 and 22,125 pairs. Evans was also able to give some indication of the movements of the birds following breeding.

Unlike other auk species they do not show any marked migration, (though there maybe some movement from Iceland to Greenland (Peterson 1982)). Many remain in the breeding areas throughout the winter in areas of open water (such as leads in the ice), though some disperse, mainly southwards. Ringing recoveries indicate that the Upernarvik population winters in Umanaq District and Disko Bay (where it can apparently cope with heavy ice cover), whilst some have been recovered across Baffin Bay and south to Hudson Strait, eastern Canada; the Umanaq population moves south to winter mainly in southern Egedesminde, but also in Disko Bay; birds from Disko Bay tend to move south to the coast between Holsteinsborg and Godthab. Where there is open water throughout most of the winter (for example in Sukkertoppen District), the population appears to be fairly resident (Salomonsen 1967). Many young birds first move north after the breeding season, probably assisted by the north-going current along the coast. These return to the breeding grounds rather later than older birds, some remaining through the summer in areas to the south. Ringing recoveries suggest that 12% of the population (71% of these being first-year birds) are shot, mainly in September and October when the young birds are dispersing (Salomonsen 1967). They also fall victim to gill nets, becoming entangled and drowning in them when they are along the coast during the salmon fishery in autumn (Christensen and Lear 1977).

Buckley and Buckley (1984) thought that around 2,700 pairs of black guillemots were breeding along the north and middle Atlantic coast of the USA in 1977 and pointed out that the species:

... at present breeds only on rocky islands in Maine and Isles of Shoals ... in the last ten years has increased southward in winter to the sandy shores of Cape Cod and Nantucket Isle and birds seen in summer in likely locations in northern Mass. may presage a modest breeding range extension. Prior to 1900 there were no usable data for Maine, and even thereafter, counts varied widely (although usually within an order of magnitude) so that estimates for the 1900 'baseline' population ranged from 85 to perhaps 600 pairs; better estimates were 1350 pairs at 24 sites in 1945 and 3,400 pairs at 123 sites in the early 1970s (Drury 1973–4) but not even these resulted from complete surveys.

Buckley and Buckley went on to point out that the 1977 figure of 2,675 pairs present at 115 sites was probably on the low side. North of Maine, black guillemots breed right up through the Canadian Arctic into the polar basin.

Behaviour and Breeding

In the early spring adults gather on the sea quite close to their breeding sites and begin communal displays which can be very exciting to observe and were first described by Armstrong in 1940. Modern ornithologists have made efforts to describe these ritualised movements in behavioural terms and to give each of them names. The pair swim around together in a circle becoming more and more excited, their mouths opening and closing to reveal the bright red interior. They may partially submerge as they chase each other and at these times their cocked-up tails can resemble a miniature shark fin. On occasions groups of birds may engage in these splashing displays which involve sailing gracefully first one way then the other, then on the surface now below. The purpose of these mass displays is to bring the pairs into breeding condition at the same time which is of vital importance, even in species like the black guillemot which is only loosely colonial. Lines of displaying birds can also be seen in winter and especially in August and September when young birds take part. The precise function of these displays is not known but they may be concerned with feeding.

Uspenski (1956) was of the opinion that some birds at least remained as a pair, perhaps within a small flock, throughout the winter, which would certainly make pair-bonding easier during the short Arctic breeding season. Both Kaftanovski (1951) and Bianki (1967) reported that pairs tended to return to the same nest site and Preston (1968) postulated that most of the courtship and all subsequent breeding behaviour was confined to the often fiercely-defended territory around the nest site. Whilst fierce in defence of territory, the black guillemot becomes less aggressive in the communal roosts which may be on the sea or on cliffs and to which off-duty birds come to 'relax'.

At the beginning of the season the nest sites are tentatively examined, usually early in the morning, and some display, even leading to attempted or actual copulation, may occur at this time, but there is a return to the sea before nightfall. Mass flights are also a typical feature of these rafts, especially if potential predators, such as the *Larus* gulls or even a hungry peregrine (*Falco peregrinus*), put in an unwelcome appearance. Mild alarm is expressed by dipping the bill in the water until the eyes are almost covered. This behaviour seems to me to be in preparation for a crash dive, which actually happens if the threatened danger materialises, and should not be considered as a displacement activity. Bill-dipping may also be associated with a high-pitched piping alarm call.

At the nest, defence of territory may take the form of threat which, if ignored, may lead to actual fighting. The initial reaction to an intruder is to hunch the back and to open the bill wide, thus exposing the red gape. If this fails the head may be tossed and the territory-holder squats down flat onto its tarsi, cocks its tail and opens and closes its mouth whilst producing a hiss-like alarm call. At this stage the bird resembles a coiled spring. If this fails, then the bird adopts what has been termed the oblique-hunched posture, during

A pair of black guillemots, their white wing patches clearly obvious even in poor light.

which the territory-defender may stand still or actually advance towards the intruder. The bill is opened so that the intruder can see the gape and the neck is withdrawn and, if a movement is made, the wing tips may be trailed along the ground, although no noise is usually made. As the threat increases, the bird adopts the oblique-upright posture during which it stands up on the tarsi, stretches the neck, points the bill downwards and lifts the wings. This can be seen from quite a distance as the white on the wing is shown off to its best advantage in this position. It is quite rare for this to fail, but if the intruder persists then an all-out attack is launched, accompanied by the alarm call. The bill is used to inflict painful nips, wings batter the foe and the sharp nails are also brought into play. These aggressive actions have been observed to take place on water but are most typically seen when breeding territory is being defended. Preston (1968) observed one of the most amusing displays in the whole of the avian world which he accurately describes as 'leap-frogging' and involves gliding over a potential intruder before crash-landing on the water in front. This may or may not be part of the sexual display but it is certainly used by established pairs to prevent adolescents approaching too close.

Pair-bonding begins by a pair of birds *strutting*, a term used to describe the exposure of the white wing patches, and this may take place either on water or on land. As the season advances the pair may indulge in *head-bobbing*, which Drent (1965) whilst describing the closely related pigeon guillemot (see below), referred to as *billing*. Witherby *et al.* (1941) described both the head-bobbing and the interlocking of the bills of the partners. On land this behaviour is also accompanied by a raising of the tail. Copulation, which always occurs on land, may follow a session of head-bobbing, the male circling the female whilst producing a series of staccato calls until she permits him to mount.

NEST AND EGGS

With such a wide geographical range, the date of the onset of breeding will obviously vary and laying may begin as early as May to as late as August. Some eggs are laid directly onto rock but the majority are laid into a depression. The nest sites may be either solitary or colonial, the preferred situations being areas with plenty of talus or crevices in fairly low cliffs. Petersen (1981) reported the frequent use of holes, either natural or artificial. The nest sites which I discovered on the Scottish Slate Islands were certainly man-made and the birds could be seen incubating well out of arm's reach among the fractures in the exploited slate beds. It was whilst watching these nest sites that I first heard the incubating adults produce a snake-like hiss. During 'Operation Seafarer', Cramp *et al.* (1974) reported that:

Cavities in man-made structures are used in some areas, for example harbour walls . . . a hole in a wooden pier . . . the great stone brock on Mousa (Shetland) and ruined buildings on North Ronay (Outer Hebrides).

I visited the latter site in 1982 and found 11 nests in the ruined buildings and also found 17 nests in old quarry buildings on the Slate Islands. Asbirk (1979) examined 411 nests in Denmark and calculated that 57% were among stones, under driftwood and washed-up fish-boxes.

The normal clutch is two, although nests with only one and as many as three eggs have been recorded. Very occasionally, four eggs have been found in one nest and this is certainly due to two females laying in the same site. All other auks breeding in the British Isles lay only one egg but both the Atlantic puffin and the razorbill have two brood patches which may well be an indication that at some time in their evolution they also produced two eggs. The brood patch, also known as the incubation patch, is an area of skin on the bird's abdomen which becomes modified during the breeding season to allow the eggs to be efficiently incubated. The area concerned may actually lack feather tracts (*apteria*) but it is more usual for contour and down feathers to be deliberately plucked to reveal an area of bare skin. This becomes thickened due to an increase in the number of blood vessels and is then pressed close to the egg. The lost feathers are then replaced during the post-nuptial moult, an event which is vital to such sea-based birds as the auks. There may be one large patch, as in the song birds (passerines), but there are never more than three. In the gannets and boobies, cormorants and anhingas, pelicans, tropic birds, frigate birds and pelicans, brood patches are absent and alternative methods of incubating the eggs have to be found.

In the gannet (*Sula bassana*) for example, the egg is warmed on the webs of the feet. The crested auklet (*Aethia cristatella*) is the only member of the auk family not to have a brood patch.

The ground colour of the pointed oval eggs of the black guillemot varies from white to bluish green, spotted or blotched with dark red and ash grey. They are never glossy and have average dimensions of 6 by 4 centimetres ($2\frac{5}{16}$ by $1\frac{19}{32}$ inches) and weigh around 50 grams ($1\frac{3}{4}$ ounces). Not all birds lay two eggs, although in the USSR, Bianki (1967) calculated the average clutch size to be exactly 2.0. The corresponding figure for Shetland was estimated by Broad to be 1.43 but Petersen (1981) showed that first-time breeders produced smaller clutches. Preston (1968) thought that the interval between the laying of the first and second eggs was 3 days and Hyde (1937) postulated a period between 2 and 5 days. Once incubation is well advanced a repeat clutch is unlikely.

Both sexes share in the incubation, each 'shift' lasting less than an hour. The incubation period is difficult to calculate but does not usually begin until the second egg has been laid. Witherby *et al.* (1941) gives the following estimates: 'about 21 days (A.C. Bent), $3\frac{1}{2}$ weeks (B. Hantsch) 24 days (F. Faber), about 4 weeks (W. Bond)'. In the light of recent work, particularly by Asbirk (1979), the period appears to vary from as short as 23 days to as long as 40 days, the precise time possibly being dependent upon the ambient temperature. The eggs usually hatch within a day of each other, an event which is rendered more likely by the fact that the first egg takes 2.15 days longer to hatch than the second.

THE YOUNG AND FLEDGING PERIOD

The young, which are cared for and fed by both parents, although there is some evidence to suggest that the male may do rather more of the feeding, are semi-altricial and nidicolous and require close-brooding during the first few days. The soft thick down with silky tips is dark brown on the dorsal surface but paler on the ventral surface. The bill is black with a pale pink gape, whilst both the legs and feet are dark brown. The young are fed on fish which the adults bring to them singly, carrying them crosswise rather than parallel to the bill, as is the case with the common guillemot and Brunnich's guillemot. Edward A. Armstrong (1940) in his book *Birds of the Grey Wind* suggested that the prey was always carried with its head to the right. This led to a fascinating study by P.J.B. Slater which was published in *Bird Study* (1974, Volume 21). During August 1972, 28 tysties were observed at a colony of 14 pairs on Fair Isle, Shetland. Out of 444 occasions on which adults were seen carrying fish, 208 held the prey with its head to the right and 236 with the head to the left. Clearly the fish, which can measure up to 20 centimetres (8 inches), must be balanced in the bill and which side the head of the prey hangs out would seem to be a matter of chance rather than choice. Slater's work shows clearly that this is in fact the case. The actual size of the prey given to the young will obviously increase with age, as will the number of feeds, although Petersen's work (1981) would suggest that feeding periods show a peak between 0500 and 0600 and 1900 and 2200 hours. This fish may either be forced down the chick's gullet or dropped in the nest. As they near fledging, the chicks may meet the parents at the entrance to the nest site. Unlike many auks, the young do not leave the nest site until they are fledged, which occurs between 34 and 40 days following hatching. The idea that parents tempt the young with fish to get them to move seawards does not seem to be true and adults do not seem to be involved in the dispersal of their offspring.

Attempts have been made to assess the breeding success, particularly by Asbirk (1979) in Denmark and Petersen (1981) in Iceland. Asbirk followed the fortunes of 683 eggs and found that only 59% hatched and, of the chicks which emerged, only 54.8% fledged. Eggs were lost to predators, especially gulls of the genus *Larus*, and also many were 'flooded' by high tides. Chicks were also predated but many died of starvation. Older birds appeared to be more efficient parents and colonial breeders appeared to have more success than solitary pairs, although the hatching rate was similar. It may be that predators find it harder to run the gauntlet through the colony than to pick up isolated chicks. In contrast, Preston (1968) thought the reverse to be true whilst Cairns (1980) thought that it made no difference one way or the other! Petersen's work would seem to suggest that Icelandic birds are much more efficient as parents. He followed the fortunes of 935 eggs and found that 79.5% hatched successfully and of these 89.2% of the young were successfully fledged. Mink (*Mustela vison*) and black and brown rats (*Rattus rattus* and *Rattus norvegicus*) were important predators but some eggs and young were lost to *Larus* gulls and to flooding. It would be wrong to place too much emphasis on the differences between these two studies, which were carried out at different times and in different places. The success of any breeding bird will depend to a large extent upon the prevailing local weather conditions and the food supply.

Food and Feeding

In the south of its range, the tystie feeds mainly on fish whilst, in the Arctic regions, it exists mainly on crustaceans (krill). There is also a great difference in diet between one colony and the next and it may be more accurate to refer to the black guillemot as an opportunistic rather than a selective feeder. There is also evidence to suggest that birds from the same colony may have different feeding areas. Both Preston (1968) and Petersen (1981) suggested that the state of the tide also affected the diet, high water enabling the birds to move into the littoral area and take prey like the butterfish (*Centronotus gunnellus*) which, unlike the majority of the fish caught, is usually brought alive to the young. Unlike many auks which can travel long distances in search of food, black guillemots feed mainly around inshore areas. Summerhayes and Elton (1928) mentioned that black guillemots had been seen hunting in freshwater lakes, which fits in closely with my own observations on the Slate Islands, where several birds were seen diving after prey in an old flooded quarry in the centre of the island. In the breeding season the foraging distance does not exceed 4 kilometres (2½ miles) and is invariably much less. In winter they feed closer to the pack ice, icebergs and glaciers than other auks. Stover (1952) and other workers have pointed out that there is great variation in both the time of submersion and the actual depth reached. Because of the variety in the diet, both these events can hardly be regarded as surprising. On the Slate Islands I timed 100 feeding dives, the longest being 68 seconds, the shortest 17 seconds and the average time 43.4 seconds. This fits in closely with the range noted by other observers.

Black guillemots favour sheltered areas where they dive expertly for fish.

Black guillemots usually hunt alone but there are records on one hand of them robbing their neighbours whilst on the other hand there are occasions when a line of birds gradually swim around a shoal of fish and 'close the net' before moving in for the kill. During the breeding season the young are fed almost entirely on fish, which makes sense because a relatively large amount of energy can be delivered in a single journey. The list of species taken is obviously very long but there is a distinct bias towards the butterfish (*Centronotus gunnellus*) in Scotland. Slater and Slater (1972) for example identified 544 food items delivered by 13 pairs of black guillemots and found that these were made up of 46.9% butterfish, 18.4% members of the cod family Gadidae, 17.4% sand-eels (*Ammodytes tobianus* and *Hyperoplus lanceolatus*), 8.1% sea-scorpions, 7% flat-fish and the remaining 2.2% were unidentified. Asbirk (1979), investigating the diet of young birds in Denmark, found it to consist of almost 99% fish, of which 67% were butterfish, 22% sand-eels, 7% wrasse (*Ctenolabrus rupestris*) and 4% viviparous blenny (*Zoarces viviparus*). In the Baltic where the viviparous blenny is more common, it is an important part of the nestlings' diet. Bergman (1971a & b), working in Finland, found that the viviparous blenny made up 95% of the nestlings' diet with the other 5% consisting of sand-eels. At this stage, the dependence upon crustaceans is very small but the few studies made of the contents of adults' stomachs show that they do have a greater dependence upon crustaceans.

In 1957 Madsen investigated the contents of 26 stomachs from birds shot in Denmark. He found approximately 66% fish and 33% crustaceans, including crabs (in nine stomachs) and shrimps and prawns (in eight). Crabs of the genera *Eupagurus*, *Portunus*, *Hyas*, *Carcinus* and *Porcellana* are all taken. The animals are not usually swallowed straight away but are given a good shaking and the claws and carapace (shell) removed. Around the Icelandic breeding grounds, the adults feed on a combination of fish and invertebrates, including the annelid worm *Nereis diversicolor*, the mollusc *Onoba striata*, the crustacean *Anonyx nugax* and the shrimps *Pandalus* and *Spirontocaris*. Belopol'ski (1957) examined the stomach contents of 88 birds from the Barents Sea and found (by number of specimens) 73.3% fish and 20.7% crustaceans, minor items including 3.0% molluscs, 1.5% polychaetes and 1.5% insects. In Spitzbergen, Hartley and Fisher (1936) noted a far greater dependence upon crustaceans which made up 61.2% by number of the diet of the 21 adults examined whilst fish and molluscs were each present in 19.4% of stomachs. Demme (1934) looked at the stomach contents of 28 birds killed in Franz Josef Land between March and May and found that 43% by number contained annelids of the class of polychaete (mainly *Nereis diversicolor*), 37% amphipod crustaceans and only 20% fish.

The winter diet is very difficult to ascertain with any certainty but, in the more northerly areas, there is likely to be an increasing dependence upon the crustaceans which form such a large part of the Arctic plankton.

PIGEON GUILLEMOT (*Cepphus columba*)

This species may be regarded as the Pacific equivalent of the black guillemot and the two are certainly similar in appearance and in behaviour. The pigeon guillemot can be distinguished by the fact that the white wing patch is divided into two or three separate patches by transverse lines of black. The wings are sometimes totally black in winter. In the black guillemot, the axillary feathers and also the underwing coverts are white whilst those of the pigeon guillemot are brownish grey. The tail of the pigeon guillemot consists of 14 feathers whilst the black guillemot has only 12. The Pacific bird tends to be slightly larger and measures 36 centimetres (14½ inches) with a wing length of up to 17.5 centimetres (7 inches). This compares with figures of 32.5 centimetres (13 inches) and 16.2 centimetres (6¹³⁄₃₂ inches) for the black guillemot. The inside of the mouth and the legs and feet of both species are bright vermilion. The pointed bills of both species are black.

The range of the pigeon guillemot extends from the Bering Sea to adjacent areas of the Arctic Ocean and down into the North Pacific. In winter the species can reach as far south as Japan and lower California. It breeds from the Santa Barbara Islands in California and to the north of this site to the Aleutian Islands and also along the Kamchatkan and Siberian coasts to Wrangel Island and Herald Islands. Birds within these parameters belong to

Distribution of the pigeon guillemot (*Cepphus columba*).

Pigeon guillemot, Round Island, Alaska.

the sub-species *Cepphus columba columba*. The second sub-species, *Cepphus columba snowi*, breeds along the coast of southern Kamchatka and the Kuril Islands. The latter sub-species, as indicated in Chapter 1, was once thought to be a separate species and went under the name of Snow's guillemot. Although there is some overlapping of measurements, it tends to be rather smaller. This is yet another example of Bergmann's rule as Snow's guillemot ranges further south than *Cepphus columba columba*. The variations seem to be purely physical and the behaviour patterns do seem to be identical.

The two eggs are laid in a cavity similar to that of the black guillemot between May and July depending upon latitude and the details of the cycle are again similar to those of the black guillemot. The clutch is invariably two eggs with average measurements of 6.0 by 4.0 centimetres ($2\frac{13}{32}$ by $1\frac{9}{16}$ inches). The markings are very similar and even the green inner shell membrane is the same shade in the two species. Both parents share the incubation period which lasts for around 28 days. The nestling is semi-precocial and the down which covers its body is thick and soft, being dark brown above but much paler brown on the ventral surface. It is only when the feathering is disturbed by wind that paler feathers can be seen and, when they are sleeked down or wet, the youngster seems to be black. It is thought that the young fledge when between 35 and 42 days old and tend to stay within the 'burrows', where they can become quite active, often coming to the entrance to snatch fish from the adults. Both parents play an active part in feeding but their duties end at or soon after fledging.

SPECTACLED GUILLEMOT (*Cepphus carbo*)

This species has a very restricted range and therefore has no sub-species. It

The spectacled guillemot (left) is closely related to the pigeon guillemot (right) but lacks the white wing patch. Its white eye ring is also a distinguishing feature.

Distribution of the spectacled guillemot (*Cepphus carbo*).

is found around the coast of Okhotsk and the seas around the Japanese islands and reaches the Commander Islands. Breeding occurs on the coast of Kamchatka, the Okhotsk Sea, Kuril Islands, northern Japan and Korea. Its breeding range thus overlaps with that of the pigeon guillemot to which it is obviously very closely related. The breeding behaviour and body structures are remarkably similar but there are obvious physical differences, three of which are taxonomically important. The main feature is the white ring around the eye of birds in summer plumage, and the lack of any white areas on the wing. It is also much greyer on the back than the pigeon guillemot. The bill is black and the legs are red, colours which are maintained throughout the winter, when the plumage becomes paler and decidedly less attractive. The chin, throat and undersurfaces are white during this season and the underwing coverts shade to brownish. Immature birds resemble an adult in winter plumage except that the foreneck is distinctly greyer.

8

MURRELETS

This term 'murrelet' embraces six species all but one of which, the Japanese or crested murrelet, breed along the Pacific coast of North America. With the exception of the ancient murrelet and the crested murrelet, which have some facial ornamentation during the breeding season, the murrelets do indeed resemble small guillemots of the genus *Uria*. In North America these species are referred to as murres and hence we have an explanation for the term murrelet. It is however in their breeding behaviour that the murrelets (pronounced mer-lit) differ markedly from other auks.

Kittlitz's murrelet (left), the marbled murrelet (centre) and ancient murrelet (right) all require a great deal more study if their complex life cycles are to be fully understood.

Xantus' murrelet (*Brachyramphus hypoleucus*) and Craveri's murrelet (*Brachyramphus craveri*) are considered by some workers, but not by me, to be conspecific and breed further to the south than any other auk. Craveri's murrelet nests on islands in the Gulf of California and actually moves north into its wintering range.

Kittlitz's murrelet (*Brachyramphus brevirostris*) is even less auk-like in its reproductive biology and breeds high in mountains, often far from the sea and way above the tree-line. The egg, however, is deposited on bare rock which cannot be much different from a sea cliff and there may well be safety from the traditional auk-predators at this altitude. As if this was not remarkable enough the marbled murrelet (*Brachyramphus marmoratus*) often selects a nest site high in a tree. Near the Russian coastal city of Okhotsk, a nest was found 6 metres (20 feet) up a larch tree, (*Larix decidua*). This was 'beaten' by a nest found to the south of San Francisco in 1974 which was 45 metres (nearly 150 feet) up in the branches of a Douglas fir (*Pseudotsuga menziesii*).

The murrelets have not proved easy to study and there are many gaps in our knowledge of their life history. The six species described in this chapter are the marbled, ancient, Kittlitz's, Xantus', Craveri's and crested.

MARBLED MURRELET (*Brachyramphus marmoratus*)

Murrelets are quite small alcids and this species is around 25 centimetres (10 inches) long. They are chubby little birds which seem to lack a neck and have very thin bills. The marbled murrelet can be distinguished in summer by its evenly dark brown back and comparatively long black slender bill. It is also heavily barred on the ventral surface, another unique feature which makes the species easily recognised. In winter it is the only member of the auk family to have white scapulars. These show up as a strip of white between the back and the wing. There is also a white ring around the eye and a white band across the nape. When the bird is resting on the water, the bill and tail are both cocked-up, producing a most alert-looking posture and there is also a white band on each side above the wings.

The breeding range includes Kamchatka and the Kuril Islands in the western Pacific, as well as the west coast of North America from Unalaska to Vancouver Island. Two sub-species have been recognised. In his book *Birds of the Ocean* W.B. Alexander (1955) wrote that the range of the marbled murrelet took in the:

... *Sea of Okhotsk and North Pacific Ocean, south in winter to the Liu Kiu Islands and San Diego California. Breeds in Kamchatka, the Kuril islands and Yezo (*Brachyramphus marmoratus perdix*) and on the American coast from Unalaska to Vancouver Island (*Brachyramphus marmoratus marmoratus*).

This division into sub-species seems to have been made on very slender evidence and Alexander went on to say that this is:

... the commonest small auk on the coasts of south-eastern Alaska and British Columbia. Though a few eggs have been obtained, the breeding habits are not properly known. It probably lays its eggs on the ground high up in the mountains. Egg dates: April–June.

By the 1980s very little more information had been added. The cryptically-coloured eggs are either laid on the ground or on moss- and lichen-covered branches of conifers, often as high as 30 metres (100 feet) above ground-level. The nests may be as much as 10 kilometres (6 miles) inland but this figure was only based on five nests. Despite the fact that the species is not uncommon, its nests have proved to be extremely elusive.

In *The Status and Conservation of the World's Seabirds*, published by the International Council for Bird Preservation (1984a), a table was published giving the population size and status of Californian seabirds based on the work of Sowls *et al*. (1980). The entry for the marbled murrelet is fascinating to say the least. It reads: 'Number of Colonies?, Breeding population (birds)? 2000, and Status Decreasing?' What is obviously needed is a method of

Distribution of the marbled murrelet (*Brachyramphus marmoratus*).

censusing the species both at sea and in the breeding areas. The work of Lensink (1984) first reviewed and then gave details of populations in Alaska. The highest populations are found in Prince William Sound where Dwyer *et al.* (1975) thought that the population of marbled and Kittlitz's murrelets was around 100,000 and the work of Isleib and Kessel (1973) suggests that the former is the more common by a factor of about ten. Lensink thought that logging operations were likely to reduce populations in south-eastern Alaska but there were still 100,000 Kittlitz's murrelets with perhaps as many as 1 million marbled murrelets. The species is so very solitary in the nesting season that the discovery of its habits, the threats it faces and the essential conservation methods which are obviously required to protect it are difficult to identify.

In the same volume mentioned above, the International Council for Bird Protection published an article by Sealy and Carter (1984) who set out to study the population of marbled murrelets in British Columbia. These two workers also favour the division into the two sub-species mentioned by Alexander, *Brachyramphus marmoratus perdix* being the Asiatic-based sub-species. Their account of the search for an occupied nest of the marbled murrelet makes fascinating reading and is a clear indication that modern scientific research can still be fun, even if not successful.

*Fervent interest in the Marbled Murrelet arose in the early 1900s in British Columbia. The prospect of collecting eggs of this species attracted the attention of numerous naturalists and oologists. Early accounts portrayed these searches as being extensive but discouraging (see Guiguet 1956). Several nests were reportedly found but none was subsequently authenticated. One such egg apparently taken by C. de B. Green and A. Brooks on Cox Island, Queen Charlotte Islands (Bowles 1920; Taylor 1921) was described (Bowles 1920) as smaller than an Ancient Murrelet (*Synthliboramphus antiquus*) egg and intermediate in colour between this and Xantus' Murrelet (S. hypoleucus). However, the whereabouts of this specimen is not known. Young (1930, 1931) mentions an egg found also by C. Green on Banks Island, B.C. However, Grinnell (1921) and Brooks (1923) indicated that Green had been unsuccessful in that area and the location of this egg is also unknown. S.J. Darcus (1927) secured four single eggs, three from burrows and one from a deep rock crevice, on Cox Island where he estimated a colony of 20 pairs. Several authors discredited this record (see Drent & Guiguet 1961: Sealy 1974) and Kiff (1981) examined one of these eggs and considered it to be of an Ancient Murrelet. Kiff (in litt.), however, could not discount the possibility that Darcus took no Marbled Murrelet eggs since not all were examined. However, Ancient Murrelets once nested on Cox Island (Drent & Guiguet 1961) and it is therefore likely that these eggs were indeed of the Ancient Murrelet. Young (1930, 1931) reported an egg (now housed in the B.C. Provincial Museum, Victoria) collected by C.F. Newcombe on Marble Island, Queen Charlotte Islands, which he considered to be 'doubtless of this species'. Carter examined this egg and considered it to be an Ancient Murrelet* *egg based on colour and shape. He also compared it to eggshell fragments (housed in the B.C. Provincial Museum) of a known Marbled Murrelet (see also Drent & Guiguet 1961) which match the descriptions of color provided by Kiff (1981). Young (1930, 1931) mentioned two other eggs brought to him from the Queen Charlotte Islands, but which he doubted were Marbled Murrelet eggs (but see Baily 1931).*

The difficulty of finding the nest of the Marbled Murrelet, and the few discoveries of single nests mentioned earlier, have prompted several workers to suggest that Marbled Murrelets nest solitarily in B.C. (Brooks and Swarth 1925; Drent & Guiguet 1961: Sealy 1975a) and throughout their breeding range (Gabrielson & Lincoln 1959: Simons 1980). Since the initial failures to find the nest, the only evidence of nesting in B.C. has been obtained through the collection of Marbled Murrelets with eggs in their oviducts, discoveries of juveniles at inland localities (see Drent & Guiguet 1961: Sealy 1972 for reviews) and the two probable nest discoveries during logging operations. The efforts to find the nest of the Marbled Murrelet have therefore ended with a sense of futility. Unfortunately, this has resulted in an apparent lack of concern for the species, to the point where it has been ignored. Its present and past status in B.C. is unknown, although many authors have commented on its abundance at sea (e.g. Brooks & Swarth 1925; Guiguet 1971b).

Since the normal techniques of censusing auks at their breeding colonies are of little use in estimating the population of a species whose nests are well nigh impossible to find, other measures must be adopted. They are, however easy to count at sea and this has been done in Alaska by Isleib and Kessel in 1973 and Gould *et al.* in 1982, in British Columbia by Robertson in 1974, in Washington State by Manuwal in 1979 and Wahl in 1981, and in California by Sowls *et al.* in 1980. Sealey and Carter (1984) expressed the opinion that these censuses did not take into account that the species is seldom distributed evenly around the coast during the breeding season. They have instead a clumped-at-sea distribution pattern which could easily be counted from inflatable dinghies. The counts around Vancouver Island in British Columbia were made from 0500 to 1400 hours between the 1 and 25 June when breeding was at its peak and adults not incubating were thought to be taking a rest on the water. Sowls *et al.* (1980) pointed out that marbled murrelets are usually clumped at sea in areas opposite coastlines dominated by mature coniferous forests.

The work of Binford and his co-workers had already suggested (in 1975) that marbled murrelets prefer old-growth coniferous forests in which to site their nests and he further speculated that the open crowns typical of old trees were the ones most likely to be preferred. Thus logging, which is the main industry of British Columbia, may well be threatening the breeding habitat of what is arguably the world's most elusive sea bird. Some evidence that this may be the case was indicated by an observation made by Guiguet in 1956. An adult bird complete with a brood patch, and therefore presumably incubating, and an egg-shell showing evidence of having been at an advanced stage of incubation were found among the twisted branches of a felled western hemlock (*Tsuga heterophylla*) on Queen Charlotte Island. Harris related a similar discovery which took place in 1961 when Vancouver Island loggers felled a mature western red cedar (*Thuja plicata*) and out fell a couple of flightless young. Old-growth forests are being cut down at an alarming rate and it is certain that, even with generous replanting programmes, the regeneration will take several hundred years. For marbled murrelets, which do seem to demand mature trees, such felling programmes could be disastrous. But how does one protect a species when one knows so little of its biology? The problem facing the marbled murrelet in British Columbia (and almost certainly in other areas where its habitat requirements are similar) was succinctly put by Sealey and Carter in their answer to the following question.

Are Existing Efforts to Conserve Seabirds in British Columbia Relevant to the Marbled Murrelet?

Most seabirds that nest in British Columbia including the Marbled Murrelet, are federally protected by the Migratory Birds Convention Act of 1916. Additional protection is afforded seabirds in British Columbia through several provincial acts: Wildlife, Museum, Parks, Ecological Reserves and Firearms Acts. The Ecological Reserves Act of 1971 has been particularly important with regard to the protection of seabirds in British Columbia. Many important nesting colonies of nearly every seabird species have been set aside as ecological reserves. However, most seabirds nest colonially on small islands, which are well-defined units of habitat that are usually free of commercial concerns and therefore more easily established as reserves (Terborgh 1974).

Because murrelets nest solitarily in forested areas along most of the coast they have largely escaped protection. At present it is not possible to isolate important nesting areas nor to set aside large tracts of coastal forest due to commercial logging concerns. In future, if murrelet populations are found to decline in certain patterns at sea relative to logging patterns in adjacent forested areas, it may be possible to identify smaller tracts of coastal forest to be set aside.

The Marbled Murrelet presents a formidable problem of conservation and may even be of special concern (see Weber 1980) although it was not included in the proposed list of rare and endangered species in British Columbia. Existing seabird conservation efforts in British Columbia are not relevant to problems confronting the Marbled Murrelet at sea or in nesting areas. Efforts in the future should be directed toward: (1) obtaining adequate baseline data on murrelet distribution at sea along as much of the coast as possible. (2) monitoring murrelet populations at sea adjacent to forested areas that will be logged and (3) investigating the possibility of protecting areas where aggregations of feeding murrelets and gill-net fishing operations co-occur.

To this must be added the hope that some skilled field-worker will successfully complete a study into nest-site selection, where breeding occurs and also make some progress in unravelling the elusive life-cycle of the marbled murrelet.

KITTLITZ'S MURRELET (*Brachyramphus brevirostris*)

This is rather a small species around 24 centimetres (9½ inches) long, recognised in its summer plumage by its pale buff cheeks, chin and neck. The upper parts are much more dusky, but there is a great deal of buff streaking. It can be distinguished from the marbled murrelet by its much lighter upper parts. The ventral surface is almost white but with bars of black showing clearly on the chest and sides. The axillary feathers (also called *axillers* and situated in the 'arm pits') and underwing coverts are both dark brownish grey. The winter plumage is also very attractive with the dorsal surface being slate-grey but spotted with white and there is also a white collar on the nape. There is a grey crescent in front of the eye and grey bars on the side of the breast. Other white patches are found on the sides of the head whilst the ventral surfaces are also pale. The tail is also edged with white. The bill is black and the legs pale brown.

The species ranges from the Arctic coasts of Siberia and Alaska as well as

Distribution of Kittlitz's murrelet (*Brachyramphus brevirostris*).

along the coastline of the Bering Sea, whilst in winter it can be found as far south as Japan. Breeding is well established from Cape Yakan, Siberia, to Kamchatka, the Kuril and Aleutian Islands and also from Alaska east to Sitka. It breeds high on mountains usually very close to the summit and some sites can be several miles from the sea. The nest is sited on bare ground almost always above the tree-line and snow may still be present when the single egg is laid in a slight depression. The eggs have average dimensions of 6 by 4 centimetres ($2\frac{13}{32}$ by $1\frac{19}{32}$ inches) and are bluntly rounded at both ends. The background colour is olive-buff, covered with dark brown and black blotches, specks and spots. The laying season begins in late May and goes on through June, depending upon local conditions. This is true of auks in general where latitude has some effect on egg-laying, but what is unusual about this species is that altitude is also an important factor.

The incubation period has not been calculated with any certainty and the young which hatch are probably semi-precocial and are certainly downy. The head and throat is yellowish buff liberally spotted with black and the bill is black. The body down is mid-grey although, when ruffled by the wind, the black bases show up clearly. The neck is dark grey and becomes lighter on the abdomen. The legs and feet are pink at the front but much darker, almost black, at the back and the nails are also black. The precise nesting period is still the subject of debate but it is known with certainty that the young are present at the nest sites for at least 14 days when they have lots of down but the wing quills are well-formed.

XANTUS' MURRELET (*Brachyramphus hypoleucus*)

Perhaps about to be renamed *Eudomychura hypoleuca*, this species measures around 22 centimetres ($8\frac{1}{2}$ inches) and is found around the coasts of southern California. It also breeds in this region from Monterey Bay to Cape San Lucas as well as on Santa Barbara Island and Los Coronalow Island. The favourite nesting habitat appears to be on rocky offshore islands, some of the colonies being defined as 'huge'. Once more we find loose terminology in the assessment of auk populations and more research is urgently required. Sowls *et al.* (1980) did census the species in California and estimated around 3,500 pairs breeding in between eight and ten colonies. They further pointed out that this figure represented something of a recovery.

The actual nest site is in a cavity, usually in a cliff crevice or in the corner of a cave. Hollows beneath dense foliage have also proved popular sites. A natural hollow seems to be preferred but some birds will deliberately scrape a hollow; they never provide a lining. As Xantus' murrelet breeds further south than most auks, breeding can often be in full swing by the middle of March. Eggs are still being laid in July and this has led to speculation that two broods may be laid. It seems, however, that the season is merely a protracted one, a feature also typical of Cassin's auklet (*Ptychoramphus aleuticus*). The clutch consists of either one or two eggs which often differ

Distribution of Xantus' murrelet (*Brachyramphus hypoleucas*).

markedly in colour. The average dimensions are 5.5 by 3.5 centimetres ($2\frac{3}{16}$ by $1\frac{13}{32}$ inches). Each is smooth and slightly glossy with a background colour of pale blue-green through various shades of olive or brown. Brown and purple spots, blotches and spots add to the amazing variations in egg colouration. It may well be that each individual egg can be recognised by the parents. Both sexes take part in the incubation and they almost always change over at night. Although the precise period has not been calculated with any certainty, 3 to 4 weeks would seem to be the parameters. The nestling is precocial and covered with a thick down which is particularly dense on the undersurface. The dorsal surface is soot-black but with a small white mark both above and below the eye. The ventral surface from the throat downwards is creamy white. The young, as with the last species, only remain in the nest for a maximum of 4 days before making a night-time trek, still in full-down plumage, down to the sea and swimming away with their parents. From the beginning, they dive and swim with great efficiency and are able to catch their own planktonic food.

Once known as Scripps's murrelet, Peterson (1941) wrote that:

... the original Xantus's Murrelet came from Guadalupe Island, Mexico, and that the birds off the California Coast were quite different, so it was proposed

131

that the California bird be designated by the name Scripps's murrelet and the other one retain the name Xantus.

The present view is that there are no sub-species and Scripps's murrelet has now faded into history.

Xantus' murrelet has a slate-grey dorsal surface and flanks, although it is a great deal darker on the wings. The ventral surface and the underwing coverts are white. It can be distinguished from the ancient murrelet by the absence of any black on the head. The clearly visible white underwing coverts enable Xantus' to be distinguished from Craveri's murrelet.

CRAVERI'S MURRELET (*Brachyramphus craveri*)

Like the last species, recent 'taxonomic gymnastics' have resulted in the designation of the scientific name *Eudomychura craveri*. It is suggested that the two species be included in the genus *Eudomychura* and both are confined to the north-east Pacific. At sea, separation between the two is all but impossible and only at close range can definite distinctions be made. The bill proportions differ, as do the colour tones of the dorsal surfaces and the colour of the underwing coverts. Craveri's murrelet ranges from the lower regions of California as far north as 28°N on the west coast and 24°N on the east coast. Breeding takes place on Isla Raza in the Gulf of California. Hellmayr and Conover (1948) point out that breeding also occurs on 'various islands on the Gulf of California' but no details are given of populations. The same workers also point out that the Craveri's murrelet also 'occurs in post breeding season on the Pacific coast from Monterey Bay south along the Lower California Peninsula'.

The differences between this species and Xantus' murrelet have already been described and the difficulties indicated but some authorities still feel that it should be regarded as a sub-species of Xantus' murrelet. For the present we shall consider it to be a separate species and an important one at that since it is the most southerly of the auks and the only species which regularly penetrates into the Tropics.

The dorsal surface is dark slate-grey with the ventral areas white. The flanks and underwing coverts are lighter grey than the back and thus there is a gradual transition from dark dorsal to light ventral surfaces. The black tiny slender bill is ideally designed for a plankton-eating bird of about 21 centimetres ($8\frac{5}{16}$ inches) in length.

Its almost tropical distribution is reflected in the timing of the breeding season, which can begin as early as February, and egg-laying is almost always complete even in the northermost parts of the range by early July. As a breeding species it is restricted to islands in the Gulf of California from Cape San José Island and Ildefonso Island penetrating as far north as Isla Raza. Apart from the fact that one egg is laid and the cycle is similar to that of Xantus' murrelet (about which very little is known) there are huge gaps in

Distribution of Craveri's murrelet (*Brachyramphus craveri*).

our knowledge of this species. When breeding is over the birds disperse in all directions. Those moving north regularly reach the waters of southern California during the period between late August and October and, in years following hot summers, when the water is warm, the occasional pioneer may reach the Bay of Monterey and there was once a record of Craveri's murrelet reaching Oregon. Others drift south and are seen off the western coast of Mexico. There is then a gradual drift back to the breeding grounds, all movements dictated by their diet of shrimp-type crustaceans.

ANCIENT MURRELET (*Synthliboramphus antiquus*)

This species is one of the easiest of the murrelets to identify because of the contrast between the blue-grey back and jet-black head and very pale bill. It measures around 27 centimetres (10½ inches) long and has a wing span of 43 centimetres (17 inches). During breeding the throat, face, head and neck are all black but a white stripe is clearly visible on each side of the crown. These delicate white plume feathers account for the species often being called 'the old man', an obvious reference to white hair associated with those human beings of mature years. The sides of the neck are also white.

In winter the throat becomes white and the chin greyish and during this period the ancient murrelet is often recorded bobbing gracefully on the waters off the western coast of North America from California and points north as far as Alaska and the Aleutian Islands. The species also occurs in corresponding latitudes on the opposite side of the Pacific Ocean off the coast of Korea, China and Japan. To some extent it is an easy bird to census on the sea since it prefers not to fly, but dives efficiently and can travel some distance under water. The half-open wings enable the bird to 'fly' under water. It can also swim quickly on the surface. Both these efficient methods of locomotion enable the species to obtain its food which consists mainly of crustaceans found in the surface plankton. They have also been observed scraping off animals attached to drifting wood and the keels of boats!

In winter, ancient murrelets tend to keep fairly close to the coast and in spring the birds from the south move north to breed. As the ancient murrelet takes up its breeding sites in the extreme north Pacific, the southern islands of Japan where it wintered are taken over by breeding crested murrelets. At the time of writing, little is known about the breeding population of the western coastline of the Pacific, but those in the Aleutians and north-eastern Pacific Oceans are thought by Sowl *et al.* (1978) and Vermeer *et al.* (1983) to be in the order of 535,000 pairs, more than half of these being on the Queen Charlotte Islands, British Columbia.

Distribution of the ancient murrelet (*Synthliboramphus antiquus*).

Lensink (1984) noted that breeding in Alaska is restricted to the Gulf itself and the Aleutian Islands. 33 colonies with a total of 110,000 birds were found around the Gulf with a further 2,500 birds in nine colonies. Nysewander *et al.* (1982), however, showed that breeding on the Aleutians was more widespread, especially on islands which were free of the Arctic fox (*Alopex lagopus*). He found an additional 30,000 birds in 27 colonies whilst Bailey and Faust (1980) found a correlation between declining fox populations and improvement in numbers of the ancient murrelet.

Some accounts of the nesting behaviour state that steep hillsides within 65 metres (200 feet) of the sea are preferred. The work of Vermeer *et al.* (1984), however, suggests that they nest in burrows under the canopies of mature trees and goes on to postulate that clearcut logging is likely to reduce populations. Thus commercial forestry poses just as much of a threat to ancient murrelets as to the more elusive marbled murrelet discussed above. The burrows are usually just less than 1 metre (3 feet) deep and end in a cavity in which the eggs are laid. Although some nests are lined with dry grass, most are left bare and eggs have even been found laid on a layer of ice in rocky crevices.

Depending upon latitude, the birds are present around the breeding colonies from late March onwards and, in British Columbia, the clutch of two eggs is being incubated by mid May and the young hatch from late May onwards, although the actual period of incubation is difficult to establish. Each egg (some birds lay only one) is long and sub-elliptical in shape measuring 6 by 4 centimetres ($2\frac{13}{32}$ by $1\frac{19}{32}$ inches). It is almost glossy, the base colour of creamy buff being finely and evenly marked with speckles and spots but with some brownish and grey blotches. Although there may be an interval of several days between the laying of the first and second eggs, incubation does not begin until after the second has been laid. This means that the chicks hatch out within a few hours of each other. Although the precise time of incubation has not been established, it is probably between 16 and 23 days and seems to be shared by both sexes. The incubating bird seems to be relieved by its partner during the hours of darkness. As the breeding grounds are often shared with other species, including other small auks and petrels which also tend to be at least partially nocturnal, the noise can be almost deafening.

How each bird finds its own nest has been the subject of speculation without any firm conclusions being drawn. It may be that the incoming bird recognises the low shrill whistle of its mate waiting the change-over of incubation duties. These notes certainly appear to be of a different pitch to the usual piping calls. One wonders also if the shape of the nest hole may be detected by a series of ultrasonic sounds employed in the manner of bats. The precise period of incubation has not been established with any certainty but is probably around 3 weeks or so.

Once hatched, however, the chicks have a most unusual appearance. They are precocial and downy, the upper parts, including the head as far as the lores and the lower edge of the ear-coverts, are black. If the light strikes the plumage, a blue-grey tinge can be detected and there is also a whitish patch on the hinder of the ear-coverts. The underparts are yellowish. Both parents tend the young at night but the precocious little creature is ready to leave the nest when it is under 4 days old. In response to the piping calls of its parents, the tiny bundle of feathers follows them to sea and swims with surprising strength away from the breeding grounds. The majority of young make the journey to the sea at night scuttling over rocks, tumbling over the talus and cascading like water over rock crevices. Eventually they are called into the pounding surf by the parents and the young plunge in with no apparent fear. This early baptism of the chicks gives the murrelets a genuine claim to be the most marine of all sea birds. Similar behaviour patterns have also been noted for the crested, Xantus' and Craveri's murrelets and thus the precocious behaviour of the young must have a real evolutionary advantage.

CRESTED OR JAPANESE MURRELET
(*Synthliboramphus wumizusume*)
This rare and poorly-documented species measuring 26 centimetres ($10\frac{5}{16}$ inches) long is restricted to the islands off Japan. It is assumed, but not

Distribution of the crested murrelet (*Synthliboramphus wumizusume*).

confirmed, that its breeding biology is similar to that of the ancient murrelet, with which its breeding range overlaps. It is known to breed on the Iza-shietito Islands from whence Dementiev and Gladkov (1951) reported its dispersal to areas of sea off the mainland from Sakhalin and points south into Korea. The sexes are alike but, in contrast to Craveri's murrelet, the crested murrelet does show seasonal variations. The mainly black head bears a prominent crest and there is also a thin pale stripe running along the sides of the head and meeting on the upper nape. The upper surface of the body is dark grey, but it still looks quite pale in contrast to the head. The flanks are a subtle mixture of grey and black feathering whilst the lower parts of the body are almost pure white. The underwing coverts are also white and show up well against the grey flight feathers. In winter there is little, if any, change in body feathering but the crest and white feathering on the head are both moulted out. Juvenile birds are centainly much browner than winter adults but there is such a paucity of data that detailed descriptions are almost totally lacking.

As this chapter indicates, there is confusion in almost every aspect of murrelet natural history. The taxonomy is far from settled and the life-cycles are many years away from being unravelled. The same is true of the auklets which form the subject of the next chapter.

9

AUKLETS

Under this heading come five species of auk, three of them being allotted to the genus *Aethia*. These are the crested auklet (*Aethia cristatella*), the least auklet (*Aethia pusilla*) and the whiskered auklet (*Aethia pygmaea*). The other two species considered in this chapter are Cassin's auk (*Ptychoramphus aleuticus*) and the parakeet auklet (*Cyclorrhynchus psittacula*). All auklets except Cassin's have breeding adaptations of the bill and also often have distinguishing head plumes. They all nest in crevices within rocks, again with the exception of Cassin's which excavates a burrow rather like the puffin. This leads me to a consideration of the rhinoceros auklet (*Cerorhinca monocerata*) which also excavates a burrow as well as being far too large to fit the diminutive title of auklet. There is no doubt that this species should be classified with the puffins and I have therefore described it in Chapter 10. We therefore consider only five auklets in this chapter whilst many workers may well be inclined to describe six. It should also be mentioned that the word auklet has no taxonomic integrity and is used as this chapter heading (and by ornithologists generally) merely as a convenience.

The crested, least and parakeet auklets are a fascinating trio and demonstrate how three very similar species can have an overlapping distribution and yet avoid direct competition by each having its own unique life style. Studies conducted on St Lawrence Island in Alaska, where all three breed, have been invaluable in postulating the theory of the ecological niche. They all breed on, in and around the scree slopes which are so much a feature of the island. The least auklet is the most numerous species and the colonies can be as large as 100,000 pairs, although most are substantially less than this and there can be as few as 3,000 pairs. The crested auklet colonies can contain as few as 2,500 pairs and seldom exceed 5,000 pairs. Both species site their nest among the scree, but they each choose boulders of differing size. The crested auklet goes for large irregular boulders, in contrast to the least auklet which is far happier among the smaller pebbles of the rather uniform-looking areas of scree. This leaves the parakeet auklet with the problem of finding a suitable niche. This it does by nesting in much smaller numbers among the rocky ridges opened by the combined action of frost, wind and the heat of the sun. Their colonies are never large and nests are often fairly widely separated. Thus we have each of the three species breeding in its own niche.

The only possible area of conflict remaining concerns the food supply

A crested auklet with its unique feathering and white eye line.

and even this has been solved during the course of evolution. All feed upon plankton, but they take prey either of different sizes or from different depths. The least auklet is only 14 centimetres (just over 5½ inches) long and is therefore able to live off tiny species which are of little use to the two larger species, which would seem to be in direct competition since both the crested and parakeet auklets are around 26 centimetres (10¼ inches) long. They do, however, penetrate to different depths and there are also subtle, but nevertheless significant, variations in bill shape which means that they take different prey and avoid direct competition.

CRESTED AUKLET (*Aethia cristatella*)

This attractive and alert-looking species measures around 27 centimetres (10½ inches) and is recognised by its dark grey upper parts and a rather darker crest which curves forwards from the forehead. This stands out clearly from the grey-brown feathering of this area but even more prominent are the white elongated plumes which originate from behind the eye and bend across the cheeks. The short bill (designed for plankton-eating) is red in colour during the summer. In winter it is yellow and even smaller due to the shedding of parts of the bill. There is usually a white tip to the bill. The summer bird, with its small bill and head plumes, as well as its flight pattern, is thought by many observers to resemble the California quail (*Lophortyx californica*).

The range of the crested auklet extends from the Bering Sea across parts of the Arctic Sea and along the North Pacific. It is a common resident in south-western Alaska and finds suitable breeding areas on islands such as the Shumagins, Pribilofs, Commanders, Kurils and the Aleutians. Lensink (1984) provides population estimates of 650,000 on the Pribilof, St Matthew and St Lawrence Islands in the central Bering Sea, 440,000 on Buldir and Gareoli Islands in the western Aleutians and 172,000 on Diomede and King Islands and Fairway rock in the Bering Straits. Lensink also states that the populations appear to be relatively stable. In winter the birds tend to remain rather close to the breeding areas, providing they remain free of permanent ice, in which case the birds do wander and may reach the north-western seaboard of the USA, Amurland, northern Japan and Kodiak Island. There is a unique record of a crested auklet 'collected' from the waters to the north of Iceland in August 1912 (Hörring, 1933).

Breeding birds return to their natal colonies early in May, depending upon local conditions, but laying seldom begins before June and, in the northern part of the range, this may still be going on into August. The colonies are sited amongst boulders quite close to the high-water mark. The birds show an uncanny knack of judging the height of the tide, although the occasional pair tempt providence and become flooded out. It is surprising

Distribution of the crested auklet (*Aethia cristatella*).

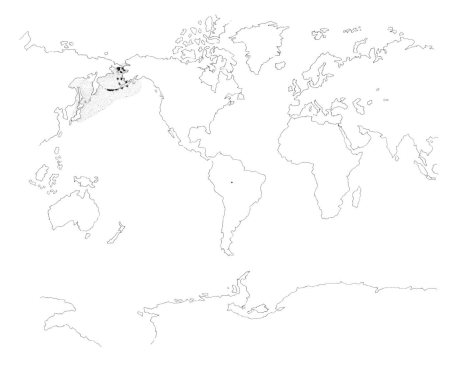

A group of crested auklets.

how often the colonies are sited on headlands and other exposed spots. Perhaps this allows the birds easier access to the nest sites and an escape route from predators such as the larger gulls. The crested auklet is a particularly vociferous species with a surprisingly varied vocabulary based upon grunts and honking noises. The alarm call, often uttered from below ground, can resonate around the breeding site and the total effect in a large colony can be deafening. This noise appears to be the main line of defence because, unlike the parakeet auklet, which is much 'braver' or as some workers put it 'tamer' and sits tight, the crested auklet runs away across the scree and soon takes flight.

A single white egg is laid, usually in quite a deep recess. It is laid directly onto the bare ground with no nesting material used. It is oval in shape, quite smooth although never glossy and measures around 5.5 by 4.0 centimetres ($2\frac{3}{16}$ by $1\frac{19}{32}$ inches). It is known that both sexes share the incubation but the precise period of incubation has proved difficult to establish with any certainty. The present author would favour a period of between 35 and 45 days. The nestlings are covered in dark brown down above and are much paler below. On hatching they are semi-precocial. They are thought to be ready to leave the nest in about 35 days, up to which time both parents feed them. This has presented more of an evolutionary problem for the auklets than has been the case with the fish-eating auks. All the latter have to do is to bring in large fish which are pushed into the larger open gullets of the young. With the plankton-eating auklets it is difficult if not impossible to carry sufficient food in the bill to satisfy the appetite of the nestling. Auklets have evolved an extendable gular pouch in which the plankton soup can be carried and evacuated into the open bill of the youngster.

They really are specialist divers and can go quite deep in search of prey if the plankton is not to be found at the surface. This is quite possible during rough weather and it is also well documented that many species making up the plankton show what is known as vertical migration (see page 55). Crested auklets in pursuit of deep-moving plankton have occasionally been recovered from the stomach of the cod (*Gadus morhua*) which usually feeds in deep water. A group of crested auklets diving for food is perhaps as near as one can get to poetry in motion, unless one prefers the mass flights of birds driving low across the water. The flight pattern of the crested auklet is certainly much more direct than those of other auklets and their sheer grace is breathtaking. The crested auklets buzzing about among the larger auks, especially guillemots or murres, have been delightfully compared to 'slow battleships and the buzzing aeroplanes around them'.

LEAST AUKLET (*Aethia pusilla*)

This tiny species, once known as the knob-billed auklet, measuring only 16.5 centimetres (6½ inches) is smaller than any other auk and therefore not likely to be confused with any other species except perhaps the whiskered auklet which measures some 18.5 centimetres (7½ inches). The least auklet can, however, be distinguished by its black dorsal surface with conspicuous white marks both on the wings and the scapulars. The tiny dusky bill plus white feathers and head plumes are other equally diagnostic features which render confusion between the two most unlikely.

The range of the least auklet extends from the Bering Sea and areas around the North Pacific, the evolutionary home of the species. Breeding in large colonies occurs on islands in the Bering Sea and the Aleutian Islands, the eggs being laid, depending upon latitude, between the months of June and August. The least auklet, although difficult to census is certainly the most abundant Alaskan seabird, being found in vast numbers in the western Aleutians and on islands in the Bering Sea. The total population is an estimated 6 million birds in just over 30 colonies. In winter some birds, but by no means a majority, wander far from the ice floes and can reach the Okhotsk Sea, the Liu Kiu Islands and Washington.

The dorsal surface of the adults is slate-black with the scapulars partly white. Scapulars are the easily-seen feathers found along the area above the shoulders and overlap the feathers of the upper surface of the wing and those of the back, thus providing the essential smooth transition from the feathers of these two regions. The secondary feathers of the wing are also usually tipped with white. The throat and ventral surfaces are mainly white but there are dark blotches, especially around the neck where they are often prominent enough to form a band around the foreneck. The underwing

Distribution of the least auklet (*Aethia pusilla*).

coverts are also white. Covert feathers also play a vital role in avian efficiency. Coverts are contour feathers which overlap the primary and secondary
feathers of the wing and also those of the tail (called the retrices) and serve to
keep the shape of the wing constant. This is essential if it is to function as an
efficient aerofoil and, in the case of the auks, as a stiff paddle for swimming.
The main feature of a least auklet in breeding plumage, however, is the row
of long facial plumes which extend from behind the eye and run downwards
across the dark cheeks, against which they are outlined to perfection. Another row of white plume feathers extends from the corner of the small
red stubby bill. In summer there are a series of white pointed feathers on
the forehead which give the little bird a very quizzical and often amusing
expression.

In winter the species retains its alert posture, but the bill fades from bright
red to black and all white plumes are moulted out, although the dark dorsal
surface and contrasting white scapulars remain diagnostic features.

Breeding occurs both on offshore islands and rocky promontories of the
mainland, colonies often being 'very large' but difficult to census. Each nest
is usually sited in the crevices of weathered rocks or among fallen boulders
on talus slopes. No actual nest construction would appear to take place but
the single egg, measuring about 4.0 by 3.0 centimetres ($1\frac{19}{32}$ by $1\frac{3}{16}$ inches) is

Least auklets breed in considerable numbers on the Pribilof Islands.

laid often on bare rock. It is smooth but not glossy and incubated by both sexes. The precise period is not known but would seem to fall within the period of 29–36 days, once more almost certainly dependent upon latitude. The nestling, like most auks when hatched, is semi-precocial and covered with blackish brown down on the dorsal surface with the head being the darkest area. Beneath the down feathers are much paler, the majority being greyish. The young are again tended by both parents but the precise fledging period has proved difficult to establish with certainty. The young do not leave the nest site until fully fledged but the wing feathers do develop with surprising speed. Spencer G. Sealy (1981) postulated the reasons for variations in fledging weight pointing out that:

It is often thought that birds' breeding seasons are timed so that the young are raised when food is most abundant or easily obtained. There is evidence now (Perrins 1965, 1966, Harris 1969, Hedgren 1979) that in some species early breeders leave more progeny that are in better condition in a season, than those that breed late.

Plate 1   Little auks on their breeding ledge.

Plate 2   A pair of razorbills, one going through its wing-stretching routine.

Plate 3   Guillemots show great aerial dexterity prior to landing on the crowded breeding ledges.

Plate 4   Brunnich's guillemot can be distinguished from the common guillemot
by the rather more substantial bill and the white area on the inner edges of the mandibles.

Plate 5   Black guillemots are efficient fishers and are easily recognised by their bright red feet and white wing patch.

Plate 6   The pigeon guillemot is the Pacific equivalent of the black guillemot.

Plate 7   A mixed group of crested and least auklets on their breeding grounds.

Plate 8   Rhinoceros auklet in non-breeding plumage.

Plate 9   The stout bill is an easily recognisable feature of the parakeet auklet.

Plate 10   The tufted puffin is one of the most colourful of the auk family.

Plate 11   The horned puffin on its breeding grounds.

Plate 12   More at home on the sea than in the air, the puffin's whirring flight
makes fascinating watching during the breeding season as the birds seek control prior to landing.

Sealey's reasoning is broadly in line with that of Hedgren (1979) who was working on the fledging weights of the common guillemot, and also that of O'Connor (1976) who studied nestling blue tits (*Parus caeruleus*). C.M. Perrins working on the Manx shearwater (*Puffinus puffinus*) is also in broad agreement. Sealey's chosen area of research certainly provided a rich supply of information on auklets which he clearly indicates in what ought to be regarded as a classic paper, published in 1973.

Sevuokuk Mountain (63°47′N, 171°36′W) in the northwest Cape area of St Lawrence Island Alaska holds one of the largest mixed auklet colonies in the Bering Sea . . . . About 72,000 Least Auklets breed there most of them in crevices in talus slopes (Bedard 1969a). When the auklet chicks leave their nest crevices to go out to sea at about 29 days of age and at about 87% adult weight they can fly and apparently are independent of their parents.

Female auklets lay their single egg remarkably soon after the snow and ice have melted from the nesting slopes each year . . . . Egg laying in this colony spanned 13 days (24 June to 6 July) in 1966 and 14 days (12–25 June in 1967). The nestling period occurred over 42 days in both years (21 July to 7 September in 1966 and 15 July to 26 August in 1967).

The work of Perrins, O'Connor and Bedard mentioned above prove that the heaviest fledglings are the ones which have the best chance of survival and, in the context of the little auklet, Sealy was able to show that females that breed early in the season would tend to be more successful breeders. With many species the optimum laying period would tend to be at a time to ensure that the young are growing at a time when food is at its most abundant. In the case of the little auk it is not food but snow and the fact that it melts at different times each year, at least on St Lawrence Island. Certainly Sealy's work shows that the eggs are laid almost immediately after the ice and snow has melted. Food supply is still something of a factor, however, since it can influence the weight of the egg and the quality of the yolk within it. The young hatching from these eggs may well have more than a head start over those hatching from lighter eggs produced under conditions of relative food shortage.

WHISKERED AUKLET (*Aethia pygmaea*)

Around 19 centimetres (7½ inches) long, the whiskered auklet ranges from the southern regions of the Bering Sea, where it breeds on the Aleutian Islands, to the west of Unalaska to the Commander and Kuril Islands, egg-laying beginning during May. In winter the species ranges some distance southwards, the occasional bird reaching northern Japan.

Adults in breeding condition can be recognised by the dusky grey of the dorsal surface, head and neck whilst on the forehead and curving forwards are tufts of white plumes which, when a wind is blowing, are inclined to blow across the eye. When 'at rest' these plumes seem to follow three lines. One group runs down across the cheeks, one passes upwards and bends forward from the forehead while the third bends downwards and backwards. The chest is a rather dull grey blending into the white of the lower abdomen and undertail coverts. The underwing coverts are greyish brown. The short bill is bright red, but obviously tipped with white and in summer there is a bluntly-shaped knob at the base. The white undertail coverts and the knob on the bill are points of distinction from the least auklet. In young birds and in winter adults the crest is lacking as are plumes and the knob on the bill changes colour from red to dull brown.

In their *Field Guide to the Birds of the USSR*, Flint *et al.* (1981) note that the whiskered auklet is nomadic rather than strongly migratory and also that it seems to prefer seashores with precipitous cliffs. In these conditions it is described as common and in places numerous although more precise, indeed any, figures are lacking. The nest site is in the crevices of inaccessible ledges, often beneath overhanging ledges. As can be imagined this makes accurate censusing a very tall order indeed although some nests are sited beneath rocks and are therefore much easier to count. The species is colonial although often associated with storm petrels (*Oceanodroma furcata*) and crested auklets (*Aethia cristatella*). It can be distinguished from the latter by

Distribution of the whiskered auklet (*Aethia pygmaea*).

The whiskered auklet can be recognised by its attractive head pattern.

its smaller size 22 centimetres ($8\frac{23}{32}$ inches) compared with 27 centimetres ($10\frac{19}{32}$ inches), lighter-coloured belly and the three sets of longer white feathers on the head. There is also a distinct white patch underneath the tail.

The single white egg is laid directly on the ground, usually in May or early June, and although the precise incubation period is not established it is probably between 3 and 4 weeks. The egg is incubated and the young fed by both parents on plankton carried in the throat pouches. Feeding appears to take place both by day and night and the depths reached by the auklets in pursuit of prey depends upon the vertical movements of the zooplankton discussed earlier in this chapter. It may be an advantage for flocks of birds to feed together and so large numbers are often found feeding in close proximity. Things are, however, far from peaceful because whiskered auklets are extremely garrulous and their piercing cries and frequent bouts of wing flapping and threatening postures are a constant part of their behaviour.

W.B. Alexander (1955) described the species as the rarest and least known of the auklets which is as true today as it was then. Some important work has been carried out by Sowls *et al.*(1978). He noted that this was the rarest alcid in Alaska, but breeding was known to take place on ten islands in the Aleutian chain from Buldir East to at least the islands of Four Mountains. The largest known colony was some 3,000 pairs on Buldir Island and the total population was thought to be around the 20,000 mark. Lensink (1984) pointed out that the whiskered auklet had the most restricted distribution of all Alaskan seabirds. The work of Nysewander and his co-workers (1982) and also as yet unpublished work by Forsell suggest that populations, particularly in the central and western Aleutians may have been seriously underestimated. The total population is almost certainly in excess of 50,000.

CASSIN'S AUKLET (*Ptychoramphus aleuticus*)

Cassin's is another plankton-feeding auklet measuring only about 23 centimetres (9 inches) and ranging along the Pacific coast of North America from the Aleutian Islands to lower western California down to latitude 30°N and tends to remain fairly static. It also breeds throughout its range. Easily recognised by its alert mannerisms, either on land or sea, this stubby little bird can be recognised at all times of the year by its rather obscure dark colouration on the dorsal surface with a very dusky throat and flanks. There are a series of tiny pale spots both above and below the eye and also a distinct white cresent can be seen above the eye. The underparts are white. The conical-shaped bill is rather long and mainly black although there is a pale area on the underside of the lower mandible. The legs and feet are blue.

Throughout the year the species tends to be gregarious and can often be seen far out to sea, feeding in large rafts, usually on planktonic crustaceans, especially shrimps. When alerted the auklets rise easily and delicately off the surface with a whizzing blur of the blunt wings but the flight is surprisingly direct. The dusky plumage is also apparent in flight although there is a rather small white patch on the abdomen which shows up surprisingly clearly. Although feeding often tends to be a deep-water exercise, the work of Stallcup (1978) suggests that the majority of birds prefer to return to sheltered bays to roost at night.

At the breeding grounds Cassin's auklets tend to be almost totally nocturnal which is bound to make accurate censusing a little difficult. Since it is

Distribution of Cassin's auklet (*Ptychoramphus aleuticus*).

Cassin's auklet (top) can be recognised by its short bill whilst the least auklet (bottom) is a most attractive species.

one of the most widespread of the Pacific auks some considerable effort has gone in to locating colonies and counting populations. Sowls *et al.* (1978) was able to list at least 21 sites and estimate that the Alaskan population was around 600,000. Sowls also investigated the population on the Farallon Islands which lie off San Francisco. Here Cassin's auklet is the most numerous sea bird, with a population in excess of 100,000, and has the very unusual behaviour pattern of returning to the islands at night, even in winter, to roost. It is indeed unusual for a population of auks to be so static. Jehl Jr (1984) reported a Californian population of 131,000, a figure which was increasing. At one time Cassin's auklet was thought to be rare in Alaska, a situation not helped by the predation of Arctic foxes (*Alopex lagopus*). Nysewander *et al.* (1982) founds 13,000 pairs in the Aleutians and Trapp noted a large colony at Chagulak Island also in the Aleutians. It may be that the demise of the fox is allowing the population of both Cassin's auklet and the marbled murrelet to make substantial recoveries. Wherever they winter the birds are back around the colonies by March, the eggs being laid between this time and early July. The single white egg is laid in a crevice in rocks or at the end of a burrow. Little is known of the incubation and fledging periods, but by August the winter dispersal has begun, birds drifting generally southwards, but never apparently reaching Asiatic shores. The main wintering grounds seem to be off the Washington coast down as far as Baja California.

PARAKEET AUKLET (*Cyclorrhynchus psittacula*)

Around 25 centimetres (10 inches) long this attractive species is found in the

North Pacific Ocean its range overlapping with several other alcids, especially the least and crested auklets. There are, however, many physical
features which render confusion with any other species quite impossible.
In contrast with many auklets the parakeet (once known as the paroquet) is
comparatively large and its red, stubby, turned-up bill and white underparts
are easily seen, even from long distance. The most obvious feature in the
breeding season is a thin white plume running behind the eye. The bulk of
the head is dull sooty black with the area around the chin and throat and
foreneck white but with a few brown speckles. The rest of the underparts
are white but there is a greyish mottling on the throat. The upper wing is
soot-black and the undersurface is dark dusky grey, but they can look
surprisingly pale against the darker upper surface. It differs from both the
crested and whiskered auklets by the lack of crest on the head and by white
on the breast and the belly. In winter the bill becomes duller, almost fading
to dull red-brown and the plumes are lost. The legs are light bluish grey at
all seasons.

In the USSR, the species is reported to breed on seashore cliffs and in
winter to wander the seas, keeping clear of frozen seas. It is described as
common and nomadic rather than migratory. The nests are grouped in small
colonies and they tend to be less gregarious than other auks. It walks well on

Distribution of the parakeet auklet (*Cyclorrhynchus psittacula*).

The parakeet auklet resting on a lichen-covered rock.

dry land and, although it seems to prefer to keep quiet, it can generate a series of low-pitched whistles which can be linked together to produce quite an attractive trill. The actual nest site is mainly in crevices and under fallen rocks. It breeds along the shores of the Chukotskiy and Kamchatka Peninsulas, the Sea of Okhotsk, Commander and Kuril Islands whilst in winter it can reach the coasts of Japan. Breeding also takes place from Cape Lisburne on the Bering Strait southwards through the Bering Sea, including the St Lawrence, Pribilof and Aleutian Islands and thence eastwards through the Kodiak archipelago as far as Prince William Sound. The breeding range also stretches westwards as far as the Commander Islands.

Few population studies have been published although Sowls and his co-workers (1978) have once more carried out pioneer studies. In Alaska they reported breeding at some 90 sites with a total population of around 800,000. Some 150,000 of these are reported to breed on George Island which must therefore be regarded as the centre of the Alaskan population. Lensink (1984) updated these statistics but sensibly pointed out that:

... nesting behaviour also precludes accurate censussing of breeding birds, estimates of numbers may be substantially in error. Currently this auklet is known to breed at about 127 locations.

He then goes on to agree with Sowls' figure of more than 800,000 but still regards the available data as insufficient to assess population trends. He does, however, suggest that populations seem to be stable, and that the activities of man do not appear to have any effect upon these.

Birds begin to return to the breeding colonies from April onwards depending upon the volume of ice. Once more there is a scarcity of precise data but most eggs are laid between June and August which means that fledging and dispersal is likely to be in full swing by September.

Like their Russian counterparts, North American ornithologists have found problems plotting the winter movements. Sowls and his co-workers (1978) agree with the Russians that most parakeet auklets remain in ice-free areas within the breeding range, using them as winter refuges, but as yet there is no proof to support this. Stejneger spent the winter of 1885 on the Commander Islands and failed to see a single parakeet auklet. Forsell and Gould (1981) conducted a thorough winter search around the breeding grounds on the Kodiaks and again came up with a blank. Perhaps we should be looking for a more likely explanation, perhaps in line with that recorded in the horned puffin (*Fratercula corniculata*) as a result of a survey by Robertson (1980). This would suggest more of a pelagic disposition drifting south to reach California and Japan. It may well be that the southerly drift will be influenced by temperature and perhaps also by salinity. We have already seen how salinity can affect the distribution of the larger alcids, especially the common guillemot (thin-billed murre), Brunnich's guillemot (thick-billed murre) and the razorbill (*Alca torda*).

I am aware, as indicated at the beginning of this chapter that many, probably most, taxonomists would expect this chapter to conclude with a description of the rhinoceros auklet but I prefer to classify it with the puffins which are the final group of Alcids and which are the subject of the next chapter.

10

PUFFINS

This chapter concerns itself with three genera and four fascinating species. The genus *Cerorhinca* consists of only one species, the rhinoceros auklet (*Cerorhinca monocerata*). The genus *Fratercula* is made up of two geographically isolated species of very similar appearance: the horned puffin (*Fratercula corniculata*) is confined to the North Pacific Ocean whilst the Atlantic puffin (*Fratercula arctica*) is restricted to the Atlantic waters. Finally we have the tufted puffin (*Lunda cirrhata*), another Pacific-based species.

RHINOCEROS AUKLET (*Cerorhinca monocerata*)

The head is the most distinctive feature of this species being basically brown but with two pairs of long facial streaks, one pair running backwards from the eye to the nape and the second leading from the throat forwards to the gape of the mandibles. The body has been described as sooty black, but many specimens are quite brown-looking, with many feathers having pale edges, giving the impression of delicate scaling. The upper breast is also quite dark but, after a mid-ventral zone of mottling, the belly becomes almost white. The upper surface of the wings is brown but the coverts also have pale edges, which add to the feeling that the species is almost as scaly as the reptiles from which birds evolved. The underwing is of a much lighter shade of brown, merging in some specimens into a soft grey. The tail is also brownish and Alexander (1963) mentioned that the number of retrices can vary from 16 to 18. If this is true one may wonder why there has been no move to separate the rhinoceros auklet into two subspecies. The length of the species is around 35 centimetres (14 inches) which surely suggests auk rather than auklet and the bill is remarkably 'puffin-like'. It is long, orange yellow and with a pale horny projection at the base of the upper mandible which is only present in summer. It is also a feature of puffins that part of the bill is moulted at the end of the breeding season. The legs are yellowish grey with black webs.

Rhinoceros auklets have a somewhat discontinuous breeding range extending from Korea, Japan, Sakhalin, Kuril and the Aleutian Islands. It also breeds from southern Alaska through British Columbia, where it is quite rare, to California and especially at Farallon Island, Castle Rock and Prince Island. Its distribution has been mapped by Sowls *et al.* (1980) and, two

Distribution of the rhinoceros auklet (*Cerorhinca monocerata*).

years earlier, the same team reported the results of a census of the Alaskan population which was estimated at around 200,000 birds. The main concentration was at Forrester Island where there were 108,000, the remaining birds being found in 11 other sites. This fragmented distribution would suggest that there may be other colonies although they are hardly likely to be large ones. This was confirmed by Lensink (1984), who noted a colony of only 30 birds on Buldir Island, and also reported birds on the Near Islands which are even further to the west but was unable to confirm breeding in this area. In the USSR, the species is reported breeding on the Kuril, Shantarskiy and Sakhalin Islands and wintering as far south as Japan.

Favoured nesting habitats are usually on small grass-covered islands and if there is a gentle slope with a thick covering of soil then so much the better. The single white egg is laid at the end of a tunnel lined with dry grass and which is usually 2 or 3 metres ($6\frac{1}{2}$ to 10 feet) deep which the bird can dig itself, another piece of behaviour which indicates that here we have a puffin rather than an auklet. Both sexes may join together to dig the burrow and there are records of tunnels of 6 metres (20 feet) in length being constructed. The egg is often lightly speckled with purple, which suggests that tunnel-nesting may have come late in the evolutionary history of the species and the ancestral species nested in the open and produced cryptically-coloured eggs.

There is strong evidence to show that the species is single-brooded, but a second egg is laid should the first be lost early in incubation. Each egg measures about 7 by 4.5 centimetres (2¾ by 1¹³⁄₁₆ inches). Incubation takes about 32 days and the semi-precocious youngsters are hardly ever brooded by the parents. They are dark grey-brown above and much paler below and are active quite soon after hatching. They come to the entrance of the burrow to defaecate and in around 40 days they are ready to leave the burrow whilst far from fully grown and still partially covered in down.

The adults are usually back in and around the colonies by April and, in suitable weather conditions, laying can commence very soon, although it can continue well into June. Fledging is at the end of July and onwards. Most of the breeding activities and the feeding of the young take place under the cover of darkness, but once the season is over there is a gradual drifting to the south, a behaviour pattern which has been recorded on both sides of the Pacific. They do tend to roost together at night, usually seeking out a sheltered bay. Stallcup (1976) recorded flocks of several thousand rhinoceros auklets taking refuge in Monterey Bay. When swimming, the bird floats low with the head drawn back along the line of the back, thus adding to the mistaken impression that the alcids are birds without necks. At this time confusion with the immature tufted puffin can arise but the larger triangular bill of the latter should prevent this. In flight the rhinoceros auklet has much more pointed wings and flies more directly than either the tufted or the horned puffin.

The rhinoceros auklet earns its name because of its very prominent bill, with a horn-like structure on the upper mandible.

TUFTED PUFFIN (*Lunda cirrhata*)

Of all the Alaskan sea birds the tufted puffin is the most widely distributed and, according to Lensink (1984) it is the fourth most abundant alcid in this area. The shortage of reliable fieldwork has often been mentioned in the course of this book, but perhaps I may have failed to pay tribute to the sheer physical problems of conducting the necessary work in harsh conditions. Imagine moving from one Alaskan island or inlet to another in a small boat tossed on the waves of the grey sea and buffeted by an icy wind. Think of focusing binoculars on mist-shrouded cliffs and with gloved hands numbed with cold. Then think of getting some sleep in the land of nearly 24 hours sunlight before beginning the next day's sail and counts. Perhaps now when we read an extract from Lensink's work we may appreciate not only its value but the effort it took to obtain it. He tells us that:

A total of 559 breeding sites with a population of 2,500,000 birds has been identified. Undoubtedly, numerous smaller colonies exist and the total population probably approaches 4 million birds. The largest colonies and the center of abundance are in the vicinity of Uminak Pass, the eastern Aleutians and the western Gulf of Alaska. These areas support almost half the known population. Nesting colonies of this species were no doubt devastated by introduction of foxes;

Distribution of the tufted puffin (*Lunda cirrhata*).

The head pattern of the tufted puffin makes it instantly recognisable.

present abundance of this seabird indicated that its numbers may have increased in recent decades.

From Siberia the breeding range extends southwards down the coast of America to Santa Barbara Island, California, but the bird's hold on the latter area seems very feeble and Jehl Jr (1984) suggests a decreasing population of 250 birds in five colonies. The species also occurs around the shores of the Chukotskiy Peninsula, Kamchatka, Commander and Kuril Islands; Sakhalin also holds some colonies and others are found fringing the Sea of Okhotsk.

The tufted puffin is described as nomadic and non-migratory remaining in the open sea where a supply of food, which consists mainly of small fish, is guaranteed. The diet is occasionally supplemented by crustaceans and sea urchins, but the young are fed totally upon fish. Breeding takes place on grassy slopes, some of the colonies being described as 'large' although, as with all alcids, difficult to census. The nest is sited at the end of a burrow, the majority of which penetrate quite deeply, often as much as 2 metres ($6\frac{1}{2}$ feet) into soft earth but in some rocky areas a shallower hollow may have to suffice. Some birds bring in lining material, which may be dry grass or even feathers, but other pairs (both birds assist in burrow-digging and collecting any materials thought to be necessary) leave their hollow unlined. Once again latitude affects the time of laying which may begin in April in the south but not until July in the far north of the range. The single egg averages 7 by 5 centimetres ($2\frac{13}{16}$ by 2 inches) in size and is usually white but can be speckled with pale violet, an evolutionary throwback already discussed above with reference to other tunnel-nesting alcids. Tufted puffins are diurnal in their habits and change-over at the nest is usually in the hours of daylight. Adults approach the nest sites at greater heights than other auks before swooping down to their burrows. The incubation period is about 30 days and the nestling is semi-precocial and covered in long silky down, dull black on the dorsal surface and sooty grey beneath. Both parents are attentive and the youngster grows quickly, but when about half fledged the chick is persuaded to leave the burrow and accompany the parent to sea.

The breeding bird is a magnificent-looking creature measuring 34 centimetres ($13\frac{5}{16}$ inches) and often to be seen drifting about in large feeding rafts. It is thus larger than the Atlantic puffin and recognised by its chunky appearance and huge triangular bill. The overall colour is blackish but, with the white cheeks, the red bill with an olive-green base and yellow ear tufts, there is no bird anywhere in the world which can be confused with a tufted puffin. In winter, with all its 'wedding dress' moulted away and its white cheeks also gone, we are left with an all-black bird with a deep red bill which is still large enough to show up very well in profile. The feet are bright red. Immature birds are very similar to the adults in winter dress except that their bills are substantially smaller.

HORNED PUFFIN (*Fratercula corniculata*)

This large auk averages around 32 centimetres ($12\frac{19}{32}$ inches) and looks at first sight like the Atlantic puffin but it is rather larger, has white cheeks in summer, and the basal section of the large bill is yellow and the tip red. It thus lacks the almost multicoloured bill which is so typical of *Fratercula arctica*. The horned puffin also has a small erectile horn over each eye which is purely a breeding decoration and from which it derives its vernacular name. In winter the bird is far less spectacular, the yellow fading from the base of the bill which moults plates to become significantly smaller; the chicks are much greyer than the adults. The crown is of an attractive grey-brown set against the much darker neck and dorsal surface whilst the chin is brownish grey and the underparts are white. It is not necessary to distinguish this species from the Atlantic puffin since the two do not share the same range, but the tufted puffin does occur in the same zone. The horned puffin has a white belly and also lacks the feathery growths on the sides of the head.

Horned puffins, which are basically diurnal, range from the shores of Chukotskiy and Kamchatka Peninsulas, the Commander, Kuril, Shantarskiye and Sakhalin Islands. They are reported to winter on the open seas quite close to the nesting areas. Lensink (1984) reported the species to be common throughout the Gulf of Alaska, Aleutians and Bering Sea with 80% of the known total population being centred at the western end of the Gulf of Alaska. The largest single breeding population, according to Hatch, is on the Semidi Islands which support some 370,000 birds. Lensink himself was very aware of the problems facing the observer and noted that:

Distribution of the horned puffin (*Fratercula corniculata*).

As the behaviour of this species makes it difficult to census accurately, the estimated total population of 1.5 million birds may be conservative. Population may have been depleted by introduced foxes, although not as severely as those of many other species. Data are inadequate to assess trends in populations which are assumed to be stable.

The preferred breeding habitat is around rocky headlands and offshore islands where usually small colonies are established in cliff crevices or burrows. Occasionally there are larger breeding aggregations but in any event these are difficult to census as Lensink clearly indicated following his Alaskan researches. The nest itself is usually at the end of a tunnel between 1 and 3 metres long (about 3¼ and 10 feet). The shallow nest cup at the end may be used without lining or a few wisps of dry grass may be added to cushion the single egg. Usually this species is surprisingly quiet but it can deliver an impressive variety of sounds at the breeding grounds, all based on a rather muted 'orr-orr'.

The dull white egg is described as sub-elliptical to oval and although quite smooth it lacks a glossy consistency. It quickly becomes stained with mud and guano which tends to obscure the faint pale grey or purple spots which, as with other species, probably indicates an ancestral habit of laying a well camouflaged egg out in the open, as do other alcids. The average measure-

The horned puffin on its breeding ground.

ments of the egg are 7 by 5 centimetres (2$\frac{13}{16}$ by 2 inches). The breeding season begins in early June but eggs are still being laid as late as the end of July, depending upon latitude. It is known that both species share the incubation period; although the precise period has not been recorded it would seem to be between 30 and 40 days.

The nestling is downy and semi-precocious, a youngster in the typical alcid mould. It is covered in long, soft pale greyish down, fading gradually in colour from back to belly and tending to be a yellowish white on the lower abdomen. Both parents play their part in feeding the youngster on a diet of fish. The adults themselves are mainly fish-eaters but supplement their diet with crustaceans and also molluscs. Although by no means as precocious as some of the murrelets, young horned puffins seem to be drawn like magnets towards the sea and are only partly feathered and a long way short of maximum body size when they flutter down to the water and swim away in the company of their parents. Horned puffins, however, are nomadic as opposed to migratory and do not wander far from the breeding grounds unless particularly cold conditions cause build up of ice. Compared with the Atlantic puffin, *Fratercula corniculata* spends much more time on land (or even ice) when its habit of bracing itself on its tarsi often gives it the appearance of a museum specimen inexpertly mounted.

The bill pattern of the horned puffin is quite distinct from that of the Atlantic puffin.

As we have already seen with the auklets and murrelets, there is a great deal of work to do both on the breeding biology and ecological interactions of the puffins. Since *Fratercula arctica* is never in contact with either the horned or the tufted puffin there is no chance of them being in competition. There are areas of contact between the two Pacific species but these have not been deeply studied. To some extent, however, the pair are geographically separated. They both breed on both sides of the Bering Sea and on many of the islands in between but the horned puffin is much more of an Arctic species and occurs on the Wrangel Islands and on the Chukotskiy Peninsula where conditions can be very harsh indeed. The tufted puffin does not breed further north than the west coast of Alaska where conditions are still often far from pleasant. In summary then we can say that all puffins are tough, but some are tougher than others.

ATLANTIC PUFFIN (*Fratercula arctica*)

Few birds have a more attractive, not to say comical, appearance than the puffin. More words have been written about and more photographs taken of the 'sea parrot' than any other sea bird. Breeding as it does so close to human settlements it is not surprising that it has been used for food and abused for 'sport' for centuries, both activities being brought to a fine art because of the puffin's fatal curiosity. Several books have been written about the behaviour of the puffin including splendid and detailed monographs by R.M. Lockley (1953) and M.P. Harris (1984).

Habitat

The puffin is a much more wide-ranging species than other Alcidae and can be found in winter from just outside regions of pack ice to areas of the Mediterranean which can almost be described as sub-tropical. It also ventures further out to sea and tends not to gather in dense flocks close inshore. This makes it less vulnerable to oil pollution than other species, particularly the common guillemot. The greatest concentrations are found in waters where the temperature varies from 0° to 15°C (32° to 59°F).

The breeding habitat is also quite flexible. In areas of the high Arctic where the ground is gripped by perma frost, even the efficient burrowing technique of the puffin is defeated and the birds resort to siting their nests in crevices and cracks. In these situations puffins often breed close to little auks and Brunnich's guillemots. Further south, in the low Arctic, the puffin may resort to breeding among the talus and rocks quite close to sea level, in which case it has black guillemots for company. Puffin colonies, however, are seen at their busy best on grassy islands or headlands where holes can be burrowed into the ground below the soft earth dominated by thrift (*Armeria maritima*), sea campion (*Silene maritima*), scurvy grasses (*Cochlearia officinalis*) and an assortment of salt-tolerant grasses of the genera *Poa* and *Festuca*. Unfortunately the brown rat (*Rattus norvegicus*), since the eighteenth century, when it was introduced to the British Isles and other areas on board ships, has proved to have a devastating effect upon many colonies. The puffins themselves have also had a detrimental effect upon some islands where there is only a thin layer of soil above the bed rock. The nest holes, when blasted by the winter winds, may add to the erosion problem. To compensate for this, however, the guano produced by thousands of birds fertilises the soil and allows a luxuriant vegetation to develop, the roots of which may act as a stabilising influence upon the soil.

Description

The size of the puffin varies from 26 to 30 centimetres (10¼ to 12 inches) and the wingspan varies from 45 to 63 centimetres (17¾ to 24¹³⁄₁₆ inches). The male is, on average, slightly larger than his mate. It is on the basis of these statistics that the puffin is divided into three sub-species (see page 164). In summer the tubby little bird is shiny black above and pure white below but

Atlantic puffin: adult in summer plumage (left) and winter plumage (right).

its whole stately presence in breeding dress is its huge and so colourful bill, which is almost as deep at its base as the head itself. The bill is compressed laterally and does bear a distinct resemblance to that of a parrot. The basal section is pale blue followed by a yellow band and the tip is red. There is also a patch of yellow at the hinge of the bill. It is fascinating to find that the red area of the bill bears a number of grooves and these can be used to determine the age, or rather the maturity, of the puffin. These lines increase both in length and number as the individual matures. A breeding adult at around 5 years old will have two complete grooves and the puffin must be one of few birds with such markings in courtship. The situation with the razorbill (*Alca torda*) appears to be similar. The head and neck are black but between them on either side of the head is a prominent white patch. The large dark eye is surrounded by a red ring whilst above and below the eye are bluish horny-looking patches, usually triangular in shape but occasionally crescent-shaped. The powerful orange coloured legs end in webbed feet with sharp black claws. These can be up to 1 centimetre ($\frac{3}{16}$ inches) and are very efficient excavating organs during the construction of the burrows.

When winter sets in the puffin becomes a very much duller creature. The lovely blue-grey base of the bill falls off and the structure therefore looks much smaller and can lead to mistaken identity when viewed by in-experienced birdwatchers. Even the red area at the end of the bill fades to a dull yellow, the yellow wattle at the hinge of the bill withers away and the horny triangle over and under the bill falls off. The red eye ring disappears also and the white face patches turn grey. Even the shiny black plumage becomes greyer and duller and the white abdomen becomes distinctly greyer. It is small wonder that the winter puffin often goes unrecognised, especially when in the company of other alcids, especially razorbills. Albin-ism seems to be more common in puffins than in other alcids, although this must be regarded as a subjective opinion not based on any reliable scientific data.

Distribution and Populations

Wherever Atlantic puffins are found there are no differences in plumage which would justify separating them into sub-species. There are, however, differences in size which have led various workers to suggest three sub-species. The comparatively large *Fratercula arctica naumanni* is a high-Arctic species and separated (in museum skins at least) from the smaller *Fratercula arctica grabae* which is the species found in Britain and points south to France and eastwards to southern Norway. *Fratercula arctica arctica* is intermediate in size and is found in North America and Iceland, and in Norway apart from the south.

In this book, Bergmann's rule has frequently been mentioned to explain why northern birds tend to be larger than those of the same species from the south of the range. Many feel that the puffin should therefore be lumped rather than split. Harris (1984) in his excellent monograph on the species summarised all the arguments for and against the division into sub-species. He also pointed out a curious and as yet unexplained anomaly in which

Distribution of the Atlantic puffin (*Fratercula arctica*).

puffins breeding on the east coast of Scotland are significantly larger and heavier than birds which breed on the west. He gave the average comparative figures as 379 grams against 374 grams ($13\frac{11}{32}$ ounces against $13\frac{3}{16}$ ounces) and wing length of 16.2 centimetres against 15.8 centimetres ($6\frac{3}{8}$ inches against $6\frac{1}{4}$ inches). There we must leave the problem of sub-species without being able to come to any firm conclusion. More work remains to be done to measure birds in all areas of its range.

In North America puffins are found from around 55°N in Labrador down to New Brunswick and eastern Maine. As many as 60% may breed on islands dotted around Witless Bay. Nettleship's work suggests some 52 colonies with a total population of 338,000 pairs and Harris (1984) is certain that these figures represent a serious decline which he attributes to human persecution, especially shooting. In the New World, Newfoundland is certainly the centre of population with around 250,000 pairs whilst Labrador holds 77,000 pairs in 17 colonies all of which have shown serious declines due to man's greed (see Chapter 11).

In Greenland the population has never been high and the situation was summarised by Evans in 1984, and only a few thousand pairs occur. These are mainly centred on the west coast. The main colonies are at Rifkol Island where a 'large' colony was identified in the 1940s, and other 'large' colonies were listed at the Skerries at Satsigsunguit which is the north of Godthab and around the Naujarssuit islet. The total population of Greenland does not exceed 5,500 pairs and it is not possible to calculate if there have been any significant population changes. Salomonsen (1950), however, seemed to be convinced that there had been a decline because of the collection of eggs for food and that several burrows had been deserted. Some legislation may have resulted in a temporary improvement, but having laws is one thing and actually applying them is another problem altogether. The puffins of Greenland, like the rest of its protein-rich wildlife, are still very much under threat.

To some extent the same is true of the puffins in Iceland, where human hunting, and especially the introduction and subsequent escape of the North American mink (*Mustela vison*) has made significant inroads into the once huge populations. This lovely land still remains the centre of the puffin population but the colonies are scattered around the indented and often inhospitable coastline and among hundreds of tiny islands often impossible to land upon due to a combination of wind, tide and swell. Lockley (1953) thought there might be something in the order of 5 million pairs, but Petersen (1982) thought that there may well be twice this number. So far Petersen has been the only worker to brave the Icelandic seas in search of a reliable estimate of the population. He noticed that in some cases the birds were their own worst enemies because their extensive burrowing into ecologically-delicate island soils may result in massive erosion with the subsequent forced abandonment of the site. In the mid-nineteenth century, bird-fowling with nets reduced the populations but sensible laws insisting that immature birds were caught rather than mature adults reduced their effects. Present-day evidence, mainly based on the work of Petersen would suggest that the puffin is at least holding its own and may even be increasing slightly.

In the British Isles, where many of the colonies are within comparatively easy reach of the mainland, efforts have been made to arrive at reliable estimates. The burrow-nesting habit, however, has made things difficult. Manx shearwaters, which have the confusing scientific name of *Puffinus puffinus*, have an even more confusing habit of also nesting in burrows. There are instances of burrows which have several branches and one entrance may be shared by shearwaters, rabbits and puffins and, in these instances, censusing is almost impossible, especially when we consider that each puffin burrow is often longer than the human arm.

Many colonies these days are far removed from human activities and especially from grazing although there are some islands which seem to be able to support both. Perhaps the soil is firmer in these instances. In the south of England many colonies have certainly decreased very sharply indeed. These may be due to the burrowing activities of the birds themselves, to various pollutants or to the activities of introduced brown rats.

In the mid 1970s ornithologists were pointing to catastrophic declines in British puffin populations without being able to offer any explanation to account for this in the more remote colonies in places like the Hebridean Shiants and St Kilda. It would seem safe to assume that there have been peaks and troughs in puffin populations over the centuries and by the mid 1980s there were firm indications of an improvement in numbers. In 1969–70, the 'Operation Seafarer' put the total population at around 500,000 pairs, making the puffin Britain's second most numerous alcid after the guillemot. During the 1950s, Fisher and Lockley were reporting populations of puffins at *individual sites* of around the figure of 500,000 and there must be some way to go before these populations are restored. Careful censusing most be continued and methods improved but it cannot be easy as Harvie-Brown in 1888, working on Mingulay, now an uninhabited island off Barra in the Hebrides was well aware when he wrote:

The Puffin has complete hold over the whole upper crust .... Later in the year the whole surface is one sticky compound of mud and dung, feathers, bad eggs and defunct young puffins, ankle deep or deeper – waiting perhaps to be scraped way some day from the rocky follor on which it rests, and be spread far and near over the worn-out pastures by future generations of farmers – truly a filthy if a fruitful compost.

On my last visit in 1985 the island was deserted but it was still a heaving heap of breeding puffins and Harvie-Brown's remarks were as fresh and accurate as on the day they were written.

The decline of the puffin in the southern counties of Britain is reflected in

Part of an active colony of puffins.

the figures for France where Pasquet (1982) reported only 250 pairs compared with the 10,000 pairs on the island of Rouzic in 1912 which had been halved by 1950. The decline has continued since and was accelerated by the Torrey Canyon oil spill of 1967 which affected 85% of the breeding population, and the Amoco Cadiz disaster 11 years later was also particularly disastrous. According to Guermour and Monnat (1980) and Penicaud (1980) these falls could be mainly due to climatic changes rather than as a result of human activities. This may also account for falls in Channel Island populations. It is thought that the effect of climate on the puffin's food supplies has been a more important factor in the decline in Britain than either oil or other forms of pollution (Harris, 1976a). The Channel Island population which Lockley thought might have been as high as 100,000 birds in 1953 is now less than 500 pairs and showing no sign of any substantial improvement. The situation is nowhere nearly as bad to the north and Harris (1976b), although reporting significant declines during the early years of the twentieth century, suggested a halt to the problem. The population has now probably stabilised at between 400,000 and 1 million pairs, the wide range between maximum and minimum reflecting the problems of making a reliable census.

In Norway, Brun (1966) thought that the population might be between 1½ and 2 million pairs concentrated mainly in the north of the country. Little is known of population trends but they are thought to be relatively stable. Puffins have probably never been particularly numerous in Spitzbergen and Løvenskjold (1964), who knew the area well, did not know of any colony larger than 100 pairs. These all belonged to the large race *Fratercula arctica naumanni* which may give them a little extra strength to dig through the perma frost. The same is true of both Bear Island and Jan Mayen whilst in the USSR the situation is similar with Norderhaug *et al.* (1977) reporting less than 100 pairs but Skokova (1962) indicating a population of between 15,000 and 20,000 strung out in small colonies along the coast of Murmansk.

Behaviour and Breeding

Puffin-watching has doubtless been an enjoyable human pastime since the hungry hunters of past civilisations worked out how to get near enough to them to kill them and add their nutritious flesh to the pot. Scientists with a desire to unravel their sign language have enjoyed many an hour in their company and the sheer joy of this experience is echoed in the writings of Perry (1946), Lockley (1953), Myrberget (1962), Harris (1984) and Taylor (1984). Armed with lists of postures worked out by these workers, the present author has spent many happy hours sitting among the puffin colonies around the coastline of the British Isles and attempting to translate the body language of the birds.

It would be a shame to waste the massive bills and 'evolution is not wasteful of energy'. Anyone sitting amid the puffins will find it hard not to watch the attractive antics of the lovely birds, but give your eyes a rest and listen for a while with your eyes closed. You will soon become aware of the clashing of bills during the process of billing. This is a mutual activity and is very important in building up the pair bond. The approaching bird swings its head from side to side and gives its mate (or potential mate) a quick nibble on its bill. The response may be a sharp rebuff or a session of mutual billing during which the sound of clashing bills may be audible over quite a distance. If billing takes place on the sea it may form part of a pirouetting water ballet and, if land-based, one partner stretches up to allow the one crouching to administer the most efficient billing. The pair may spread the webs of their feet wide and do a land-based, and therefore much more clumsy, pirouette. When this behaviour is witnessed by others in the flock they all start to bill and the whole procedure is a subtle mechanism to bring the birds into breeding condition at the same time. During billing one bird seems to be more active than the other and the behaviour is therefore different from the allopreening seen, and already described, for the razorbill (*Alca torda*). The yellow rosettes may play some part in the billing behaviour even if it is only as an 'aiming point'.

Myrberget (1962) also described both sexes forming a bowing movement which he thought could be a threat display or even an invitation to the mate to begin billing. This is not a very common form of behaviour but I have observed it particularly at the beginning of the breeding season when the head is inclined by birds swimming around and also on land when the legs can be seen to bend so that the puffin seems to be looking backwards through its legs. It certainly seems to be a part of the pair-bonding behaviour and would therefore tend to be seen early in the season.

The full details of pair bonding can sometimes be obscured by the fact that old-established pairs may know each other well enough for the processes to be carried through quickly. Harris (1984) described head-flicking and wing-fluttering which the male uses to pursuade the female to copulate. The head is quickly jerked up and down, the breast raised out of the water (successful copulations in puffins are aquatic-based) and is followed by

Display movements of the Atlantic puffin.

mating. Conder (1950) noticed that mated birds with their pair bonds well and truly cemented tended to remain closer together within the raft than those not already 'spoken for'. The desire to mate may thus spread through the whole raft during which the female remains passive, unlike in the common guillemot where the female responds to the male by tossing her head.

Having mated, the pair are ready to lay claim to a burrow in which to lay the fertilised egg. They are prepared to fight for territory but prefer to threaten, which they do by opening their bills wide and 'gaping' at intruders, the yellow interior flashing like a flag. Its meaning is clear: 'This is our territory – keep off'. Both sexes defend their nest site and if the gape fails then the birds may fight, which they do by gripping bills and the contestants squirm about in a twisting, writhing, animated bundle of stiff feathers. Puffin vocalisation is not well advanced (or perhaps not well documented) but their anger is obvious from the low growling noises issuing from the fighters.

In huge colonies birds landing and wishing to make their way through the mass of aggressive puffins to their own nest hole certainly require some sort of 'white flag' or policy of appeasement. When I watch puffins I am reminded of a drunken human trespasser tip-toeing past a forbidden area. This has rightly been called the low profile walk (Taylor, 1984) and the anxious bird takes up a hunch-backed position and then moves in jerks before stopping suddenly and having a quick look round before walking quickly on. Think of your own movements in unfamiliar territory and you may perhaps understand the low profile walk and as you move into home territory you will also understand the pelican walk, during which the bird raises each foot deliberately and stamps towards its own burrow. Once it has arrived it may walk on the spot, keeping the high-stepping movements with its foot webs spread wide. The period of greatest danger comes at the point of landing and some movement is needed fairly quickly. Puffins landing well away from other birds fold their wings as soon as they land, but if they feel they are too near to the territory owner, the landing posture with wings raised is maintained and seems to say: 'I'm only visiting and will soon be on my way and I don't wish to be attacked'. This behaviour has been described by both Danchin (1983) and Taylor (1984). Having established how puffins first claim a mate and then a breeding territory we can now briefly examine the breeding cycle of the species.

The Breeding Cycle

In Britain, puffins tend to arrive back in the areas around their colonies during February or March but it is later in the year in the northern parts of the range. They tend not to spend much time on land but lounge about in rafts just off shore, building up and cementing pair bonds as discussed above. During this time birds 'mill about' in the water with their bodies pressed low into the water and necks stretched up. This is one of the few occasions during which ornithologists may realise that auks actually do have necks.

Gradually more and more time is spent on shore and displaying birds engage in wheeling flights, turning and twisting around the stacks, precipitous cliffs and over the grassy islands. Taylor (1974) is of the opinion that wheeling is one method of prospecting for nest sites although it does seem as if the birds are enjoying the experience and it may help to cement the pair bond.

The single egg is laid at the end of a burrow which may be over 2 metres (6 feet) deep and often lined with dry grass, feathers or even sprigs of thrift, scurvy grass or sea campion. The average size seems to be 6.5 by 4.5 centimetres ($2\frac{19}{32}$ by $1\frac{13}{16}$ inches) and weighing approximately 60 grams (about 2 ounces). Ashcroft (1976) found that eggs laid earlier in the season tended to be heavier and once again we find in the alcids that the early breeders within a given population tend to be the most successful. Occasionally there are faint spots of reddish brown on the eggs although, as incubation proceeds, these are lost under a coating of mud and guano. It does show, however, that puffins once nested out in the open like other alcids. Occasionally two eggs are produced which some workers have suggested may be due to two females laying in the same nest. There is anatomical evidence which suggests otherwise. Puffins have two brood patches, situated on either side of the breast bone and this surely indicates descent from an ancestor which laid two eggs. A replacement egg is laid should the first be lost soon after laying. Both male and female take their share of incubation sitting in shifts of about 30 hours the change-over taking place mainly at night. Lockley (1934) thought that the female did more incubating than her mate. The time does seem to vary from colony to colony, Ashcroft calculating an average of 39 days for Skomer, in Wales, and Myrberget calculating almost 42 days for birds at Lovunden, Norway.

The young are described as semi-altricial and are covered in long soft down. The upper surface is dark brown with the base of each feather being grey. The underparts are white. The bill is not recognisable as that of a puffin, being quite small with the upper mandible being black and the lower one a great deal paler. There are records of puffins feeding their young 24 times in one day but Harris thinks that between four and five feeds per day, depending upon the weight and quality of fish delivered, is nearer to the truth. The period of fledging is also variable and may depend partly upon latitude and also upon the quantity and quality of food which both parents are able to bring to them. Harris conducted fascinating studies of the food brought to young puffins and found that almost any species of mid-water fish would be accepted, but that, if there was a choice, then sand-eels and sprats were the favourite (see page 174 for diet). Harris found that young birds fed upon sand-eels around the Isle of May thrived better than those around St Kilda which were fed upon whiting. It does not seem reasonable to argue against Harris's theory that this diet accounts for the fact that the St Kildan population is steady whilst that of the Isle of May birds is increasing rapidly. There does seem to be a higher food value in sand-eel flesh than in that of whiting. Contrary to early opinion that young puffins reached a certain size and were then starved until they left the nest, it now seems that they are fed right up until leaving the burrow, which they do of their own accord.

The first journey of a young puffin is a real baptism of fire as they run the gauntlet through predatory gulls. The little creatures are not altogether ill-prepared since they spend two or three evenings at the entrance to the burrow looking around before they choose a usually moonless night, preferably with a curtain of mist, during which to make the journey to the sea and try to get as far from land as possible before dawn. Ashcroft suggested that fledging (and independence from parents) was around 38 days, Myrberget calculated nearly 48 days in Norway whilst Harris (1984) found the period varied between 34 and 50 days on the Isle of May and between 35 and 60 days on St Kilda.

The young puffins then enter upon a period of pelagic existence and for the first 2, or even 3 years of their lives they may undergo a wing moult at the time when the mature adults are breeding. It is this wanderlust, which is lacking in adults of other species, which makes ringing puffins a rather unrewarding business since so many birds die in mid ocean, their heavy bodies then sinking beyond recovery. Some birds attempt to breed at the age of 4 years, but they are not likely to be successful until the 5th year. Because of the low recovery rate of rings placed on puffins (less than 1%), calculations of life expectancy are likely to be somewhat speculative but Mead (1974) did suggest that, for adults, the survival rate (based on colour-ringed adults returning to their colonies) could be higher than 90%. Harris further estimated that, for the 2 years following birth, the death rate could be as high as 25% and then, in the 3rd year, the birds were becoming more experienced and the rate fell to around 19% and then to 8% during years 4 and 5. Those few rings which were returned seldom indicated the precise cause of death, but prominent causes would seem to be from oiling, shooting and by becoming entagled in fishing nets (see Chapter 11).

All workers point out the potential errors in working out the areas and directions of winter dispersal from ringing returns because most puffins which die in deep water are likely to sink without trace. The southern populations of the subspecies *grabae* ringed in Britain showed some dispersal as far to the south as the western Mediterranean and eastern Italy. The evidence, however, consists of only 175 recoveries up to the end of 1982 but it does seem that puffins breeding on the eastern coasts of Britain are less inclined to wander than those which breed on the western coasts. It could be that the temperatures of waters in this area are within the puffins' range of 0°C to 15°C (32°F to 59°F) and that they have therefore less incentive to move. Such recoveries as there have been (see Mead, 1974, and Harris, 1984) have been around the North Sea basin with smaller numbers reaching the Bay of Biscay. It would also seem that birds in their first year tend to

A puffin colony is a place full of sound and movement.

wander further than at other periods in their life. This wanderlust, taking them into deeper and often warmer waters, is reflected in ringing returns of birds from British auk colonies, i.e. 2.7% for the guillemot, 3.0% for the razorbill and a mere 0.7% for the puffin.

Birds of the sub-species *naumanni* breeding in the high Arctic also seem to be dispersive, although there are very few returns and the evidence must be regarded as speculative rather than concrete. One specimen was found as far south as Vesteralen in Norway and reported by Haftorn in 1971. It may be that puffins have to be aware of closing ice, but the food supply in the area may be rich enough to keep some birds near the home base. The birds breeding around Thule in Greenland do seem to move southwards and Salomonsen (1967) reported that wintering birds did not penetrate northwards beyond Sukkertoppen in the southern Davis Strait.

The nominate sub-species *Fratercula arctica arctica* appears to wander southwards to around 55°N and both Salomonsen (1967) and Tuck (1971) indicate that those breeding in Canada and western Greenland tend to winter around Newfoundland. It is not a coincidence to find that these areas are also rich fishing grounds. There has also been an extensive, although very labour-intensive, ringing programme in Norway which indicates more birds breeding in the south wintering in a southwesterly direction towards Skagerrak and occasionally beyond into the North Sea as far as Scotland. Northern-based Norwegian puffins tend towards the Faroes, Iceland and Greenland with Myrberget (1973) reporting one such bird actually reaching Newfoundland. Tuck (1971) had 21 returned rings from the Newfoundland area of which 18 were first winter birds from Iceland. Whilst these movements would seem to be typical, with so few returns to go on it would be wrong to do other than make tentative suggestions and yet another alcid is in need of more research.

Food and Feeding

Many of the early studies on the puffins' diet were carried out on the breeding grounds and it was found to consist almost totally of fairly small fish, particularly the sand-eels of four species: *Ammodytes marinus*, *Ammodytes lancea*, *Ammodytes tobianus* and *Hyperoplus lanceolatus*. At one time sand-eels were not important in human commerce but increasing numbers are now being netted for making into fish meal which is used both as fertiliser and animal food. The effect upon puffin populations has yet to be established, but it could well become a real problem in the not too distant future. Three fish of the Clupeidae family are also taken, especially the sprat (*Sprattus sprattus*), herring (*Clupea harengus*) and the capelin (*Mallotus villosus*). Other species commonly taken include the whiting (*Merlangius merlangus*), red fish (*Sebastes marinus*) – but not in Britain, saithe (*Pollachius virens*), haddock (*Melanogrammus aeglefinus*) and the three rocklings – the five-bearded (*Ciliata mustela*), northern (*Ciliata septentrionalis*) and three-bearded (*Gaidrosparus vulgaris*).

As puffins dive for their food they will obviously take whatever species comes their way and so a great many species are eaten from time to time but the species appearing regularly in the diet are found in the above list. Most species of sea bird are only able to carry one fish at a time. Puffins are able to carry over 20 but the number depends upon weight of fish and the numbers available. The precise method of capturing so many fish is not known but it is easy to understand how the fish are held. An examination of the mandibles reveals them both to be sharp edged and, on the roof of the mouth, there are backward-pointing tooth-like projections which dig into and hold firmly onto the slippery struggling prey. The tongue is also cornified which helps to grip the fish. The puffin also has a short but very tough quadrate bone between the upper and lower jaws which allows the mandibles of the bill to be held parallel as the mouth opens. Thus a number of fish can be held firm whilst what amounts to a pair of double-jointed jaws can be opened and snatch another fish.

Puffins on the hunt for food usually search around by dipping their heads into the water and diving, although they do not penetrate very far below the surface. Harris and Hislop (1978) reported that puffins fish only during the day. One technique is to crash-land over a shoal of fish and as many as 100 birds may join together in a communal frenzy of feeding, although the average number of participants is nearer to 15. Although the fish are carried crosswise in the bill, the old idea that heads and tails were arranged alternately has now been finally discounted. For those of us who love our natural history to be poetic as well as scientific it is perhaps a pity that Perry's description written in 1946 cannot now be accepted. After stating that puffins arrange fish in a head-tail sequence nine times out of ten he described the puffin weaving about under the water and: 'Progressing thus he will first take a fish to the left, the right, then left.' Feeding is obviously disrupted by stormy weather, but despite Lockley's opinion, expressed in the 1930s, the state of the tide has little effect upon the activity. During the breeding season the majority of birds remain close to their colony and Harris and Hislop estimated the journey to the feeding grounds as between 2 and 10 kilometres ($1\frac{1}{4}$ and $6\frac{1}{4}$ miles). Ashcroft (1976) studying the colony at Skokholm found that the majority of birds fished within 8 kilometres (5 miles) of the colony. Belopol'ski (1957), reporting on Russian colonies, pointed out that puffins breeding in the Barents Sea fed close to the colonies but birds from the Ainov Islands, particularly the males, were thought to travel a distance of between 15 and 25 kilometres ($9\frac{3}{8}$ and $15\frac{5}{8}$ miles).

As already indicated, the diet of puffins has been worked out on the evidence of prey carried to the young. Adults on their way to their burrows have been trapped in mist nets and, in their struggles, release the fish which can be counted and identified. Very little seems to be known about the diet of the adults although a few pioneer workers have examined the contents of

stomachs. The digestive juices of puffins are particularly strong and the food is quickly broken down, and many stomachs have been found to be empty, even shortly after having visited the feeding grounds. One such worker was Belopol'ski (1957) who examined 124 stomachs taken from puffins in the Barents Sea. He found 67% of these stomachs to contain fish, 24% sponges, 4% crustaceans, 4% polychaetes, 0.8% molluscs with just a few insects and a little vegetable matter presumably taken by accident. When percentages are calculated by weight a much more accurate figure is obtained. In East Murmansk for example the contents of 100 stomachs showed 56.8% sand-eels, 21% capelin, 19.7% herring and 2.5% cod. Examination of 39 stomachs from the Ainov Islands yielded 50% herring, 43.7% capelin, 6.3% sand-eels. Belopol'ski also found that the sexes appeared to have different diets. Only females seemed to feed upon sand-eels, the males relying more upon a diet of capelin. This may perhaps relate to the male's rather larger size and may be yet another example of the ecological niche theory operating to reduce intra-specific competition.

At the same time Belopol'ski pointed out that the winter diet, although not properly investigated, was likely to include a higher percentage of crustaceans, an opinion supported, and to some extent substantiated, by Harris and Hislop (1978) and by Harris himself in 1984. Normally puffins do not seem to dive deeper than 15 metres (nearly 50 feet) and are not often under for longer than 5–10 seconds (Bird and Bird, 1935). They may need to dive deeper in winter when the diet includes marine worms and crustaceans, which almost certainly means that quite large volumes of salt water may be taken in during this period. As mentioned in Chapter 2 most marine-based birds are able to drink sea water and excrete the excess salt *via* nasal salt glands. Hughes (1970) found that a puffin's kidneys were twice as heavy compared with body weight as those of sea ducks, but the bulk of the excess salt was still removed by the salt glands. The speed of salt removal is as high as in any other bird. Thus the puffin is ideally adapted to handle the marine environment, but like the rest of the alcids there are many problems to solve, especially in the modern world which places more and more pressure on all the world's environments, not least the sea. These will be discussed in the final chapter.

A puffin at the conclusion of a successful fishing expedition.

11

AUKS IN THE MODERN WORLD

Throughout the history of mankind, auks with their massive colonies and nutritious flesh and eggs must have been a natural target. One could almost add primitive man to the list of the birds' natural predators. The threat posed by modern man is, however, much more subtle, as industries add their chemicals to the waters and atmosphere of the world. Modern auks have six problem areas, each of which will be considered in turn. These are: natural predators, predators introduced by man, man himself, the effect of his domestic animals, commercial fishing and finally pollutants, including oil. The latter is often spoken of as if it were the only problem facing auks at the present time. Indeed it may be well down the danger list in a global context.

NATURAL PREDATORS

The sheer density of many auk colonies means that predators are able to gather in some numbers and their activities are relatively easy to observe. The predation may often involve the stealing of food rather than the destruction of eggs, young or even adults. Kleptoparasitism has been studied by Anderson (1976) who found skuas to be particularly adept at this form of aerial piracy around the bird colonies on the Shetlands whilst Arnason and Grant (1978) observed the effect of Arctic skuas (*Stercorarius parasiticus*) in Iceland. They found that, early in their breeding season, the skuas fed mainly by harrying kittiwakes (*Rissa tridactyla*) until they dropped their food, which the skuas usually managed to retrieve in mid air. The skua eggs do tend to hatch around the same time as those of the puffins and so the pirates switched their attacks onto *Fratercula arctica*. The success of the skuas depended to some extent on the distance between the puffins' feeding grounds and the nesting cliffs and also upon the height of the cliffs themselves. This is because the skuas prefer to attack high enough in the air to allow themselves time to catch the fish before it falls either into the sea or onto the ground. In these cases the fish tended to be eaten by scavenging birds, particularly herring gulls (*Larus argentatus*) or glaucous gulls (*Larus hyperboreus*) and ravens (*Corvus corax*). Birkhead (1975) found that jackdaws (*Corvus monedula*) can also be a problem amongst colonies of common guillemots.

My own researches among the auk colonies of the Hebridean Islands and on the west coast of England and Wales indicate that both carrion crows and hooded crows (*Corvus corone*) can also be a problem in the sense that they not only harry for food but also consume both eggs and young birds.

In Alaska, Lensink (1984) found that the glaucous gull and the raven were both significant predators, as were the bald eagle (*Haliaeetus leucocephalus*), and Peal's peregrine falcon (*Falco peregrinus pealii*). Mammals can also be a problem in Alaska and listed among the most destructive are the brown bear (*Ursus arctos*) and both the Arctic and red foxes (*Alopex lagopus* and *Vulpes fulva*).

In Greenland, Evans (1984) points out that the Arctic fox, glaucous gull and raven are important predators as is the Gyr falcon (*Falco rusticolus*) and skuas, including the great skua (*Stercorarius skua*), pomarine (*Stercorarius pomarinus*) and the Arctic skua, which is well named *Stercorarius parasiticus*. In addition to these species, there are also the herring gull, the great blackbacked gull (*Larus marinus*) and Iceland gull (*Larus glaucoides*).

Salomonsen (1950) pointed out that the birds adapted to the predators by resorting to areas difficult for the predators to reach. In the case of Brunnich's guillemot, and doubtless other species, the greatest danger comes as the young make the perilous journey from nest site to sea through often large numbers of predators waiting for a meal. This is where the advantage comes of large colonies breeding at the same time because large numbers of young birds heading for the open sea means that a significant number are able to slip through the net.

Whilst man cannot be directly blamed for the inroads made into auk populations by predators there is no doubt that larger numbers of gulls survive because of our throw-away society. Rubbish dumps full of decaying food allow many gulls to survive the winter and so more are waiting to kleptoparasitise the auks and feast upon their young during their breeding season. This, according to Nettleship (1972, 1975), has adversely affected the populations of Atlantic puffins in the south east of Newfoundland. The increased number of gulls around areas of high human populations may well have had a considerable effect upon the colonies of auks sited on islands close to these areas. There is often also the added problems caused by predators introduced as a result of man's activities. These may have been either deliberately or accidentally introduced but the effect is the same – often catastrophic.

INTRODUCED PREDATORS

The effect of brown rats (*Rattus norvegicus*) on many British auk colonies, especially those of puffins on the west coast has been profound and, in some cases, disastrous. Colonies of puffins on both the Isle of Man, especially the Calf and the once well-named Puffin Island off the Welsh coast, have been brought to the point of extinction. Murie (1959) and Jones and Byrd (1979) drew attention to the reduction in Alaskan auk colonies by brown rats and also by red and Arctic foxes which were introduced into many islands to meet the demands of the fur trade which peaked towards the end of the eighteenth and the beginning of nineteenth century. The trade flourished until World War 2 brought it to a sudden end. Comparisons between bird populations free from foxes and those where they still thrive shows clearly their adverse effect. Alcids suffering most are the ancient murrelet, Cassin's auklet and the tufted puffin. The population of a predator does not need to be great to have an effect. This was clearly described by Petersen (1981) who documented the effect of one pair of marooned red foxes on Shaiak Island. Many birds suffered, including the common eider (*Somateria mollissima*) and black-legged kittiwake (*Rissa tridactyla*) as well as common guillemots, whilst the population of tufted puffins was reduced by 6,600 birds, an estimated 8.3%. Once fox-farming ceased the foxes quickly disappeared from the smaller islands as they destroyed their food supply and the subsequent recovery of the bird colonies was spectacular. This suggests that if foxes on the larger islands were eradicated many alcids would soon revert to former population levels. This information ought to prove beyond question the danger of farming predatory animals close to vulnerable bird colonies.

This does not seem to deter speculators and there have been several attempts to institute the farming of North American mink (*Mustela vison*) on remote islands, especially in the Hebrides, Scotland. A few of these cunning predators would be bound to escape and breed. In view of the effect on the birds of one pair of foxes in Alaska the effect on Hebridean colonies after a year or two cannot be imagined without a shudder of apprehension. In Norway, mink farming is already well established and Barrett and Vader (1984) point out that escaped animals are already a threat, especially to the black guillemot. The Icelandic black guillemot colonies have also, according to Petersen (1981 and 1982) suffered from the attentions of escaped mink. Cats escaping from sinking ships have also adapted to island life and become something of a problem on islands situated close to regular trade routes. Folkestad (1982) also noted the effect of mink on western Norwegian auks and other sea birds.

THE HUMAN IMPACT

Adult auks, their eggs and their young are all highly palatable and have been invaluable and easily accessible sources of protein for centuries. Immigrants are thought to have arrived in Greenland in about 2500 BC and have hunted birds ever since, especially Brunnich's guillemot, the population of which is still being reduced by hunters, despite efforts to protect it. Hunting of this species and the common guillemot may still be carried on during the Newfoundland winter and as many as 450,000 birds may be the annual cull according to Wendt and Gooch (1984). When one considers that illegal hunting also goes on, then the annual kill must still be enormous. Traditional hunting techniques, such as snaring and netting, were all carried on at a local level and had little effect on population levels. Many primitive societies had a surprising degree of in-built conservation and literally farmed the breeding cliffs. The introduction of firearms and an increased commercially-minded approach by visitors as opposed to residents has caused the extinction of many colonies and one entire species, the great auk, which was the subject of Chapter 2.

The exercise they affect most is climbing of steep rocks, He is the prettiest man who ventures upon the most inaccessible, though all they gain is the eggs of the fowls and the honour to dye, as many of their ancestors, by breaking of their necks.

Thus wrote Sir George Mackenzie of Tarbat in 1675 in his description of the inhabitants of the remote island group of St Kilda. Almost always hidden by a shroud of mist St Kilda lies 55 kilometres (34 miles) WNW of the western headland of North Uist in Scotland's majestic Hebrides. St Kilda is not an island but a fascinating group of stacks and small islands. There are three main islands: Boreray, Soay and Hirta, the latter being the only one to have been inhabited. Dun is a tiny islet, which has always been home to large numbers of puffins, and which is easily reached from Hirta. The group is completed by the three lowering stacks of Levenish, Lee and Armin, all of which are thriving sea-bird cities with the world's largest gannetry (*Sula bassana*). Hirta is peaked by the towering cliffs of Conachair which tower 431 metres (almost 1,400 feet) above the sea and are riddled with sea-bird ledges. Breeding here are vast numbers of fulmars (*Fulmarus glacialis*). The St Kildan economy was totally based upon sea birds, with gannets and fulmars providing the main crop from a financial point of view. Oil, feathers and food were all obtained in huge quantities. By the time alternative sources of these commodities had been found, the St Kildan way of life, which cannot have altered for centuries, came under pressure and, in 1931, the population deserted the island and there have been no permanent residents there since, although the army now maintain a small base and ornithologists are frequent visitors.

Williamson and Morton Boyd (1960) and Harris (1984) all recount the thrill of this remote spot and their descriptions of the clamour of birds, the dripping fog which invariably surrounds it and the ruins of a once-thriving human community never fail to stir my own memory of days spent on St Kilda, once called 'the islands at the end of the earth'. If you sail past St Kilda it is next stop North America and in the heart of a storm the swell and fetch of the Atlantic is terrifying.

To the St Kildans, gannets and fulmars brought bargaining power and functioned as currency to trade with the outside world, but it was the auks which provided the bulk of their food. Eggs of the guillemot and the razorbill were eaten, but the most numerous bird on the island group was always the puffin which was, and still is, centred on Dun. They knew them as popes, tammie norries, bougirs and coulternebs and looked forward to their arrival in March and felt the pangs of hunger after their departure in late August.

The first thing visitors to St Kilda notice is the *cleitans*, which look like small houses in the shape of igloos and are made out of rough stone but with no windows. These were the St Kildan equivalent of a deep freeze where the carcasses of birds were hung. The stones of which the cleitans were built were arranged so that they filtered out most of the rain and damp but allowed the wind, which always seems to be blasting this treeless island, to pass through and dry the flesh. Some birds were also salted. Although there are accounts of the mould having to be scraped off the flesh, the hanging fowls kept body and soul together on an island where frost is virtually unknown. All the St Kildans had to do was catch their birds.

The St Kildans trained dogs to crawl down the burrows and, when they emerged, protesting puffins were usually hanging on to the fur and were then grabbed and killed. They also used an ingenious device, called a *fleyg*

The island of St Kilda, showing the stone-built *cleitans* used in drying the bodies of sea birds captured and killed in the summer and eaten in the winter.

St Kildan catching puffins using a long thin pole with a running noose at the end.

or fowling rod, which was often made of bamboo (traded with mariners for fulmar oil) and usually about 5 metres (16 feet) long with a running noose at the end made of horse hair and held open with a quill feather taken from a gannet. The operator crept slowly along the narrow ledges with the heavy sea far below him and then dangled the rod above the puffins. A sudden movement and a puffin was secured and wriggling in the noose. A skilled man could catch between 100 and 200 in a day. Fowling gins were also used and these consisted of horse-hair nooses, often as many as 30, attached to a long rope and laid down on rocks used as loafing areas by puffins. Once the birds settled down the rope was pulled and several birds were captured.

Guillemots, which the St Kildans called *lavy*, were pupular both because of their taste and because of the fact that they arrived back on the breeding ledges as early as February when fresh meat was in short supply. In 1837 the village records show that 3,750 guillemots stripped of their feathers helped to pay the rent. The birds were caught by using an amusing strategy, during which the fowler was lowered over the cliff at night with a white sheet over his head. (Think of how much courage this must have taken!) When the birds returned to their ledges in the early morning the dim light meant that they confused the fowler with a guano-stained rock and a skilled operator could catch as many as 100 birds before it became too light for the ruse to work.

Folk who have not been lucky enough to visit this remote island often ask why the St Kildans did not live on fish. A couple of days spent watching the swell and the towering waves and feeling the might of an Atlantic breeze quickly dispels any thought of fishing and one turns ones eyes to the hills (or should it be cliffs?) and hungers and thirsts after birds and nothing but birds. Young puffins were also eaten and were considered to be a great delicacy, not only in St Kilda but in other parts of its range, especially on the Scilly Isles, Isle of Man and the east-coast colonies at Flamborough head. Digging out or crawling after puffin chicks is both time-consuming and dangerous and so they were never a regular item of diet, the adults being much easier to catch. Fowling for puffins is not a thing of the past in some areas, especially Iceland, Norway and the Faroe Islands, where fowlers still kill thousands of birds each year although there has been some reduction in recent years. If the birds killed are expressed as a percentage of the total population then the slaughter can be considered to be going on unabated. Alaskan Indians and Eskimos have also used alcids and other sea birds as food since prehistoric times and some killing is still allowed in regions under the control of the conservation-minded 'civilised' governments of the USSR, USA, Canada, Mexico and Japan.

Much more worrying than birds being killed for food is the increased disturbance at the once remote colonies as transportation becomes more efficient. Prospecting for oil and minerals, acquisition of remote land and expanses of sea for military exercises and, above all, tourism may all be threatening the delicately-balanced sea-bird populations. On Pine Island, British Columbia, a study of dead birds in the region of the lighthouse revealed large numbers of rhinoceros auklets. Also in British Columbia, tufted puffins on Triangle Island deserted their burrows because of helicopters landing.

Writers like the present author, as well as those fascinated by ornithological research, should beware that in our desire to find out more about species with complex life histories we do not disturb them to such an extent that they slide even more quickly along the road to extinction. We have also seen in the case of marbled murrelet how the logging of timber can have a potentially devastating effect upon breeding populations. The effect of man's domesticated animals can also cause problems.

DOMESTIC ANIMALS

In his account of the sea birds of Alaska, Lensink (1984) noted that the introduction of the European rabbit (*Oryctolagus cuniculus*) to Middleton Island (Rausch, 1956) and also onto the Aleutians (Nysewander *et al.*, 1982) has meant the reduction of cover and an increase in erosion which is likely to prove detrimental to several species of sea birds, including alcids. Domestic cats and dogs have also caused problems by living ferally whilst cattle, sheep and reindeer (*Rangifer tarandus*) can disturb nesting birds, cause the collapse of burrows and crush eggs. It is now illegal to introduce domestic animals onto the islands of Alaska.

On Pine Island, British Columbia, the dogs kept by lighthouse keepers have been reported to kill large numbers of rhinoceros auklet chicks, and domestic cats escaping into the wild are a problem in many bird colonies. Leaving aside the escape of predators whose effect is obvious, the impact made by 'harmless farm animals' is probably much greater. Disturbance at breeding colonies is a crucial factor little studied and, in view of the vested interests involved, is bound to be difficult, if not impossible to eradicate.

COMMERCIAL FISHING

The effect of fishing on alcids can be considered as either direct or indirect. Direct competition between birds and man for diminishing fish stocks is now fierce, whilst the birds which become entangled in the nets seems to be the main worry. In the long run, however, it may be food shortages caused by man's overfishing which will affect bird populations more than the loss of thousands of birds trapped in narrow-mesh gill nets. The Danish gill nets, however are known to have drowned 500,000 to 750,000 Brunnich's guillemots every year between 1968 and 1973. Since this peak, numbers so killed may have fallen slightly, but the human demand for such fish species as capelin, sand-eel and sprats has increased, partly due to the production of fish meal for pet-food and fertiliser and partly due to the diminishing stocks of larger fish, such as cod. After all a fish finger can be made from any species which tastes good when crushed and covered with batter. The North Atlantic puffin is now in direct competition with Danish trawlers catching sand-eels. Around the North Pacific area, Japanese salmon-fishing fleets around Alaska are known to affect adversely Brunnich's guillemot and both horned and tufted puffins. Exactly how these are affected is not known but, at the time of writing, the USA and Japan are jointly embarked on a joint study of the problem.

In British Columbia, Sealy and Carter (1984) reported that 200 marbled murrelets drown each year in gill nets operated in Berkeley Sound which is situated on the west coast of Vancouver Island. Whilst this figure does not appear to be high it becomes important when we realise that this is some 10% of the breeding population. Other British Columbian alcids affected by gill nets include ancient murrelets, rhinoceros auklets and common guillemots. Joseph R. Jehl Junior (1984) reviewed the effect of gill-net fisheries around the coast of California and the Pacific North-West. He noted that, of 22,000 birds washed ashore, some 90% had been drowned in gill nets and that the species involved were mainly sooty shearwaters (*Puffinus griseus*), common murres (*Uria aalge*), cormorants (*Phalacrocorax* sp.), pigeon guillemots (*Cepphus columba*) and marbled murrelets (*Brachyramphus marmoratus*). Jehl went on to point out that:

The shearwaters are sufficiently numerous that the losses are probably not significant on a population basis. That does not seem true for the alcids, and the problem is considered sufficiently severe that a Bill regulating the gill nets is now before the California State Legislature.

In western Greenland and eastern Canada, where some Greenland birds join the native breeders, monofilament drift-netting for salmon and cod has become increasingly common since the 1960s. Tull *et al.*(1972) thought that as many as half a million alcids, especially guillemots, were drowned in nets whilst Christensen and Lear (1977), in a paper relating to the period 1970–72, thought that a maximum of 350,000 were destroyed, and they further pointed out that the birds were most at risk from night-fishing.

Migrating birds of several species, including Brunnich's guillemot, little auk, Atlantic puffin and black guillemot often escaped the fishing fleets operating between September and October because they had not arrived in the danger area. In 1976, Salmon fishing quotas were imposed because they halted fishing by the middle of September and gave the alcids some respite. Recently however fishing is being practised in deeper water with more efficient equipment and over the whole 24 hours.

Off Newfoundland, Greenland birds fall foul of the gill nets between May and December, the greatest mortality occurring in the last 2 months of the year. The nets sample water between 50 and 200 metres (163 and 650 feet). Little auks and Atlantic puffins are both trapped but both common and Brunnich's guillemots tend to dive deeper and are therefore more at risk.

POLLUTION

Whenever modern-day biologists observe falls in avian populations their natural tendency is to blame pollution without being any more specific than this. In the case of sea birds, oil pollution is often the scapegoat, although it is doubtless a problem in some areas.

Oil affects sea birds in three main ways. Firstly the oil may coat the plumage and increase the body weight to such an extent that the bird cannot fly and merely sinks out of sight. Birds which do not seem so badly affected still have their insulation efficiency reduced as individual feathers are clogged with oil. A combination of wind and water therefore increases the

Red-throated diver, guillemot and razorbill killed by oil pollution.

chill factor, the body temperature falls and the bird dies of hypothermia. Thirdly the bird, recognising that something is amiss, preens the feathers and in doing so ingests the oil. Depending upon the type of oil, it can either be an unpleasant irritant or a quick-acting poison. This means that not all oil spills are equally dangerous. What happens to birds depends upon many factors, including the type of oil, the volume involved, the locality, time of year and which bird species are present.

The weather also plays an important part and cold calm conditions would appear to be the most dangerous. High temperatures cause volatile elements in the oil to evaporate and rough weather breaks up the spill. Disasters such as the *Torrey Canyon* and *Amoco Cadiz* tend, naturally and quite correctly, to make the headlines. In the *BTO News* of May 1978, P. Hope-Jones reported on the *Amoco Cadiz* disaster in the following emotive words:

A fortnight in France? The prospect dimmed slightly when I realised that it would entail long days of working with birds killed by oil from the Amoco Cadiz, but the RSPB had sent me over to Brittany to help and, in the circumstances, the recording of dead birds seemed the most constructive activity.

Immediately after the wreck, French birdwatchers thought the French equivalent of 'here we go again', because this was the fourth major oiling incident in Brittany in eleven years. At Brest, they were quickly off the mark in setting up a centre for rehabilitation of live birds and for reception of oiled corpses. The co-ordinator of scientific work on this incident was Jean-Yves Monnat, who very kindly looked after me during my stay in Brest; between us we examined several hundred auks and good numbers of Shags.

By the 17th April, a total of 2,700 birds of 34 species had been brought in to the Brest centre, either direct from beached-bird teams or via local collection centres on the coast. Only 103 of these birds were alive when found. As usual, the auks had been badly hit; 681 Puffins, 513 Razorbills, and 379 Guillemots were collected, though there were also high numbers of Shags (417) and of divers – 49 Black-throated and 54 Great Northern.

For the auks we measured winglength, together with bill length and depth, then opened up the corpses to check the sex by gonadal inspection. Some of the corpses were then passed to a group for post-mortem scrutiny, and samples were taken for future examination.

The data have not yet been analysed, but we suspect that many immature birds were involved. As well, we found that about 30% of the Puffins were in wing moult, and I brought back four sackfuls of their heads and wings for further study by Mike Harris. Plymouth Customs Officer: 'Have you anything to declare, sir?' Jones: 'Only 150 Puffin heads'.

It will be a while yet before the full impact of this oilspill on bird populations can be assessed, but once again the declining breeding populations of the Channel seabird colonies may be hard hit, and the recovery map shows that some of the affected birds were from the 'Celtic Fringe' colonies of South Wales and S.E. Ireland northwards. As with Torrey Canyon, we will never know the full extent of the casualty toll, but we must try to salvage some scientific facts from the carnage, and must continue pressing for better safeguards against oil spillage.

Horrific although these figures are they are but the tip of the iceberg. Many more birds die and sink without trace than are recovered, others swim off to die miles away from the incident. The other point which is well known to workers in the field is that the total deaths caused by small spills, which are never recorded, together add up to a greater kill than the isolated incidents which grab the publicity. In April 1985 the International Maritime Organisation issued a press release which described just this problem in West Germany where a two year study reported that: The report states: 'Among the 8,750 birds which were found dead between August 1983 and April 1984, 3,208 were covered with oil. Out of a sample of 158 oiled birds which were found dead, 126 contained oil in their digestive tract, which proves that the oil coverage happened before the birds' death.'

Out of a sample of 375 dead birds found without oil coverage 120 contained

188

oil in their digestive tract. This means that at least half of the total number of dead birds died of oil pollution.

The investigation indicates that most of this oil pollution came from shipping rather than off-shore oil production in the North Sea, says the report. A total of 112 oiled sea birds was examined between December 1982 and April 1983, but crude oil could be identified as the cause of death in only 11 samples.

The rest originated from shipping, with tank-washing operations and heavy fuel oil as the main sources. Tanker accidents do not appear to have contributed to the pollution. The Institut report states: 'All oil-induced losses of sea birds reported so far are caused by small oil quantities. There has been no oil accident in the German Bight for more than twenty years.'

The report states: 'The increase in the number of oiled birds during the last few years may originate from the increased use of heavy oil in shipping. This fuel type, which is more and more used for reasons of economy, requires an on-board separation of residues to prevent clogging of fuel pipes. It seems that these residues are often discharged into the sea.'

The report says there is no proof of a decline in sea bird population, but warns that 'long-term effects on sea bird population cannot be excluded.'

Discharges of this type contravene international treaties adopted under the auspices of IMO. The most important of these, the International Convention for the Prevention of Pollution from Ships, 1973, as modified by its Protocol of 1978 (MARPOL 73/78) introduced a series of important anti-pollution measures which are now binding on the majority of world ships. The measures include the installation of reception facilities for oily wastes in ports, requirements regarding the construction and equipment of ships, and operational procedures. The Convention applies to dry cargo ships as well as tankers.

Agreements such as these are excellent and are bound to help in the conservation of sea birds, but having laws is one thing and applying them is another. Perhaps two further laws could be brought into force. Vessels discharge oil at sea and tankers wash out their tanks for two reasons. Firstly it cuts down the turn-round time whilst in harbour and secondly it cuts the costs involved in cleaning. The problem could be solved by holding tankers in port for a limited period and by adding the cleaning bill to the harbour charges, whether they use them or not.

Even if all deliberate oil pollution was prevented there would still be accidental spills and information is needed on the effects of oil on the sea and how to clean affected birds. In *Country-Side* magazine of Summer 1982 Brian Dicks, the Director of the Oil Pollution Research Unit of the Field Studies Council, reported on the work of his unit.

In the south-western corner of Wales lies one of Europe's largest marine oil terminals, a scatter of oil tanks and refineries on the shores of Milford Haven. It is not surprising that a unit specialising in research into oil's effects in the sea should start at such a location, especially as marine life in the area is rich and a group of active marine biologists was already present at nearby Orielton Field Centre. From the humble beginnings of two research students looking at the effects of oil spills and effluents on rocky shores and in salt marshes in 1967 has grown the Oil Pollution Research Unit of the Field Studies Council – a group which now consists of 14 scientists with a wide-ranging research programme.

I think it fair to say that we would not have come into existence had it not been for the Torrey Canyon *spill, which focussed attention on oil as a pollutant in a most alarming fashion in 1967. The almost total ignorance of the damage caused by oil in the sea at that time was highlighted by the spill, and resulted in research funds becoming available for the early studies of the unit. Since then a growing environmental awareness in the oil industry and in government has allowed us to expand our research programmes to cover a wide range of oil-related problem. These have included oil spills, spill clean-up, the biological effects of refinery effluents, and of oil production offshore, especially in the North Sea.*

Offshore Work
The rapid growth of oil production offshore in the North Sea has stimulated much interest in potential biological effects, and we have carried out monitoring studies in eight North Sea fields since 1973.

The techniques used for assessing the impact of offshore fields are painstaking and laborious. Anything up to 300 seabed samples may be taken in an oilfield, in a pattern designed to measure gradients of effect away from sources of pollution. Uncontaminated reference sites are also sampled, to make it possible to discriminate between pollution-induced changes and natural variation. We concentrate these studies mainly on sedentary pollutant stress, and they act as integrators of effects over long periods of time. Mobile organisms tend to be poor indicators, as they can move away from pollution stress. The sites may be resampled every year or two, and the results compared with previous surveys in order to follow changes in impacts over the years. Samples are normally obtained by grabs, trawls, dredges or corers operated from ships, although diving may be used in shallower coastal waters or where non-destructive sampling is important. One week of field sampling usually produces six months of laboratory work – as many as 150,000 organisms or 400 or more species in some fields.

Some work has also been carried out on the cleaning of oiled sea birds although it is time-consuming, expensive and not always successful. In Britain, Newcastle-upon-Tyne University and the Royal Society for the Prevention of Cruelty to Animals have worked on the problem, the work of the latter being funded by Shell UK. The Society have a base at Little Creech near Taunton in Somerset but they have a mobile unit which can be sent to the site of an emergency. For a common guillemot, the cleaning process can take 2 hours and the detergent used destroys the natural water-proofing of the feathers. The birds are therefore fed (usually on sprats) and kept in a warm room until their preen glands have been allowed to function long enough to restore the natural oils. Their report on the subject notes:

A badly-oiled guillemot – auks, like other diving birds, are particularly vulnerable to oil spills.

Although there are many sceptics about the value of cleaning oiled seabirds a number of people in Britain continue to treat casualties, most particularly guillemots. Although it is possible to return apparently healthy birds to sea, there is very little information about what happens to them thereafter. While no news is good news, pessimists have assumed that most die fairly quickly after their release. An oiled guillemot treated at the Wildlife Field Unit of the Royal Society for the Prevention of Cruelty to Animals near Taunton (see Ma. Pollut. Bull. 1980, 11, 182) was released to sea at Portland on the south coast of England on 22 December, 1977 and has now been recovered at Crosshaven, Eire on 5 April, 1980 – 2 years and 4 months later. Ironically it has been oiled again and this time it died. This guillemot is the longest known survivor after cleaning and rehabilitation.

As indicated above, oil is the most feared form of marine pollution just because it is so visible. What about the equally dangerous but more subtle invisible pollutants? The disposal of toxic chemicals into the seas which have long been the world's sinks have not been studied in any depth and were only noticed in the 1960s and 1970s. Like oil these pollutants may work directly on the birds themselves but are also likely to affect the birds' food supplies. Most of the dangerous chemicals are destructive, even in small doses (so small that their concentrations are expressed in parts per million or p.p.m.). The chlorinated hydrocarbons are among the most dangerous and include DDT (dichloro-diphenyl-trichloroethane), but equally damaging are the PCB group (polychlorinated biphenyls) and the twin killers, aldrin and dieldrin, which belong to the chlorinated cyclodienes.

All the above are used in increasing volumes and their dispersal leaves a great deal to be desired. They enter the seas *via* the rivers, often in very low concentrations, but they are then picked up by the plankton and then passed up through the food chains to the invertebrates, fish and finally to the birds. The chemicals are fat-soluble and do not have an immediate effect on the birds, but neither can they be eliminated from the body. The chemicals therefore lie in wait dissolved in the bird's body fat and will not be released into the bird's bloodstream until it is under stress. Thus when the bird is moulting or fighting food shortage or low temperatures and draws upon its fat reserves, it is poisoned.

Heavy metals are not soluble in fat and birds do seem to have some natural tolerance, but investigations of dead birds and analyses of eggs do show that there has been a significant and worrying build-up in recent years. It is not only in the seas washing the shores of industrialised nations that the problem is being felt, as Evans (1984) found in his Greenland researches.

Analyses of birds and their eggs ... show some toxic chemical contaminations, possibly resulting from birds migrating to more industrialised regions (no pesticides are used in Greenland). Somer and Applequist (1974) found that mercury levels in black guillemots had doubled over a period of twenty years, though they were still at the comparatively low levels of about 2ppm.

Braestrup and his co-workers (1974) also found increasing levels of organo-chlorines and so lovers of alcids and other forms of wildlife cannot afford to be complacent about their future, even in areas apparently so far away from industry. Neither can we lose sight of the possibility that climatic changes might well be having more of an effect on the populations of the Alcidae than we imagine. Ocean currents are changing all the time, although very slowly compared with a human life-span. Temperatures of the sea may also be changing and causing reductions in plankton and fish stocks. These in turn affect the auks and their populations also fall.

*   *   *

It seems that, however hard we struggle to unravel the secrets of our wildlife, we have still a long way to go. The Alcidae, that most fascinating of bird families, is hanging on to a fair proportion of its secrets and we have yet only scratched the surface. Future workers are assured that there will always be a need to bob about in a small boat, feel the wind through the hair and smell the guano which hangs over the noisy sea-bird cities.

BIBLIOGRAPHY

Ackman, E.F. (1985) 'Auks in the North Atlantic' *Sea Swallow* 11: 31–33

Ainley, D.G. & Lewis, T.J. (1974) 'The history of Farallon Island marine bird populations 1854–1972' *Condor* 76: 432–446

Alexander, H.G. (1965) 'Sixty years of bird spotting' *Sea Bird Bull.* 1: 13

Alexander, W.B. (1955) *Birds of the Ocean* Putnam, London

Allaby, M. (ed.) (1986) *Oxford Dictionary of Natural History* Oxford University Press

Anderson, M. (1976) 'Predation and kleptoparasitism by skuas in a Shetland bird colony' *Ibis* 118: 208–217

Andrews, J.H. & Standring, K.T. (eds) (1900) *Marine Oil Pollution and Birds* RSPB, Sandy, Bedfordshire

Armstrong, E.A. (1940) *Birds of the Grey Wind* Oxford University Press

Arnason, E. & Grant, P.R. (1978) 'The significance of kleptoparasitism during the breeding season in a colony of Arctic skuas *Stercorarius parasiticus* in Iceland' *Ibis* 120: 38–52

Asbirk, S. (1978) *Dansk Orn. Foren. Tidsskr.* 72: 161–178

Asbirk, S. (1979) *Vidensk. Meddr Dansk Naturh. Foren.* 141: 29–80

Ashcroft, R.E. (1976) *Breeding Biology and Survival of Puffins* Ph.D. Thesis, Oxford University

Ashcroft, R.E. (1979) 'Survival rates and breeding biology of puffins on Skomer island, Wales' *Ornis Scand.* 10: 100–110

Ashmole, N.P. (1971) 'Seabird ecology and the marine environment' In Farner, D.S. & King, J.R. (eds) *Avian Biology* Vol. 1. Academic Press London

Audubon, J.J. (1827–1838) *The Birds of America* Double Elephant Folio, London

Bailey, E.P. & Fause, N.H. (1980) 'Summer distribution and abundance of marine birds and mammals in the Sandman reefs Alaska' *Murrelet* 61: 6–19

Barrett, R.T. & Vader, W. (1984) 'The status and conservation of breeding seabirds in Norway' In The Status and Conservation of the World's Seabirds. *I.C.B.P. Techn. Pub.* No. 2

Bateson, P.P.G. (1961) 'Little auk' *Br. Birds* 54: 272–277

Bedard, J. (1969a) 'Adaptive radiation in Alcidae' *Ibis* 111: 189–198

Bedard, J. (1969b) 'The nesting of the crested, least and parakeet auklets on St. Lawrence Island, Alaska' *Condor* 71: 386–398

Bedard, J. (1969c) 'Feeding of the least, crested and parakeet auklets around St. Lawrence Island, Alaska' *Can. J. Zool.* 47: 1025–1050

Belopol'ski, L.O. (1957) *Ecology of Sea Colony Birds of the Barents Sea* Moscow

Belopol'ski, L.O. (1961) 'Ecology of sea colony birds in the Barents Sea' *Jerusalem: LPST*

Bergman, G. (1971a) *Commentat. Biol.* 42: 1–26

Bergman, G. (1971b) *Ornis Fenn.* 48: 138–9

Berry, R.J. (1977) *Inheritance and Natural History* Collins, London

Bianki, V.V. (1967) *Trudy Kandalak. Gos. Zaproved* 6

Bibby, C.J. (1972) 'Auks drowned in fish nets' *Seabird Rep.* **2**: 48–49

Binford, L.C., Elliot, B.G. & Singer, S.W. (1975) 'Discovery of a nest and the downy young of the marbled murrelet' *Wilson Bull.* **87**: 303–319

Birkhead, T.R. (1975) 'Utilisation of guillemot *Uria aalge* colonies by jackdaws *Corvus monedula*' *Ornis Scand.* **5**: 71–81

Birkhead, T.R. (1976) Ph.D. Thesis, Oxford University

Birkhead, T.R. & Taylor, A.M. (1977) 'Moult of the common guillemot *Uria aalge*' *Ibis* **119**: 80–84

Birulya, A. (1910) *Ezheg. Zool. Mus. Imp. Akad. Nauk* **15**: 167–206

Blake, B.F., Tasker, M.L., Hope-Jones, P., Dixon, T.J., Mitchell, R. & Langslow, D.R. (1984) *Seabird Distribution in the North Sea* Nature Conservancy Council, Huntingdon

Bourne, W.R.P. (1968a) 'Oil pollution and bird populations' *Fld Stud.* **2** (Supplement): 200–218

Bourne, W.R.P. (1968b) 'Observations of an encounter between birds and floating oil' *Nature, Lond.* **219**: 632

Bourne, W.R.P. (1971) 'Vanishing puffins' *New Scientist* **52**, No. 772: 8–9

Bourne, W.R.P. (1972a) 'Threats to sea birds' *I.C.B.P. Bull.* **11**: 200–218

Bourne, W.R.P. (1972b) 'The decline of auks in Britain' *Biol. Conserv.* **4**: 144–166

Braithwaite, Dave (1979) 'Underwing of little auk' *Br. Birds* **72**: 344–345

Brooke, M.L. (1972) 'The Puffin population of the Shiant Islands' *Bird Study* **19**: 1–6

Brown, R.G.B. (1976) 'The foraging range of breeding dovekies *Alle alle*' *Can. Fld Nat.* **90**: 166–168

Brown, R.G.B. & Nettleship, D.N. (1984) 'The seabirds of north eastern North America: Their present status and conservation requirements' In Status and Conservation of the World's Seabirds. *I.C.B.P. Techn. Pub.* No. 2

Brun, B. & Singer, A. (1970) *The Hamlyn Guide to Birds of Britain and Europe* Hamlyn, Feltham

Brun, E. (1966) 'Hekkebestanden av Lunde *Fratercula arctica* i Norge' *Sterna* **7**: 1–17

Brun, E. (1979) 'Present status and trends in populations of seabirds in Norway' U.S. Fish Wildl. Serv. *Wildl. Res. Rep.* **11**: 289–301

Buckley, P.A. & Buckley, F.G. (1984) 'Seabirds of the north and middle Atlantic Coast of the U.S.' In Status and Conservation of the World's Seabirds. *I.C.B.P. Techn. Pub.* No. 2: 101–134

Buckley, T.E. & Harvie-Brown, J.A. (1891) *The Vertebrate Fauna of the Orkney Islands* Edinburgh

Cairns, D.K. (1979) 'Censusing hole nesting auks by visual counts' *Bird Banding* **50**: 358–364

Cairns, D.K. (1980) *Wilson Bull.* **92**: 352–61

Campbell, B. (1977) *Birds of Coast and Sea* Oxford University Press

Christensen, O. & Lear, W.H. (1977) 'Bycatches in salmon drift-nets at West Greenland in 1972' *Meddr Grønland* **205** (5): 1–38

Collinge, W.E. (1924) *The Food of Some British Wild Birds* Published privately in York

Conder, P.J. (1950) 'On the courtship and social displays of three species of auk' *Br. Birds* **43**: 65–69

Corkhill, P. (1972) 'Measurement of puffins as criteria of sex and age' *Bird Study* **19**: 193–201

Corkhill, P. (1973) 'Food and feeding ecology of puffins' *Bird Study* **20**: 207–220

Corrick, R. & Waterston, G. (1939) 'The birds of Canna' *Scott. Nat.* **1939**: 5–22

Cott, H.B. (1953–54) 'The exploitations of wild birds for their eggs' *Ibis* **95**: 409–449, 643–675; **96**: 129–149

Coues, E. (1868) 'A monograph of the Alcidae' *Proc. Acad. Nat. Sci. Philad.* **20**: 2–81

Cramp, S., Bourne, W.R.P. & Saunders, D. (1974) *The Seabirds of Britain and Ireland* Collins, London

Cramp, S. & Simmons, K.E.L. (eds) (1984) *The Birds of the Western Palearctic* Vol. 4 Oxford University Press

Dale, I.M., Baxter, N.S., Bogan, J.A. & Bourne, W.R.P. (1973) 'Mercury in seabirds' *Mar. Poll. Bull.* **4**: 77–79

Danchin, E. (1983) 'La posture de post-atterissage chez le macareux moine (*Fratercula arctica*)' *Biol. Behav.* **8**: 3–10

Darling, F.F. (1947) *Highlands and Islands* Collins, London

Dementiev, G.P. & Gladkov, N.A. (1951) *Ptitsy Sovietskogo Soyuza* Moscow

Demme, N.P. (1934) *Trudy Arkt. Inst. Biol. Moscow* **11**: 55–86

Dennis, R.H. (1966a) 'Notes on the breeding birds 1966' *Fair Isle Bird Obs. Bull.* **5**: 201–205

Dennis, R.H. (1966b) 'Notes on the breeding biology of the black guillemot *Cepphus grylle*' *Fair Isle Bird Obs. Bull.* **5**: 205–208

Dewar, J.M. (1924) *The Bird as a Diver* Witherby, London

Dickson, H. (1959) 'Puffins and burrows' *Skokholm Bird Obs. Rep.* **1958**: 427–34

Divoky, G.J., Watson, G. & Baronek, J.C. (1974) 'Breeding of the black guillemot in northern Alaska' *Condor* **76**: 339–343

Dixon, C. (1895) 'The ornithology of St. Kilda' *Ibis* **5** (3): 19–97

Dixon, C. (1896) *British Sea Birds* Bliss, Sands & Foster, London

Drent, R.H. (1965) 'Breeding biology of the pigeon guillemot *Cepphus columba*' *Ardea* **53**: 99–160

Dwyer, T.J., Isleib, M.E., Davenport, D.A. & Haddock, J.L. (1975) 'Marine bird populations in Prince William Sound, Alaska' Unpublished report of U.S. Fish and Wildlife Service Anchorage, Alaska

Dyck, J. & Meltofte, H. (1975) *Dansk. Orn. Foren. Tidsskr.* **69**: 55–64

Eggeling, W.J. (1960) *The Isle of May* Oliver & Boyd, Edinburgh

Evans, P.G.H. (1981) 'Ecology and behaviour of the little auk *Alle alle* in west Greenland' *Ibis* **123** (1): 1–18

Evans, P.G.H. (1984) 'The seabirds of Greenland: their status and conservation' In *The Status and Conservation of the World's Seabirds. I.C.B.P. Techn. Pub.* No. 2: 49–84

Evans, P.G.H. & Waterston, G. (1976) 'The decline of the thick billed murre in Greenland' *Polar Rec.* **18**: 183–287

Fairhurst, J. (1969) 'Gannets brooding guillemot chicks' *Bird Study* **1976**: 285–286

Feare, C.J. (1984) 'Human exploitation' In *The Status and Conservation of the World's Seabirds. I.C.B.P. Techn. Pub.* No. 2: 691–700

Ferdinand, L. (1969) *Dansk. Orn. Foren. Tidsskr.* **63**: 19–45

Fisher, J. & Lockley, R.M. (1954) *Sea Birds* Collins, London

Fitter, R.S.R. & Richardson, R.A. (1952) *The Pocket Guide to British Birds* Collins, London

Flegg, J.J.M. (1972) 'The puffin on St. Kilda 1969–71' *Bird Study* **19**: 7–17

Flegg, J.J.M. (1985) *The Puffin* Shire Publications

Fleming, Dr J. 'Observations on garefowl (1822)' *Edinb. Phil. J.* **10**: 96

Flint, V.E., Boehme, R.L., Kostin, Y.V. & Kuznetsov, A.A. (1981) *A Field Guide to Birds of the USSR* Princeton University Press

Folkestad, A.D. (1982) 'The effect of mink predation on some breeding seabird species' *Viltrapport* **21**: 42–49

Forsell, D.J. & Gould, P.J. (1981) 'Distribution and abundance of marine birds and mammals wintering in the Kodiak area of Alaska' *U.S. Fish and Wildl. Serv. Biol. Serv. Prog.* FWS/OBS/81/13

Franeker, J.A. van & Camphuijsen, S.J. (1984) 'Report on *Fulmarus glacialis* Expedition 11, Jan Mayen, June to August 1983' *Versl. en Techn. Gegevens* No. 32: 1–34. Instituut voor Taxonomische Zoologie, Nr 39 Plantage, Middenlaan 53, Amsterdam

Freethy, Ron (1982a) *The Naturalists Guide to the British Coastline* David & Charles, Newton Abbot

Freethy, Ron (1982b) *How Birds Work* Blandford Press, Poole

Freethy, Ron (1985) *British Birds in Their Habitats* Crowood Press, Ramsbury

Freuchen, P. & Salomonsen, F. (1959) *The Arctic Year* Jonathan Cape, London

Gaston, A.J. (1980) 'Populations, movements and wintering areas of thickbilled murres (*Uria lomvia*) in eastern Canada' (*Can. Wildl. Serv. Prog. Note* No. 110: 1–10

Gaston, A.J. & Nettleship, D.N. (1981) 'The thick-billed murres of Prince Leopold Island' *Can. Wildl. Serv. Monogr. Ser.* No. 6

Gibson, J.A. (1950) 'Methods of determining breeding-cliff populations of guillemots and razorbills' *Bird Study* 19: 7–17

Gibson-Hill, C.A. (1947) *British Seabirds* Witherby, London

Gibson-Hill, C.A. (1976) *A Guide to the Birds of the Coast* Constable, London

Gill, R. & Sanger, G.A. (1979) 'Tufted puffins nesting in estuarine habitat' *Auk* 96: 792–794

Gray, R. (1871) *The Birds of the West of Scotland* Murray London

Greenwood, J. (1964) 'The fledging of the guillemot *Uria aalge* with notes on the razorbill *Alca torda*' *Ibis* 106: 469–81

Grent, P.R. (1971) 'Interactive behaviour of puffins and skuas' *Behaviour* 40: 263–281

Grieve, Symington (1885) *The Great Auk or Garefowl* T.C. Jack, London

Guermeur, Y. and Monnat, J.Y. (1980) *Histoire et Geographie des Oiseaux Nicheurs de Bretagne* Aurillac

Gurney, J.H. (1913) *The Gannet: the Bird with a History* Witherby, London

Haftorn, S. (1971) *Norges Fugler* Universit, Oslo

Hantsch, B. (1905) *Beitrag zur Kenntnis der Vogelwelt Islands* Berlin

Harris, M.P. (1969) 'Effect of laying date on chick production in oyster catchers and herring gulls' *Br. Birds* 62: 70–75

Harris, M.P. (1976a) 'The present status of the puffin in Britain and Ireland *Br. Birds* 69: 239–64

Harris, M.P. (1976b) 'The seabirds of Shetland in 1974' *Scott. Birds* 9: 37–68

Harris, M.P. (1976c) 'Lack of a 'desertion period' in the nestling life of the Puffin *Fratercula arctica*' *Ibis* 118: 115–8

Harris, M.P. (1978) 'Supplementary feeding of young puffins *Fratercula arctica*.' *J. Anim. Ecol.* 47: 15–23

Harris, M.P. (1980) 'Breeding performance of puffins *Fratercula arctica* in relation to nest density, laying date and year' *Ibis* 122: 193–209

Harris, M.P. (1984) *The Puffin* Poyser, Calton

Harris, M.P. & Hislop, J.R.G. (1978) 'The food of young puffins *Fratercula arctica*' *J. Zool. London* 185: 213–236

Harrison, C. (1975) *A Field Guide to the Nests, Eggs and Nestlings of British and European Birds* Collins, London

Harrison, C. (1978) *A Field Guide to the Nests, Eggs and Nestlings of North American Birds* Collins, London

Harrison, C. (1982) *An Atlas of the Birds of the Western Palearctic* Collins, London

Hartert, E. (1971) 'A note on the British puffin' *Br. Birds* 11: 163–166, 235–237

Hartley, C.H. & Fisher, J. (1936) *J. Anim. Ecol.* 5: 370–389

Hedgren, S. (1979) 'Seasonal variation in fledging weight of guillemots *Uria aalge*' *Ibis* 121: 356–361

Hedgren, S. & Linnman, A. (1979) 'Growth of guillemot *Uria aalge* chicks in relation to time of hatching' *Ornis Scand.* **10**: 29–36

Heinzel, H., Fitter, R. & Parslow, J. (1972) *The Birds of Britain and Europe with North Africa and the Middle East* Collins, London

Hellmayr, C.E. & Conover, B. (1948) *Catalog of Birds of the Americas and the Adjacent Islands* Part 1, No. 3. Field Museum of Natural History, Chicago

Hope-Jones, P., Mannat, J.Y., Cadbury, C.J. & Stowe, T.J. (1978) 'Birds oiled during the Amoco Cadiz incident' *Mar. Pollut. Bull.* **9**: 307–210

Hope-Jones, P. (1980) 'Beached birds at selected Orkney beaches 1976–78' *Scott. Birds* **11**: 1–12

Hornung, M. (1976) 'Soil erosion on the Farne Islands' *Ann. Rep. Inst. Terr. Ecol.* **1975**; 57–61

Hornung, M. (1981) 'Burrow excavation and infill in the Farne Island puffin colony' *Trans. Nat. Hist. Soc. Northumberland* **43**: 45–54

Hornung, M. & Harris, M.P. (1976) 'Soil water levels and delayed egg laying of puffins' *Br. Birds* **69**: 402–408

Hörring, R. (1933) *Dansk. Orn. Foren. Tidsskr.* **27**: 103–5

Howard, R. & Moore, Alick (1984) *A Complete Checklist of the Birds of the World* Macmillan, London

Hudson, P.J. (1979a) Ph.D. Thesis, Oxford

Hudson, P.J. (1979b) *J Anim. Ecol.* **48**: 889–898

Hudson, P.J. (1982) 'Nest site characteristics and breeding success in the Razorbill *Alca torda*' *Ibis* **124**: 355–359

Hughes, M.R. (1970) 'Some observations on ion and water balance in the puffin *Fratercula arctica*' *Can. J. Zool.* **48**: 479–482

Hyde, L.B., (1937) *A. Rep. Bowdoin Sci. Stn* **2**: 30–3

International Council for Bird Preservation (1984a) 'Status and Conservation of the World's Seabirds.' I.C.B.P. Techn. Pub. No. 2

International Council for Bird Preservation (1984b) *Conservation of Island Birds. I.C.B.P. Techn. Pub.* No. 3

Irving, L. & Krog, J. (1956) 'Temperature during the development of birds in Arctic nests' *Physiol. Zool.* **29**: 195–305

Isleib, M.E. & Kessel, B. (1973) 'Birds of the North Gulf Coast – Prince William Sound region Alaska' *Biol. Pap. Univ. Alaska* **14**

Jefferies, D.J. & Parslow, J.E.L. (1976) 'The genetics of bridling in guillemots from a study of hand reared birds' *J. Zool. Lond.* **179**: 411–420

Jehl, J.R. (1970) 'Patterns of hatching success in subarctic birds' *Ecology* **52**: 169–173

Jehl, J.R., Jnr. (1984) 'Conservation problems of seabirds in Baja California and the Pacific North West' **In** Status and Conservation of the World's Seabirds. *I.C.B.P. Techn. Pub.* No. 2

Joensen, A.H. & Preuss, N.O. (1972) 'Report on the ornithological expedition to Northwest Greenland 1965' *Meddr Grønland* **191** (5): 1–58

Johnson, R.A. (1941) *Auk* **58**: 153–163

Johnston, R. (ed.) (1976) *Marine Pollution* Academic Press, London

Jones, R.D. & Byrd, G.V. (1979) 'Interrelations between seabirds and introduced animals' *U.S. Fish Wildl. Serv. Wildl. Res. Rep.* **11**: 221–226

Jonsson, L. (1978) *Birds of Sea and Coast* Harmondsworth

Kaftanovski, Y.M. *Mater. Pozn. Fauny Flory SSSR, N.S. Otd. Zool.* **28** (13): 1–70

Kampp, K. (1982) *The Thick-billed Murre* Uria lomvia *in Greenland. Movement, Mortality and Hunting; Analysis of 35 Years of Banding* Special report for the Scientific Candidate Examination at the University of Copenhagen, December 1982

Kartashev, N.N. (1960) *Die Alkenvogel des Nordatlantics* Wittenberg, Lutherstadt

Kearton, R. (1897) *With Kearton with a Camera* Cassell, London

King, J.R. (1973) 'Energetics of reproduction in birds.' **In** Farner, D.E. (ed) *Breeding Biology of Birds* pp. 78–107. Washington: National Academy of Sciences.

Korte, J. de (1973) *Nederlandse Groenland Expeditie 1973* Preliminary Avifaunistical Report 10pp

Kress, S.W. (1977) 'Establishing Atlantic puffins at a former breeding site' **In** Temple, S.A. (ed) *Endangered Birds: Management Techniques For Preserving Threatened Species* University of Wisconsin Press

Lees, D.R. (1982) 'Kleptoparasitism by herring and lesser blackbacked gulls on puffins' *Skomer Skokholm Bull.* **4**: 9

Lensink, C.J. (1984) 'Seabirds of Alaska' **In** Status and Conservation of the World's Seabirds. *I.C.B.P. Techn. Pub.* No. 2

Lloyd, C.S. (1976) 'Bird kill' *Birds* **6**: 23

Lloyd, C.S. (1979) 'Factors affecting breeding of razorbills *Alca torda* on Skokholm' *Ibis* **121**: 165–176

Lloyd, C.S. (1982) 'The seabirds of Great Saltee *Ir. Bird Rep.* **2**: 1–37

Lockley, R.M. (1934) 'On the breeding habits of the puffin: with special reference to the incubation and fledging period' *Br. Birds* **27**: 214–223

Lockley, R.M. (1938) *I Know an Island* Harrap, London

Lockley, R.M. (1953) *Puffins* Dent, London

Lockley, R.M. (1964) 'Grassholm: some facts and a legend' *Nature Wales* **3**: 382–388

Lockley, R.M. (1974) *Ocean Wanderers* David & Charles, Newton Abbot

Lockwood, W.B. (1984) *The Oxford Book of British Bird Names* Oxford University Press

Lowe, G. (1813) *Fauna Orcadensis* Edinburgh

Luttick, R. (1982) *Vogeljaar* **30**: 17–23

Macauley, Revd. K. (1764) *History of St. Kilda* London

MacKenzie, N. (1905) 'Notes on the birds of St. Kilda' *Ann. Scott. Nat. Hist.* **14**: 75–80 141–153

Macgillivray, W. (1842) 'An account of the island of St. Kilda' *Edinb. New Phil. j.* **32**: 47–70

Macgillivray, W. (1846) *Manual of British Birds Complete* Edinburgh

Madsen, F.J. (1957) *Dan. Rev. Game Biol.* **3**: 19–83

Manuwal, D.A. (1979) 'Reproductive commitment and success of Cassin's auklet' *Condor* **81**: 111–121

Martin, Martin (1753) *A Voyage to St. Kilda* London

Mead, C.M. (1974) 'The results of ringing auks in Britain and Ireland' *Bird Study* **21**: 45–86

Meltofte, H. (1976a) 'Ornithological observations in Southern Peary Land, north Greenland 1973' *Meddr Grønland* **205** (1): 1–57

Meltofte, H. (1976b) 'Ornithological observations from the Scoresby Sund areas, east Greenland 1974' *Dansk Orn. Foren. Tidsskr.* **70**: 107–22

Merckallio, E. (1958) *Fauna Fenn.* **5**: 1–181

Montagu, G. (1813) *Supplement to the Ornithological Dictionary* London

Murie, O.J. (1959) 'Fauna of the Aleutian Islands and Alaska Peninsula' *North Amer. Fauna* **61**

Myrberget, S. (1962) 'Contribution to the breeding biology of the puffin *Fratercula arctica*' *Meddr St. Viltunders* **11**: 1–51

Myrberget, S. (1973) 'Merking av Toppskarv og Lunde pa Rost' *Sterna* **12**: 307–15

Myrberget, S. (1980) 'Criteria of physical condition of fledging puffins' **In** *Proceedings of the 2nd Nordic Ornithological Congress*

Nelson, B. (1980) *Seabirds: Their Biology and Ecology* Hamlyn, London

Nettleship, D.N. (1972) 'Breeding success of the common puffin *Fratercula arctica* on different habitats at Great Island, Newfoundland' *Ecol. Monogr.* **42**: 239–268

Nettleship, D.N. (1975) 'Effect of *Larus* gulls on breeding performance and nest distribution in Atlantic Puffins' In *Proceedings of the Gull Seminar, Sackvill, N.B. 9th September 1975* pp. 47–68. Canadian Wildlife Service

Nettleship, D.N. & Piatt, J. (1982) 'Seabird mortality from gill net fisheries in Newfoundland' In *Proceedings of the Seabird Group Conference, Denstone College, Uttoxeter U.K. 12–14 February 1982* pp. 16–17

Norderhaug, M. (1970) 'The role of the little auk *Plautus alle* in arctic ecosystems *Antarctic Ecol.* (sic) **1**: 558–560

Norderhaug, M. (1974) *Norsk Polarinst Arbck* **1972**: 99–106

Norderhaug, M. (1980) *Norsk Polarinst. Skr.* **173**

Norderhaug, M., Brun, E. & Mollen, G.V. (1977) 'Barentshavets sjofuglressurser' *Medda Polar Inst.* **104**: 1–119

Nørrevang, A. (1958) *Dansk. Orn. Foren. Tidsskr.* **52**: 48–74

North, P.M. (1980) 'An analysis of razorbill movements away from the breeding colony *Bird Study* **27**: 11–20

Nysewander, D.R., Forsell, D.J., Baird, P.A., Sheilds, D.J., Weiler, G.W. & Kogan, J.H. (1982) 'Marine bird and mammal survey of the Eastern Aleutian Islands, summers of 1980–81' Unpublished report of U.S. Fish and Wildlife Service, Anchorage, Alaska

O'Connor, R.J. (1976) 'Weight and body composition of nestling blue tits *Parus caeruleus*' *Ibis* **118**: 108–112

Ogilvie, M.A. (1976) *The Winter Birds* Michael Joseph

Paludan, K. (1947) *Alken* Copenhagen

Parkin, T. (1911) *The Great Auk. A record of Sales of Birds and Eggs by Public Auction in Great Britain 1806–1910* Burfield and Pennels, London

Penicaud, P. (1979) *Terre Vie* **33**: 591–609

Perrins, C.M. (1965) 'Population fluctuations and clutch size in the great tit *Parus major*' *J. Anim. Ecol.* **34**: 601–647

Perrins, C.M. (1966) 'Survival of young Manx shearwaters *Puffinus puffinus* in relation to their presumed date of hatching' *Ibis* **108**: 132–135

Perrins, C.M. (1970) 'The timing of birds' breeding seasons' *Ibis* **112**: 242–255

Perrins, C.M., Harris, M.P. & Britton, C.K. (1973) 'Survival of Manx shearwater *Puffinus puffinus*' *Ibis* **115**: 535–548

Perry, R. (1940) *Lundy, Isle of Puffins* Drummond, London

Perry, R. (1944) 'Notes on razorbills' *Geogrl Mag.* **17**: 84–95

Perry, R. (1948) *Shetland Sanctuary* Faber & Faber, London

Perry, R. (1975) *Watching Sea Birds* Croom Helm, Sydenham

Petersen, A. (1976a) 'Age of first breeding in puffin *Fratercula arctica*' *Astarte* **9**: 43–50

Petersen, A. (1976b) 'Size variable in puffins *Fratercula arctica* from Iceland and bill features as a criteria of age' *Ornis Scand.* **7**: 185–92

Petersen, A. (1981) Ph.D. Thesis, Oxford University

Petersen, A. (1982) 'Icelandic seabirds' In Gardarsson, A. (ed) *Icelandic Seabirds. R. Landverndar* **8**: 15–60

Petersen, M.R. (1980) 'Red fox predation of seabirds at Shaiak Island, Alaska' *Pacif. Seabird Gp Bull.* **7**: 54

Peterson, R.T. (1941) *A Field Guide to Western Birds* Houghton Mifflin, Cambridge, Mass

Peterson, R.T., Mountford, G. & Hollom, P.A.D. (1954) *A Field Guide to the Birds of Britain and Europe* Collins, London

Pettingill, O.S. (1959) 'Puffins and eiders in Iceland' *Me Fld Nat.* **15**: 58–71

Plumb, W.J. (1965) 'Nesting behaviour of razorbills' *Br. Birds* **58**: 449–456

Plumb, W.J. (1970) 'Observations on the breeding biology of the razorbill' *Br. Birds* **58**: 449–456

Preston, W.C. (1968) Ph.D Thesis, Michigan University

Ralfe, P.G. (1905) *The Birds of the Isle of Man* David Douglas, Douglas

Rees, A. (1983) *Br. Birds* **76**: 454

Richardson, F. (1961) 'Breeding biology of the rhinoceros auklet on Protection Island, Washington' *Condor* **63**: 456–73

Robbins, C., Bruun, B. & Zim, H.S. (1983) *Birds of North America* Western Publishing Company

Robertson, D. (1980) *Rare Birds of the West Coast of North America* Woodock Publications, California

Roelke, M. & Hunt, G. (1978) *Pacif. Seabird Gp Bull.* **5**: 81

Ryder, J.P. (1970) 'A possible factor in the evolution of clutch size in Ross' Goose' *Wilson Bull.* **82**: 5–13

Rydzewski, W. (1978) *Ring* **96–97**: 218–62

Rydzewski, W. (1979) *Ring* **98–99**

Salomonsen, F. (1944) 'Goteborgs Kungl.' *Vetenskaps-och Vitterhets-Samhalles Handle Sjatte Foljden* (B 3 5)

Salmonsen, F. (1950) *Grønlands Fugle* Ejnar Munksgaard, Copenhagen

Salomonsen, F. (1967) *Fuglene pa Grønland* Copenhagen

Sands, J. (1878) *Out of the World; or Life on St. Kilda* Maclachlan and Stewart, Edinburgh

Scott, J.M. (1973) Ph.D. Thesis, Oregon University

Sealy, S.G. (1968) *A comparative study of the breeding ecology and timing in plankton-feeding alcids* (Cyclorrhynchus *and* Aethia *sp.*) on St. Lawrence Island Alaska M.Sc. Thesis, University of British Columbia

Sealy, S.G. (1973) 'Adaptive significance of post-hatching developmental patterns and growth rates in the Alcidae' *Ornis Scand.* **4**: 113–121

Sealy, S.G. (1975) 'Influence of snow on the egg laying in auklets' *Auk* **92**: 528–538

Sealy, S.G. (1981) 'Variations in fledgling weight of least auklets *Aethia pusilla*' *Ibis* **123**: 230–233

Sealy, S.G. & Bedard, J. (1973) 'Breeding biology of the parakeet auklet *Cyclorhynchus psittacula* on St Lawrence Island, Alaska' *Astarte*

Sealy, S.G. & Carter, H.R. (1984) 'At sea distribution and nesting habitat of marbled murrelet in British Columbia' **In**: The Status and Conservation of the World's Seabirds. *I.C.B.P. Techn. Pub.* No. 2: 737–756

Sharrock, J.T.R. (ed.) (1976) *The Atlas of Breeding Birds in Britain and Ireland* Poyser, Calton

Simpson, G.G. (1976) *Penguins Past and Present. Here and There* Yale University Press

Slater, P.J.B. (1974) 'Orientation of fish in the tystie's beak' *Bird Study* **21**: 238–240

Slater, P.J.B. & Slater, E.P. (1972) *Bird Study* **19**: 105–114

Snyder, L.L. (1957) *Arctic Birds of Canada* University of Toronto Press

Southern, H.N., Carrick, R. & Potter, W.G. (1965) 'The natural history of a population of Guillemot *Uria aalge* Pont' *J. Anim. Ecol.* **34**: 649–665

Sowls, A.L., De Grange, A.R., Nelson, J.W. & Lester, G.S. (1980) 'Catalog of California Seabird Colonies' *U.S. Fish Wildl. Serv. Biol. Serv. Prog.* FWS/OBS/37/80

Sowls, A.L., Hatch, S.A. & Lensink, C.J. (1978) 'Catalog of Alaskan Seabird colonies' *U.S. Fish Wildl. Serv. Biol. Serv. Prog.* FWS/OBS/78/78

Sparks, J. & Soper, T. (1967) *Penguins* David & Charles, Newton Abbot

Stallcup, R. (1976) *Western Birds* **7**: 113–136

Stempniewicz, L. (1981) *Acta Orn.* **18**: 141–165

Stowe, T.J. (1982) 'Recent population trends in cliff-breeding seabirds in Britain and Ireland' *Ibis* **124**: 502–509

Swennen, C. & Duiven, P. (1977) *Neth. J. Sea Res.* **11**: 92–98

Swinton, W.E. (1975) *Fossil Birds* British Museum

Talbot, T. (1886) 'Important and curious documents relating to the Isle of Man' *Manx Sun* January 30th: 3

Taylor, K. (1984) 'Chapter 7 Behaviour' In Harris, M.P. *The Puffin* pp. 96–103. Poyser, Calton

Temple, S.A. (1974) 'Winter food habits of ravens on the Arctic slope of Alaska' *Arctic* **26**: 41–46

Thompson, F. (1970) *St. Kilda and other Hebridean Outliers* David & Charles, Newton Abbot

Tschanz, B. (1968) *Z. Tierpsychol.* No. 4 (Supplement)

Tuck, G. & Heinzel, H. (1978) *A Field Guide to the Seabirds of Britain and the World* Collins, London

Tuck, L.M. (1961) 'The murres' *Can. Wildl. Ser.* No. 1

Tuck, L.M. (1971) 'The occurrence of Greenland and European birds in Newfoundland' *Bird Banding* **42**: 184–209

Tull, C.E., Germain, P. & May, A.W. (1972) Mortality of thick billed murres in the West Greenland salmon fishery' *Nature, Lond.* **237**: 42–44

Udvardy, M.D.F. (1968) 'Zoogeographical study of the Pacific Alcidae' *Pacif. Basin Biogeogr.*

Uspenski, S.M. (1956) *Bird Colonies of the Novaya Zemlya* Acad. Sci. USSR Moscow pp. 178

Vaurie, C. (1965) *The Birds of the Palearctic Fauna Non-Passeriformes* Witherby, London

Vermeer, K. (1978) 'Extensive reproductive failure of Rhinoceros Auklets and tufted puffins' *Ibis* **120**: 112 (Abstract)

Vermeer, K. (1979) 'Nesting requirements, food and breeding distribution of Rhinoceros auklets *Cerorhinca monocerata* and tufted puffins *Lunda cirrhata*' *Ardea* **67**: 101–110

Vermeer, K. (1980) 'The importance and type of prey to reproductive success of rhinoceros auklets *Cerorhinca monoceratá*' *Ibis* **122**: 343–350

Vermeer, K. (1981) 'The importance of plankton to breeding Cassins' auklets' *J. Plantt. Res.* **3**: 315–329

Vermeer, K., Robertson, I., Campbell, R.W., Kaiser, G. & Lemon, N. 'Distribution and densities of marine birds on the Canadian west coast.' *Can. Wildl. Serv. Rep.*

Vermeer, K. & Sealy, S.G. (1984) 'Status of nesting seabirds in British Columbia' In The Status and conservation of the World's Seabirds. *I.C.B.P. Techn. Pub.* No. 2: 29–40

Wallis, J. (1769) *Natural History and Antiquities of Northumberland* Newcastle

Walters, M. (1980) *The Complete Birds of the World* David & Charles, Newton Abbot

Wendt, S. & Gooch, F.G. (1984) 'The kill of murres in Newfoundland in the 1977–78, 1978–79 and 1979–80 hunting seasons' *Can. Wildl. Serv. Prog. Note* **146**: 1–10

Whitbourne, R. (1620) *Discourse and Discovery of Newfoundland* London

Williams, A.J. (1972) M.Sc. Thesis, Sheffield University

Williams, A.J. (1975) 'Guillemot fledging and predation on Bear Island' *Ornis Scand.* **6**: 117–124

Williamson, K. (1939) 'The great auk in the Isle of Man' *J. Manx Mus.* **61**

Williamson, K. (1945) 'The economic importance of sea fowl in the Faeroe Islands' *Ibis* **87**: 249–69

Williamson, K. (1970) *The Atlantic Islands* Routledge & Keegan Paul, London

Willoughby, F. (1676) *Ornithology* London

Wilson, U.W. (1977) *A Study of the biology of the Rhinoceros Auklet on Protection Island, Washington* M.Sc. Thesis, University of Washington

Witherby, H.F., Jordain, F.C.R., Ticehurst, N.F. & Tucker, B.W. (1938–1942) *Handbook of British Birds* Vols 1–5. Witherby

Wormius, O. (1655) *Museum Wormianum Historiae Rariorum* London

Yarrell, William (1843) *A History of British Birds* Vols 1–4. Van Voorst, London. 4th edition

Yarrell, William (1885) *A History of British Birds* Revised by Howard Saunders. Vols 1–4. Van Voorst, London

INDEX

Page numbers in italics refer to illustrations; colour plate numbers are in **bold**.